English Grammar
Understanding the Basics

Looking for an easy-to-use guide to English grammar? This handy introduction covers all the basics of the subject, using a simple and straightforward style. Students will find the book's step-by-step approach easy to follow and be encouraged by its non-technical language. Requiring no prior knowledge of English grammar, the information is presented in small steps, with objective techniques to help readers apply new concepts. With clear explanations and well-chosen examples, the book gives students the tools to understand the mysteries of English grammar as well as the perfect foundation from which to move on to more advanced topics.

EVELYN P. ALTENBERG is Professor in the Department of Speech-Language-Hearing Sciences at Hofstra University, New York.

ROBERT M. VAGO is Professor and Chair in the Department of Linguistics and Communication Disorders at Queens College, City University of New York.

English Grammar

Understanding the Basics

EVELYN P. ALTENBERG
Hofstra University

and

ROBERT M. VAGO
Queens College and the Graduate Center
City University of New York

Form Amaz 1/12 31.00

CAMBRIDGE UNIVERSITY PRESS
Cambridge, New York, Melbourne, Madrid, Cape Town, Singapore,
São Paulo, Delhi, Tokyo, Mexico City

Cambridge University Press
The Edinburgh Building, Cambridge CB2 8RU, UK

Published in the United States of America by Cambridge University Press, New York

www.cambridge.org
Information on this title: www.cambridge.org/9780521732161

First published 2010
3rd printing 2011

Printed in the United Kingdom at the University Press, Cambridge

A catalogue record for this publication is available from the British Library

ISBN 978-0-521-51832-1 Hardback
ISBN 978-0-521-73216-1 Paperback

Additional resources for this publication at www.cambridge.org/altenberg-vago

To my husband, Jim, my daughters, Jen and Alli,
my mother, Lilo, and in memory of my father, Hans
and
To my son, Joel, so that he might read this book and
understand what his father was trying to teach him

Contents

Contents

Introduction

Our goal in this book is to help you learn about English grammar in as simple and straightforward a way as possible. The book was inspired by our students, most of whom panic when we say words like *adjective*, *subject*, and *passive*. We believe that panic will be replaced by knowledge and confidence as readers work their way through this user-friendly book.

Who is this book for? It's for anyone who needs or wants to understand English grammar. That includes readers who: (1) want to improve their writing; (2) are studying a foreign language; (3) are or want to be teachers; (4) are learning English as a second language; (5) are or want to be professionals such as speech–language pathologists and attorneys; (6) are interested in how English works. The book is self-guided and self-paced; it can be used alone or as part of a course.

The workbook approach used here will move you beyond simply labeling words to an understanding of how the different pieces of a sentence fit together. To help you achieve this understanding, we present information in small steps, with many opportunities to apply each new piece of information in exercises before you move on to the next step.

Like all languages, English is a collection of dialects. While society views some of these dialects as having more social prestige than others, when we look at them objectively we find that all dialects are equal linguistically. That means that all dialects have grammatical rules, and the grammatical rules of one dialect are no more precise, pure, or logical than the grammatical rules of another dialect. Nonetheless, in this book we focus on the grammar of Standard American English because it is widely known and because writing requires a knowledge of formal, standard English.

We deliberately limit this introductory book in both content and complexity. Wherever possible, we provide you with a simple rule of thumb to use. However, we don't claim to cover all of English sentence structure. A clear understanding of what usually works will give you a foundation for recognizing and understanding the exceptions. Our aim is to provide you with the basics.

This book will clarify English sentence structure and provide you with a useful reference book that you can turn to long after you've completed the exercises. It will also provide you with a solid foundation for more advanced study.

So take a deep breath and turn the page. We predict that it won't hurt a bit. In fact, you may be surprised to find out how easy *English Grammar* can be.

How to use this book

What are the features of this book that will help you use it effectively?

- We assume no prior knowledge of English grammar. Depending on your background and interest, you can either work the book through from cover to cover or just read about selected topics.
- We utilize user-friendly, easy-to-understand language, avoiding excessive technical terminology.
- Information is presented in lesson format; most lessons are short, helping to make the material manageable.
- Numerous exercises allow you to test yourself after new information is presented; the exercises gradually incorporate more knowledge while building on prior information.
- Each exercise has a sample item done for you, to help you with the exercise.
- Each exercise is separated into two parts: *Getting started* and *More practice*. With each *Getting started* part, we provide a page reference to the answers, so you'll immediately know whether or not you're on the right track. For *More practice* items, answers are provided on the accompanying website.
- In addition to exercises, each lesson contains easy to find *Quick tips*. These provide convenient "tricks" to help you master the material or highlight the main concepts in each lesson.
- We've also included short sections called *To enhance your understanding*. These sections are intended for those of you who are interested in more than basic information. These sections can easily be skipped by beginners; they're not necessary for understanding any material later on in the book.
- Throughout the text, ungrammatical sentences are identified with an asterisk (*) at the beginning.

How is this book organized?

- The book has three parts: Part I deals with types of words, Part II with types of phrases, and Part III with types of sentences.
- Each part is divided into units and each unit is subdivided into related lessons.
- Each lesson contains ample *Test yourself* exercises. Each exercise has ten questions, with answer keys provided at the end of each unit and on the accompanying website.
- A review matching exercise with an answer key is included at the end of each part.
- Additional review exercises for each unit are provided on the companion website.
- For easy reference, the end of the book contains a list of all *Quick tips*, a detailed glossary, and an index.

Website: www.cambridge.org/altenberg-vago

PART I: KINDS OF WORDS

Do you shudder when you hear the words *noun* or *verb*? Don't worry – you already know all about word categories, also known as parts of speech, though you may not think you do. You know, for example, that you can say *the idea* and *the boy* but not **the about* or **happy the*. (As stated in the *How to use this book* section, an asterisk [*] is used to indicate that something is ungrammatical.) That is, you know that some words can go in some places in a sentence and others can't. A word category, or part of speech, is just a name given to a group of words that have something in common, such as where they can go in a sentence. Part I gives you a quick and easy guide to basic word categories.

Lesson 1: Identifying nouns

Nouns are commonly defined as words that refer to a person, place, thing, or idea. How can you identify a noun?

> **Quick tip 1.1**
>
> If you can put the word *the* in front of a word and it sounds like a unit, the word is a noun.

For example, *the boy* sounds like a unit, so *boy* is a noun. *The chair* sounds like a unit, so *chair* is a noun. Compare these nouns to **the very*, **the walked*, **the because*. *Very*, *walked*, and *because* are not nouns. While you can easily put *the* and *very* together (for example, *the very tall boy*), *the very*, by itself, does not work as a unit while *the chair* does. So, *chair* is a noun; *very* is not. (There is one kind of noun that cannot always have *the* in front of it; see Lesson 6 later in this unit.)

Test yourself 1.1

Which of the following words are nouns? See if they sound like a unit when you put them here: *the _____*. Check the appropriate column.

	Noun	*Not a noun*
Sample: always	....	✗

Getting started (answers on p. 20)

1. tree	....	....
2. when	....	....
3. beds	....	....
4. glass	....	....
5. said	....	....

More practice (answers on the website)

6. slowly	....	....
7. factory	....	....
8. ticket	....	....
9. boxes	....	....
10. almost	....	....

Test yourself 1.2

Underline the nouns in these phrases. Test each word to see if it sounds like a unit when you put it here: *the _____*.
Sample: all my <u>friends</u>

Getting started (answers on p. 20)

1. your red sweater
2. those boxes
3. a few men
4. many digital photos
5. his very interesting article

More practice (answers on the website)

6. their carpets

7. a hand-painted plate

8. the court stenographer

9. our psychology professor

10. two interesting museums

Lesson 2: Concrete and abstract nouns

Here's an unusual sentence: *He smelled the marriage.* What makes this sentence unusual is that we don't generally think of the noun *marriage* as something that can be smelled. Some nouns are **concrete**: they can be perceived by our senses – they are things that we can see, hear, smell, taste, or touch. Those nouns that are not concrete are **abstract**. *Marriage* is something abstract, so it's odd to say it's being perceived by one of our senses, our sense of smell.

The nouns in Lesson 1 were all concrete nouns. Other nouns, such as *marriage*, are abstract; this means that they refer to things that you cannot perceive with your senses, things you cannot see, smell, feel, taste, or touch. Here are some more concrete and abstract nouns:

Concrete	Abstract
newspaper	love
heel	honesty
glass	culture
jewelry	mind

> **Quick tip 2.1**
>
> Concrete nouns refer to things we can perceive with one of our senses. Abstract nouns cannot be perceived by our senses.

Test yourself 2.1

Decide if each noun is concrete or abstract.
Sample: discussion   abstract

Getting started (answers on p. 20)

1. muffin ....
2. violin ....
3. freedom ....
4. elegance ....
5. train ....

More practice (answers on the website)

6. friend ....
7. friendliness ....
8. economics ....
9. dormitory ....
10. capitalism ....

Test yourself 2.2

Which of the following words are nouns? See if they sound like a unit when you put them here: *the _____.* The nouns will all be abstract nouns. Check the appropriate column.

	Noun	Not a noun
Sample: confusion	**×**	....

Getting started (answers on p. 20)   *More practice* (answers on the website)

1. concept ....   6. ran ....
2. shockingly ....   7. secret ....
3. wrote ....   8. her ....
4. conversation ....   9. death ....
5. interview ....   10. job ....

An abstract noun is sometimes easier to identify if you create a sentence with it. For example, *the happiness* is a unit, as can be seen in *The happiness on her face delighted him*. Thus, *happiness* is a noun. Here are some other abstract nouns in sentences; the nouns are underlined.

1. It was not the complaint which bothered him.
2. They were attempting to stop the abuse.
3. The joy which they felt was obvious.

Another easy way to identify a noun, especially an abstract noun, is to put the word *his* (or other words like it – see Lesson 21) in front of it and see if it sounds like a unit. For example, *his complaint*, *his happiness*, *his concern* all are units; therefore, *complaint*, *happiness*, and *concern* are nouns.

> **Quick tip 2.2**
>
> If you can put *his* in front of a word and it sounds like a unit, the word is a noun.

Test yourself 2.3

Which of the following words are nouns? See if they sound like a unit when you put them here: *his* _____. The nouns will all be abstract nouns. Check the appropriate column.

	Noun	*Not a noun*
Sample: obligation	✗	....

Getting started (answers on p. 20)   *More practice* (answers on the website)

1. jumped ....   6. closed ....
2. appropriate ....   7. celebration ....
3. popularity ....   8. their ....
4. emotions ....   9. news ....
5. real ....   10. spoken ....

Test yourself 2.4

Which of the following words are nouns? These are a mix of concrete and abstract nouns. Check the appropriate column.

	Noun	*Not a noun*
Sample: while	....	✗

Getting started (answers on p. 21)

1. repair ....
2. intelligence ....
3. a ....
4. skis ....
5. us ....

More practice (answers on the website)

6. obstruction ....
7. pounds ....
8. disgraceful ....
9. complicated ....
10. since ....

Test yourself 2.5

Underline the nouns in the sentences below. In this exercise, the nouns will all have *the* or *his* in front of them. Some will be concrete and some will be abstract. Some sentences have more than one noun.
Sample: His <u>answer</u> wasn't helpful.

Getting started (answers on p. 21)

1. She read the play over again.
2. The actions became monotonous.
3. He felt that his marriage, his relationship with her, was strong.
4. The time had finally come to confess the truth.
5. He's the boy who delivers the paper.

More practice (answers on the website)

6. The glitterati always like to follow the fashion of the day.
7. They will repair his stove.
8. The arrangement was good for all of them.
9. The audience stared at the screen, fascinated by the action they were seeing.
10. The definition was in his dictionary.

The nouns are underlined in the following sentences:
    4. This <u>author</u> lives with her <u>husband</u>.
    5. Do most <u>people</u> proceed contentedly through <u>life</u>?
    6. Your <u>photograph</u> of that <u>child</u> sleeping won you a <u>prize</u>.
As you can see from these sentences, while *the* _____ or *his* _____ are ways to test a word to see if it's a noun, a noun doesn't necessarily have *the* or *his* in front of it in every sentence. Since we can say *the author, the husband, the people, his life, the photograph, his child*, and *his prize*, the underlined words in sentences 4–6 are each nouns.

Test yourself 2.6

Underline the nouns in the sentences below. In this exercise, the nouns will not all have *the* or *his* in front of them. Just test each word to see if it can be a noun.
Sample: The <u>repair</u> of my <u>camera</u> went smoothly.

Getting started (answers on p. 21)

1. I wrote every word of the letter.
2. The house was near the city.
3. Why did he get on an elevator?
4. She has my phone.
5. Your younger brother was busy.

More practice (answers on the website)

6. A group of three generals sent the troops away.
7. The flag was near your desk.
8. My mother acted in a play.
9. He called the house every day.
10. You have to give her salary and benefits.

It's important to realize that the same word can often be used as more than one part of speech. For example, *repair* can be used as a noun (example: *The repair was relatively inexpensive*), as an adjective (example: *The repair manual was not very helpful*), or as a verb (example: *He needs to repair the washing machine*). We'll talk about verbs and adjectives in Units 2 and 4, respectively.

Lesson 3: Singular and plural nouns

What's the difference between *cat* and *cats*? The noun *cat* is used when it refers to only one cat; its form is **singular**. The noun *cats* is used when it represents more than one cat; its form is **plural**. Thus, the singular and plural forms tell us about **number**. Below are some nouns in their singular and plural forms.

Singular	*Plural*
box	boxes
bed	beds
kite	kites
day	days
country	countries
man	men
child	children

Test yourself 3.1

Underline each noun in the sentences below and indicate whether it is singular (SG) or plural (PL). There may be more than one noun in a sentence.

Sample: They used her computer (SG) to download the files (PL).

Getting started (answers on p. 21)

1. He had a few good ideas.
2. The boys spoke in a quiet whisper.
3. The tourists greeted the queen with attitudes of respect.
4. My neighbor is a neurologist.
5. The exterminator found bugs in the office.

More practice (answers on the website)

6. Sharks live in water.
7. Yesterday, I caught a big trout.
8. There are many beautiful homes on this block.
9. Visitors to this country must obtain visas.
10. His cousin fought in a brutal battle to free ninety hostages.

Regular and irregular plurals

Usually, we pluralize a noun by adding an "s" to it, as in *books*; these nouns are called **regular**. There are a handful of nouns that are pluralized in other ways; these nouns are called **irregular**.

Irregular nouns form their plural in different ways. Here are some common patterns:

1. changing a vowel: *man/men*, for example
2. adding "ren" or "en": *child/children*, for example
3. adding nothing: *fish/fish*, for example
4. changing "f" to "v" and then adding "s": *knife/knives*, for example

Test yourself 3.2

Underline each plural noun in the sentences below and indicate if it is regular (REG) or irregular (IRREG) in terms of how it is pluralized.

Sample: The women (IRREG) received their education at some exclusive schools (REG).

Getting started (answers on p. 21)

1. The doctor treated most of the patients who were waiting.

2. The geese crossed the road near my car.

3. She set a trap to catch the mice that had invaded her kitchen.

4. You will have to feed the oxen most afternoons.

5. Whenever I travel to the countryside, I see many sheep, ducks, deer, and cows.

More practice (answers on the website)

6. Those husbands and wives lead interesting lives.

7. Her feet have grown since last year.

8. The back window of my apartment overlooks about a dozen roofs.

9. The salesmen surrounded me in the showroom.

10. Kenneth had to buy two bottles of disinfectant to get rid of the lice in his bathroom.

To enhance your understanding

What is the plural of the "word" *blun*? Even though you've probably never seen this nonsense word, you're likely to say its plural is *bluns*. That's because we don't have to memorize the ending of regular plurals; we simply use our plural formation rule: "add *s*." But the forms for irregular plural words, like *children* and *men*, need to be memorized since they don't follow a consistent pattern.

To further enhance your understanding

Earlier we said that we usually pluralize a noun in English by adding an "s" to it. There's actually more to it than that, when one examines the pronunciation of regular nouns more closely.

Here are some regular English nouns:

A	B
cat	dog
lip	bee
myth	car
laugh	deal

Say each word in column A out loud, adding its plural ending. (Don't whisper, or this won't work.) You'll notice that, as you expect, you're adding an [s] sound to each word. (Symbols in square brackets [ ] indicate sounds rather than letters.) Now say each word in column B out loud, adding its plural ending. If you listen carefully, you'll notice that you're not adding an [s] sound to each word to make it plural. You're actually adding a [z] sound! (If English is not your native language, you may not be doing this.)

It turns out that we learned, when we were acquiring English as children, that it is the last *sound*, and not *letter*, of a regular noun that determines whether we add [s] or [z]. Some sounds (voiced sounds) are made with our vocal cords vibrating, like the strings of a guitar. Try this: hold your hand touching your throat, about where a man's Adam's apple is, while you say and hold a [v] sound ([v v v v v . . .]). You'll feel the vibration of your vocal cords.

Other sounds (voiceless sounds) are made with our vocal cords not vibrating. Now touch your hand to your throat again and this time say and hold an [f] sound ([f f f f f . . .]); you will notice the lack of vibration.

So how do we know whether to say the plural with an [s] or [z] sound? If the last sound of a word is a voiceless sound, we add an [s] sound to make it plural. If the last sound of a word is a voiced sound, we add a [z] sound to make it plural. This is not a rule that someone has ever taught us, but part of our unconscious knowledge of English.

Notice that having an [s] sound after voiceless sounds makes sense: [s] itself is voiceless. By the same reasoning, having a [z] after voiced sounds also makes sense: [z] itself is voiced. So what you can see is that the last sound of the noun and the sound of the regular plural share the same voicing characteristic: either the vocal cords vibrate for both sounds, or they don't.

You may have noticed that there's actually a third type of regular noun. Say the following words out loud, adding the plural ending to each:

glass	garage
maze	church
wish	judge

These words all already end in sounds (again, not letters) that are either [s] or [z] or sounds very similar to them. They are all "noisy" sounds. For the plural forms of these words, we add a vowel sound (written with the letter *e*) followed by a [z] sound (but written with the letter *s*): glass_es_, maz_es_, wish_es_, garag_es_, church_es_, judg_es_. If you think about it, pronouncing a vowel between the noisy sound at the end of the noun and the noisy sound [z] of the plural makes sense: without that vowel, we would have two noisy sounds in a row, something that would be harder for the listener to hear clearly.

Wow! You may want to just pause for a moment here and contemplate the complexity of what you know about your language. And you knew how to do this before you even went to kindergarten! You just haven't known that you know it.

Lesson 4: Animate and inanimate nouns

Take a look at the following sentence:

1. *The postcard saw the mailman.*

What's strange about this sentence? What's strange is that we don't expect a postcard, which is not alive, to be able to see something; only things that are alive have the ability to see. Nouns that refer to things that are alive are called **animate**, while nouns that refer to things that are not alive are called **inanimate**. *Postcard* is an inanimate noun and using it as an animate one makes for a very unusual sentence.

> **Quick tip 4.1**
>
> Animate nouns refer to things that are alive; inanimate nouns refer to things that are not alive.

Test yourself 4.1

Decide if each noun is animate or inanimate.
Sample: apple   inanimate

Getting started (answers on p. 21)

1. word   ....
2. lizard   ....
3. glasses   ....
4. calendar   ....
5. baby   ....

More practice (answers on the website)

6. criminal   ....
7. furniture   ....
8. doctor   ....
9. mouse   ....
10. truck   ....

Now take a look at the following sentence:

2. The dog wrote a best-selling novel.

Again, there's something strange here. We know that *dog* is animate. However, only a special type of animate noun has the ability to write a best-selling novel: a **human** noun. The following sentence is fine, since *teacher* is a human animate noun: *My teacher wrote a best-selling novel*. On the other hand, since *dog* is a **nonhuman** animate noun, sentence 2 does not sound right.

To summarize: nouns may be human animate *(teacher)*, nonhuman animate *(dog)*, or inanimate *(postcard)*.

Test yourself 4.2

Decide if each noun is animate or inanimate. If a noun is animate, decide if it is human or nonhuman.
Sample: chair   inanimate

Getting started (answers on p. 21)

1. dinner ....

2. pet ....

3. friend ....

4. child ....

5. spider ....

More practice (answers on the website)

6. tablecloth ....

7. recipes ....

8. assassin ....

9. shark ....

10. freedom ....

Lesson 5: Count and noncount nouns

Let's take a closer look at the noun *hand*. Notice that you can say the following:

the hand   a hand   hands

Here are some other nouns which demonstrate the same pattern:

the store   a store   stores
the idea   an idea   ideas
the tissue   a tissue   tissues

Let's compare *hand* to the noun *furniture*. As with *hand*, we can say *the furniture*. But we can't say **a furniture* or **furnitures*. Here are some other nouns which demonstrate the same pattern as *furniture*:

the dust   *a dust   *dusts
the energy   *an energy   *energies
the biology   *a biology   *biologies

Thus, there are some nouns that can be counted, and so we can use *a* or *an* with them and can also make them plural. These nouns are called, appropriately, **count** nouns. *Hand* is a count noun. So are *store*, *idea*, and *tissue*.

There are other nouns that typically are not counted, and so we do not use *a* or *an* with them and do not typically make them plural. These nouns are called, also appropriately, **noncount** nouns. (Another name for a noncount noun is a **mass** noun.) *Furniture* is a noncount noun. So are *dust*, *energy*, and *biology*.

You may well be saying to yourself, "Wait a minute. I can count furniture. I can say something like: three couches and three chairs make six pieces of furniture." And of course, you'd be right. But notice that in this sentence, the words *couch* and *chair* can be made plural, but not the word *furniture*. And the word *piece* can be made plural, but, again, not the word *furniture*.

Quick tip 5.1

If you can pluralize a noun in a sentence, it is functioning as a count noun.

Note that a noun is considered to be a count noun if it <u>can</u> be made plural, even if it's not plural in a particular sentence. Thus, in the sentence *I ate a cookie*, *cookie* is a count noun because one <u>could</u> pluralize it to *cookies* without changing its basic meaning.

Test yourself 5.1

For each underlined noun in the sentences below, indicate if it is count (C) or noncount (NC). Use the plural test to help you.

Sample: Her <u>hairstyle</u> (C) clearly revealed her face.

Getting started (answers on p. 22)

1. The <u>lights</u> (   ) of the <u>city</u> (   ) twinkled.

2. I love eating <u>rice</u> (   ).

3. His <u>anger</u> (   ) was barely under control.

4. Her <u>job</u> (   ) was rather demanding.

5. Many types of <u>information</u> (   ) are available at the <u>library</u> (   ).

More practice (answers on the website)

6. The <u>police</u> (   ) will be here in a moment.

7. He leaned on the <u>handle</u> (   ) and cursed.

8. I was so thirsty, I needed three <u>glasses</u> (   ) of <u>water</u> (   ).

9. How much <u>money</u> (   ) do you make in an <u>hour</u> (   )?

10. By 11 P.M., the <u>train-station</u> (   ) was nearly empty.

There is also another good way to decide if a noun is count or noncount. Take a look at the use of the words *much* and *many* in the following sentences.

1. He has <u>many children</u>.
2. That man has <u>many interests</u>.
3. That will take too <u>much time</u>.
4. They have <u>many lights</u> on in the house.
5. We have <u>much furniture</u> in our store.
6. I wonder how <u>much wealth</u> is in Silicon Valley.

As you may have noticed, *many* is used with count nouns, *much* is used with noncount nouns.

> **Quick tip 5.2**
>
> If you can use *many* with a noun (when it is pluralized), it's a count noun. If you can use *much* with a noun, it's a noncount noun.

And we have still another way to distinguish count from noncount nouns:

7. He has <u>fewer children</u> than I do.
8. That man has <u>fewer interests</u> than he used to.
9. That will take <u>less time</u> than I thought.
10. They have <u>fewer lights</u> on in the house.
11. We have <u>less furniture</u> in our store.
12. I don't have <u>less money</u> in my purse than you have.

As you've probably figured out from these examples, we use *fewer* with count nouns and *less* with noncount nouns.

> **Quick tip 5.3**
>
> If you can use *fewer* with a noun (when it is pluralized), it's a count noun. If you can use *less* with a noun, it's a noncount noun.

15

Test yourself 5.2

For each underlined noun in the sentences below, indicate if it is being used as a count (C) or noncount (NC) noun in that sentence. Use the plural, *much/many*, or *fewer/less* tests to help you. Sample: Their new album (C) was a huge hit.

Getting started (answers on p. 22)

1. Algebra (　　　) was one of my worst subjects (　　　) in high school (　　　).

2. I had no idea that there were various theories (　　　), such as Euclidean and fractal.

3. The smoke (　　　) rose through the chimney (　　　).

4. Bread (　　　) is a staple in many societies (　　　).

5. She decided to push the issue (　　　) further.

More practice (answers on the website)

6. People (　　　) are funny sometimes.

7. The government (　　　) of the United States has three branches (　　　).

8. Senators (　　　) can spend money (　　　) unnecessarily.

9. It takes effort (　　　) to get a good grade (　　　) in Mr. Goodman's class (　　　).

10. The reporters (　　　) wrote the story (　　　).

To enhance your understanding

Many nouns can be used as either count nouns or as noncount nouns, depending on how they are being used in a specific sentence. Let's look at the following sentence containing the word *sugar*:

　　13. The sugar is spilling onto the floor.

In this sentence, is *sugar* being used as a count or noncount noun? Would you say: *The sugars are spilling onto the floor*? or *Many sugars are spilling onto the floor*? Probably not. So *sugar*, in sentence 13, is a noncount noun.

　Now take a look at another sentence with *sugar*:

　　14. This gourmet shop has sugars I've never even heard of.

In this sentence, is *sugar* being used as a count or noncount noun? First, notice that *sugar* here is pluralized. Second, notice that you can say *This gourmet shop has many sugars I've never even heard of*. So *sugar*, in sentence 14, is a count noun. In terms of meaning, what is important here is that the sentence is talking about different types of sugars, say, brown sugar, white sugar, confectioners' sugar, etc.

　And one more sentence type with *sugar*:

　　15. The sugar that works best in this recipe is brown sugar.

Here, *sugar*, while not pluralized, could be pluralized and refers, in fact, to a kind of sugar. For example, you could say: *The sugars that work best in this recipe are brown sugar and white sugar*. For these reasons, *sugar* is being used here as a count noun.

　Here are some more examples of sentences with nouns which, like *sugar*, are typically used as noncount nouns but can also be used as count nouns.

　　16a. I like to drink milk. (*milk* used as noncount noun)

　　16b. That store has milks with different kinds of flavoring: chocolate, vanilla, mocha, and strawberry. (*milks* used as count noun)

16c. The milk that is the healthiest is nonfat milk. (*milk* used as count noun)

17a. A plentiful supply of water is important for a community's survival. (*water* used as noncount noun)

17b. There are different kinds of gourmet waters on the market these days. (*waters* used as count noun)

17c. The water I usually order in restaurants is imported. (*water* used as count noun)

Lesson 6: Proper and common nouns

Do the following sentences look a little strange?

1. Mrs. smith took the 10th grade class of lincoln high school to france for a trip.
2. The class visited paris and was thrilled to see the eiffel tower.

Normally, we capitalize the first letter of nouns that are actual names, no matter where they are in a sentence. Let's look at the same sentences with the names capitalized:

3. Mrs. Smith took the 10th grade class of Lincoln High School to France for a trip.
4. The class visited Paris and was thrilled to see the Eiffel Tower.

Nouns that are actual names are called **proper** nouns; nouns that are not names are called **common** nouns. Notice that not only people have names: places (*Rome*), companies (*IBM*), and books (*Gone With the Wind*), among others, can have names, too.

> **Quick tip 6.1**
>
> Nouns that are actual names, for example *Mary*, are called proper nouns. Nouns that are not names are called common nouns, e.g. *girl*.

> **Quick tip 6.2**
>
> One way to identify a proper noun is to ask yourself: is this a noun I would capitalize, no matter where it is in a sentence? If so, it's a proper noun.

Test yourself 6.1

For each noun below, determine if it is a proper noun or common noun. For this exercise, the proper nouns are not capitalized.

Sample: england <u>proper</u>

Getting started (answers on p. 22)

1. seattle ....
2. crater lake national park ....
3. tissues ....
4. sofa ....
5. pepsi cola ....

More practice (answers on the website)

6. mediterranean sea ....
7. disneyland ....
8. company ....
9. british broadcasting company ....
10. television ....

To enhance your understanding

In Lesson 1 we said that words that can have *the* in front of them and sound like a complete unit are nouns. That still works. The reverse, however, is not true: not all proper nouns can have *the* in front of them. Compare the following proper nouns. Those on the left use *the*; those on the right do not.

5. a. The United States   Great Britain
        The Netherlands   France
    b. The Holy See   Holy Cross University
    c. The Jolly Green Giant   Big Foot
    d. The Bronx   Manhattan

Most proper nouns don't use *the* – just think of the names of people you know. Those few cases where a proper noun does use *the* are exceptions; we memorize those.

Answer keys: *Test yourself, Getting started questions – Unit 1*

Test yourself 1.1

	Noun	Not a noun
1. tree	✗	
2. when		✗
3. beds	✗	
4. glass	✗	
5. said		✗

Test yourself 1.2

1. your red <u>sweater</u>
2. those <u>boxes</u>
3. a few <u>men</u>
4. many digital <u>photos</u>
5. his very interesting <u>article</u>

Test yourself 2.1

1. muffin <u>concrete</u>
2. violin <u>concrete</u>
3. freedom <u>abstract</u>
4. elegance <u>abstract</u>
5. train <u>concrete</u>

Test yourself 2.2

	Noun	Not a noun
1. concept	✗	
2. shockingly		✗
3. wrote		✗
4. conversation	✗	
5. interview	✗	

Test yourself 2.3

	Noun	Not a noun
1. jumped		✗
2. appropriate		✗
3. popularity	✗	
4. emotions	✗	
5. real		✗

Test yourself 2.4

	Noun	Not a noun
1. repair	✗	
2. intelligence	✗	
3. a		✗
4. skis	✗	
5. us		✗

Test yourself 2.5

1. She read the play over again.
2. The actions became monotonous.
3. He felt that his marriage, his relationship with her, was strong.
4. The time had finally come to confess the truth.
5. He's the boy who delivers the paper.

Test yourself 2.6

1. I wrote every word of the letter.
2. The house was near the city.
3. Why did he get on an elevator?
4. She has my phone.
5. Your younger brother was busy.

Test yourself 3.1

1. He had a few good ideas (PL).
2. The boys (PL) spoke in a quiet whisper (SG).
3. The tourists (PL) greeted the queen (SG) with attitudes (PL) of respect (SG).
4. My neighbor (SG) is a neurologist (SG).
5. The exterminator (SG) found bugs (PL) in the office (SG).

Test yourself 3.2

1. The doctor treated most of the patients (REG) who were waiting.
2. The geese (IRREG) crossed the road near my car.
3. She set a trap to catch the mice (IRREG) that had invaded her kitchen.
4. You will have to feed the oxen (IRREG) most afternoons (REG).
5. Whenever I travel to the countryside, I see many sheep (IRREG), ducks (REG), deer (IRREG), and cows (REG).

Test yourself 4.1

1. word	inanimate
2. lizard	animate
3. glasses	inanimate
4. calendar	inanimate
5. baby	animate

Test yourself 4.2

1. dinner	inanimate
2. pet	nonhuman animate

3. friend   <u>human animate</u>
4. child   <u>human animate</u>
5. spider   <u>nonhuman animate</u>

Test yourself 5.1

1. The <u>lights</u> (C) of the <u>city</u> (C) twinkled.
2. I love eating <u>rice</u> (NC).
3. His <u>anger</u> (NC) was barely under control.
4. Her <u>job</u> (C) was rather demanding.
5. Many types of <u>information</u> (NC) are available at the <u>library</u> (C).

Test yourself 5.2

1. <u>Algebra</u> (NC) was one of my worst <u>subjects</u> (C) in <u>high school</u> (C).
2. I had no idea that there were various <u>theories</u> (C), such as Euclidean and fractal.
3. The <u>smoke</u> (NC) rose through the <u>chimney</u> (C).
4. <u>Bread</u> (NC) is a staple in many <u>societies</u> (C).
5. She decided to push the <u>issue</u> (C) further.

Test yourself 6.1

1. seattle   <u>proper</u>
2. crater lake national park   <u>proper</u>
3. tissues   <u>common</u>
4. sofa   <u>common</u>
5. pepsi cola   <u>proper</u>

☞ **FOR A REVIEW EXERCISE OF THIS UNIT, SEE THE WEBSITE.**

Lesson 7: Identifying verbs

What's a verb? **Verbs** are words that usually express an action. Here are two easy ways to identify a verb; you can use either one.

> **Quick tip 7.1**
>
> If a word can have *should* in front of it and the phrase sounds complete, the word is a verb. Examples: *should leave, should sail, should discover, should complain. Leave, sail, discover,* and *complain* are all verbs.

> **Quick tip 7.2**
>
> If a word can have *to* in front of it and the phrase sounds complete, it's a verb. Examples: *to leave, to sail, to discover, to complain. Leave, sail, discover,* and *complain* are all verbs. (Note that we're not talking here about *two, too,* or the *to* that indicates direction, as in *Let's go to the park.*)

Here are some examples of verbs. You can see that they all meet the test with *should* and the test with *to.*

go:	should go	to go
tell:	should tell	to tell
disagree:	should disagree	to disagree
spell:	should spell	to spell

In contrast, the following words do not pass the *should* or *to* test:

coffee:	*should coffee	*to coffee
beautiful:	*should beautiful	*to beautiful
hardly:	*should hardly	*to hardly
under:	*should under	*to under

Thus, *coffee, beautiful, hardly,* and *under* are not verbs.

Test yourself 7.1

Which of the following words are verbs? See if they sound like a complete unit when you put the word here: *should* _____ or *to* _____. Check the appropriate column.

	Verb	Not a verb
Sample: characteristic	....	**✗**

Getting started (answers on p. 41)

1. defend ....
2. include ....
3. largest ....
4. how ....
5. learn ....

More practice (answers on the website)

6. sightsee ....
7. unbelievably ....
8. look ....
9. grow ....
10. ambitious ....

Test yourself 7.2

Underline the verbs in these phrases. Test each word to see if it sounds like a complete unit when you put the word here: *should* _____ or *to* _____.
Sample: should really <u>think</u>

Getting started (answers on p. 41)

1. must not worry
2. might keep
3. wish for peace
4. may sometimes cook
5. will travel

More practice (answers on the website)

6. can usually sleep late
7. won't go home
8. would like guidance
9. could never build
10. shall do

Lesson 8: The verb base

Sometimes a verb changes its form. Let's look at the following sentences. The verb is underlined in each one.

    1. John should <u>study</u>.
    2. John <u>studied</u>.
    3. John is <u>studying</u>.
    4. John <u>studies</u>.

You certainly can't say, **John should studied*, or *John to studied*, so how do we know that *studied* is a verb? To test the word, you have to see if it can follow *should* or *to* in a different form, not necessarily in the form that you see in a particular sentence. For example, if you see *John studied*, ask yourself if there's a different form of *studied* that can follow *should* or *to*. In this case there is: *John should study* or *John decided to study*. So *study* and all its forms are verbs. The form of the verb that follows *should* or *to* is called the **base form** or **infinitive form**. The term *infinitive* is used to refer either to the base form alone (for example, *study*), or to the *to* + base form (for example, *to study*).

    Let's put each of these verbs into its base form. The base form is underlined.

    5. working: (should, to) <u>work</u>
    6. believed: (should, to) <u>believe</u>
    7. written: (should, to) <u>write</u>
    8. wore: (should, to) <u>wear</u>
    9. throws: (should, to) <u>throw</u>

Test yourself 8.1

Put each of the verbs below into its base form. Simply find the form that follows *should* or *to*.
Sample: grew: <u>grow</u>

Getting started (answers on p. 41)

1. wrote: ....
2. talking: ....
3. thought: ....
4. considered: ....
5. seen: ....

More practice (answers on the website)

6. investigates: ....
7. spoken: ....
8. married: ....
9. decides: ....
10. found: ....

Test yourself 8.2

Which of the following words are verbs? You may have to put some into their base form in order to be sure. Remember also that a verb usually indicates an action.

	Verb	Not a verb
Sample: flow	**✗**	....

Getting started (answers on p. 41)

1. danced   ....

2. sofa   ....

3. large   ....

4. gave   ....

5. stares   ....

More practice (answers on the website)

6. pushed   ....

7. goodness   ....

8. at   ....

9. carries   ....

10. them   ....

Test yourself 8.3

Underline the verbs in each of the sentences below, using the *should* or *to* tests to help you. You may have to put some verbs into their base forms in order to be sure. Remember also that a verb usually indicates an action.

Sample: She <u>grabbed</u> his arm.

Getting started (answers on p. 41)

1. The host greeted us cordially.

2. She should say that again.

3. Jonathan walked over to the car.

4. He washes dishes every evening.

5. You can't speak Vietnamese.

More practice (answers on the website)

6. My neighbor flew to Chicago.

7. The children wanted some candy.

8. Tomorrow we might go to the museum.

9. The censor usually objects to the same seven words.

10. In the afternoon I bought a present for my son.

Lesson 9: Action verbs and linking verbs

The verbs we have looked at so far, such as *go*, *sing*, and *revise*, all indicate actions. In fact, they're called **action verbs**. However, there are other verbs which don't indicate actions. These are most commonly called **linking verbs**. One example of such a verb is the word *seem*, as in the sentences, *You seem tired*, *They've seemed busy lately*. Don't worry, though: *seem* still follows our *should* or *to* rules: *Harry should seem surprised at times*; *You don't want to seem arrogant, do you?* So even though *seem* isn't indicating an action, it's easy to identify it as a verb. Other examples of linking verbs are *resemble* and *become*. Linking verbs express a relationship between the noun or pronoun that comes before the linking verb and whatever follows it. (For pronouns, see Unit 7.)

Test yourself 9.1

Which of the following words are verbs? See if each sounds like a complete unit when you put the word here: *should* _____ or *to* _____. Check the appropriate column. All the verbs will be linking verbs. You may have to put some in their base form to be sure.

	Verb	*Not a verb*
Sample: appear	✗	

Getting started (answers on p. 42)

1. tasted
2. friendly
3. shady
4. be
5. got

More practice (answers on the website)

6. look
7. huge
8. seven
9. ocean
10. sound

Test yourself 9.2

Underline the verbs in these sentences. Test each word to see if it sounds like a complete unit when you put the word here: *should* _____ or *to* _____. All the verbs will be linking verbs. You may have to put some in their base form to be sure.
Sample: She <u>looked</u> happy.

Getting started (answers on p. 42)

1. Barry will feel awful about it.
2. Melissa resembles her mother.
3. Zack sounded extremely angry.
4. The fish tasted undercooked.
5. You were not home early.

More practice (answers on the website)

6. The final exam proved difficult.
7. That dinner smells so good!
8. The firefighters remain at the station all night long.
9. They stayed indoors throughout their ordeal.
10. By noon the weather turned nice.

The most common linking verb is the verb *be*, often called the **copula**. You can see different forms of the verb *be* in the following sentences.

1. I am happy.
2. You are happy.
3. He is happy.
4. I was happy.
5. You were happy.
6. I have been happy.
7. He is being happy.

Notice how different these forms are from the base form of *be*. In fact, *be* is the most irregular verb in the English language: it has more forms than any other verb. But you can still use the *should* or *to* test to identify *be* as a verb: *You should be happy*, *They decided to be happy*. For convenience, the forms of *be* are indicated in *Quick tip* 9.1.

> **Quick tip 9.1**
>
> The forms of the irregular verb *be* are: *am, are, is, was, were, be, been, being*.

Note that *be* and *become* are two different verbs. Here are the forms of *become*: *become, becomes, became, becoming*.

Test yourself 9.3

Underline the forms of *be* in each of the sentences below. Some sentences may contain more than one form of *be*.
Sample: It is a privilege to meet you.

Getting started (answers on p. 42)

1. Paul was in power at that moment.
2. They are absolutely correct in their thinking.
3. Your suitcases were in the overhead compartment during the flight.
4. Christina has been wanting to go to Europe for a long time.
5. What is wrong with being a good student?

More practice (answers on the website)

6. The situation is getting out of hand.
7. My niece wants to be a psychiatrist when she grows up.
8. The problem is being corrected as we speak.
9. History might be being made right now.
10. I am happy to show you around town.

Often, forms of the verb *be* are said and written as contractions, as in these sentences:

8. I'm happy. (verb = am)
9. He's happy. (verb = is)
10. We're happy. (verb = are)
11. He's being happy. (verb = is)

These are all still sentences with *be*.

For more on the verb *be*, see Lessons 34 and 35.

Test yourself 9.4

Underline the forms of *be* in each of the sentences below. Some will be written as contractions.
Sample: It's unusual to see rain at this time of the year.

Getting started (answers on p. 42)

1. They're usually home by now.

2. Are you worried about anything?

3. I heard that the flight was late.

4. We're honored by your presence.

5. It's too bad that the Yankees lost last night.

More practice (answers on the website)

6. I think she's my husband's new boss.

7. The tyrant will certainly be accused of crimes against humanity.

8. You're a real good friend.

9. I'm afraid to tell you the truth.

10. It has been far too long since we last saw each other.

Test yourself 9.5

Which of these words is a verb? See if it sounds like a complete unit when you put the word here: *should* _____ or *to* _____. Check the appropriate column. Some of the verbs are linking verbs and some are action verbs. All the verbs will be in their base forms.

	Verb	Not a verb
Sample: run	✗	....

Getting started (answers on p. 42)

1. resemble	....	....
2. become	....	....
3. this	....	....
4. be	....	....
5. new	....	....

More practice (answers on the website)

6. although	....	....
7. search	....	....
8. grow	....	....
9. without	....	....
10. really	....	....

Test yourself 9.6

Which of these words is a verb? You may have to put some in their base forms in order to be sure. Some are linking verbs.

	Verb	Not a verb
Sample: orange	....	✗

Getting started (answers on p. 42)

1. appeared	....	....
2. attends	....	....
3. whenever	....	....
4. was	....	....
5. heard	....	....

More practice (answers on the website)

6. did	....	....
7. you	....	....
8. living	....	....
9. completes	....	....
10. eraser	....	....

Test yourself 9.7

Underline the verb in each of the following sentences. You may have to put some in their base forms and test each word with *should* or *to* in order to be sure of your answer. Each sentence has only one verb. The verbs in this exercise are all action verbs.

Sample: He <u>bakes</u> cookies for his son's birthday.

Getting started (answers on p. 43)

1. The car spun out of control.

2. Don't talk during the movie.

3. The doctor tied a strip of gauze around her hand.

4. Maxine spent too much money.

5. They saw the play last Sunday.

More practice (answers on the website)

6. Molly received a reply to her letter.

7. He ate on the stoop of the front porch.

8. Grandma held the kitten in her lap.

9. She never says anything.

10. They wash the windows regularly.

Test yourself 9.8

Identify the verb in each of the following sentences. You may have to put some in their base forms and test each word with *should* or *to* in order to be sure of your answer. Each sentence has only one verb. The verbs in this exercise will be either action or linking verbs.
Sample: Bridget <u>spent</u> hours in the dusty old bookstore.

Getting started (answers on p. 43)

1. That was the best meal in the world.

2. I understand your point.

3. Maybe they know each other well.

4. She is from Wisconsin.

5. Those flowers smell heavenly.

More practice (answers on the website)

6. It seemed late.

7. Johnny packed all our things.

8. Mother is always right about that.

9. She went down to the basement.

10. I felt wonderful about my decision.

How can you determine if a verb is being used as an action verb or a linking verb? There are a number of differences between them. One way is to think of a linking verb as an equal sign (=). For example:

    12. Harry resembles his brother.
        Harry = his brother.
    13. You are bored.
        You = bored.
    14. That strange looking vegetable tastes awful.
        That strange looking vegetable = awful.

Resembles, *are*, and *tastes* are each being used here as linking verbs.

    Another way to identify a linking verb is to see if you can substitute a form of *be* for it, and leave the meaning basically the same. For example, take the sentence *John seems interested in the conversation*. We can substitute a form of *be*, specifically, *is*, for *seems*: *John is interested in the conversation*. Thus, *seems* is a linking verb in the sentence *John seems interested in the conversation*. Take a look at some more examples.

    15. After a while, the hotel <u>became</u> dingy.
        After a while, the hotel <u>was</u> dingy.
    16. Annie and Janine <u>look</u> surprised.
        Annie and Janine <u>are</u> surprised.

17. Although in his eighties, he <u>remains</u> youthful-looking.

    Although in his eighties, he <u>is</u> youthful-looking.

Thus, *became*, *look*, and *remains* are being used as linking verbs in these sentences. Remember that *be* and its forms can also be used as linking verbs. While *Quick tip* 9.2 below isn't foolproof, it will usually help you identify whether a verb is an action or linking verb.

> ### Quick tip 9.2
>
> If you can substitute a form of *be* for a verb and the meaning of the sentence is basically the same, the verb is probably being used as a linking verb. The verb *be* and its forms are also linking verbs.

Another way to identify a linking verb is to see if you can substitute a form of the word *seem* for it, and leave the meaning basically the same. For example, in the sentence, *The hot shower felt soothing*, we can substitute a form of *seem* for *felt*, and leave the sentence largely unchanged: *The hot shower seemed soothing*. Note the following examples:

18a. After a while, the hotel <u>became</u> dingy.

18b. After a while, the hotel <u>seemed</u> dingy.

19a. Annie and Janine <u>look</u> surprised.

19b. Annie and Janine <u>seem</u> surprised.

20a. Although in his eighties, he <u>remains</u> youthful-looking.

20b. Although in his eighties, he <u>seems</u> youthful-looking.

Thus, *became*, *look*, and *remains* are being used as linking verbs in these sentences. Again, while *Quick tip* 9.3 below also isn't foolproof, it will help you identify whether a verb is an action or linking verb.

> ### Quick tip 9.3
>
> If you can substitute a form of *seem* for a verb and the meaning of the sentence is basically the same, the verb is probably being used as a linking verb.

Test yourself 9.9

Decide if the underlined verbs in the sentences below are action or linking verbs. In this exercise, if it's a form of *be*, it's being used as a linking verb. If it's not a form of *be*, use the *be* or *seem* substitution tests to see if the verb is being used as a linking verb.

	Action	*Linking*
Sample: She <u>laughed</u> at all his jokes.	✗	

Getting started (answers on p. 43)

	Action	*Linking*
1. The Czar <u>was</u> a person of high rank.		
2. That dog <u>barks</u> a lot.		
3. Mr. Kelly <u>watched</u> the traffic below his window.		
4. You have <u>been</u> a terrific friend to me over the years.		
5. I love the way the pillows <u>feel</u> so cozy in this hotel.		

More practice (answers on the website)

6. Jimmy is always eager to <u>answer</u> any questions. ....

7. Finding a healthy meal on the menu <u>proved</u> easy. ....

8. He<u>'s</u> not as smart as he led me to believe. ....

9. We could <u>hear</u> the neighbors arguing for hours. ....

10. That <u>sounds</u> good to me. ....

Test yourself 9.10

Underline the verb in each sentence below and decide if it's being used as an action or linking verb. In this exercise, if the verb is a form of *be*, it's being used as a linking verb. If it's not a form of *be*, use the *be* or *seem* substitution tests to see if the verb is being used as a linking verb.

	Action	*Linking*
Sample: The policeman <u>gave</u> him a ticket.	✗	....

Getting started (answers on p. 43)

1. They became best friends. ....

2. It is not nearly the same as mine. ....

3. Unfortunately, I forgot your birthday this year. ....

4. I went to the corner bakery. ....

5. Mark remains a legend to this day. ....

More practice (answers on the website)

6. Trigonometry bores me. ....

7. Babies often get hungry. ....

8. No one got a C on the midterm exam. ....

9. It's much ado about nothing. ....

10. He made such a fuss over a minor mistake. ....

Hopefully you now have a good sense of the difference between action and linking verbs. However, there are some verbs that can be used as either an action verb or a linking verb, depending on the sentence that it's in. Compare, for example, the following two sentences with *feel*:

    21. Mary <u>felt</u> tired.

    22. Mary <u>felt</u> the softness of the material.

In sentence 21, *felt* is being used as a linking verb. Note that *Mary = tired*; *Mary is tired*, *Mary seems tired* all make sense here. In sentence 22, Mary is doing an action. Also, one can't think of it as: **Mary = the softness of the material*, **Mary was the softness of the material*, or **Mary seemed the softness of the material*. That is, thinking of *felt* as an equal sign or substituting a form of *be* or *seem* for *felt* clearly doesn't work here. Thus, in sentence 22, *felt* is being used as an action verb.

Here are a few more examples:

23. The dinner at that restaurant <u>tasted</u> delicious. (linking verb)
    (The dinner at that restaurant was delicious.)
24. I <u>tasted</u> the soup. (action verb)
    (*I was the soup.)
25. The flowers <u>smelled</u> heavenly. (linking verb)
    (The flowers are heavenly.)
26. She <u>smelled</u> the fire before she saw it. (action verb)
    (*She was the fire before she saw it.)

Test yourself 9.11

Underline the verb in each sentence below and decide if it's being used as an action or linking verb.

	Action	Linking
Sample: The crowd <u>grew</u> angry.	....	.....**×**.....

Getting started (answers on p. 43)

1. He grew potatoes on his farm.	....	....
2. I looked at the mess all around me.	....	....
3. Stephen looks happy today.	....	....
4. In reality, exceptions rarely prove the rule.	....	....
5. Learning the rule proved difficult.	....	....

More practice (answers on the website)

6. I got nervous before my blood test.	....	....
7. I got a spasm in my arm.	....	....
8. The idea of having a pizza sounds real good.	....	....
9. Last night a burglar sounded the alarm.	....	....
10. You rarely become a star overnight.	....	....

To enhance your understanding

Another important difference between action and linking verbs is that a linking verb can be followed by just an adjective, while an action verb cannot:

27. She <u>is</u> tired. (*Tired* is an adjective.)
28. The mayor <u>looked</u> victorious. (*Victorious* is an adjective.)
29. *She <u>washed</u> tired.
30. *The mayor <u>voted</u> victorious.

As you can see, *is* and *looked* are linking verbs in these sentences; *washed* and *voted* are action verbs. However, since we haven't yet talked about adjectives (see Lesson 16), just keep this in mind as another difference between the two types of verbs.

To further enhance your understanding

Compare the following two sentences:

31a. She looked careful. (*careful* is an adjective)

31b. She looked carefully. (*carefully* is an adverb)

Can you sense the difference? In sentence 31a the verb *looked* is a linking verb, followed by the adjective *careful*; the basic meaning of the sentence is *She looked like she was a careful person*. In contrast, in sentence 31b *looked* is an action verb, followed by the adverb *carefully* (adverbs will be discussed in Lesson 27); the basic meaning of this sentence is *She looked around in a careful manner*. *Quick tip* 9.4 identifies yet another difference between linking verbs and action verbs.

Quick tip 9.4

Linking verbs are followed or modified by adjectives, while action verbs are followed or modified by adverbs.

Test yourself 9.12 – Grand finale

If you can do this exercise, you've achieved a basic understanding of nouns and verbs.

In each sentence below, underline the nouns and put a squiggly line under each verb. Each sentence has only one verb but may have more than one noun.

Sample: The judges were unanimous in their decision.

Getting started (answers on p. 43)

1. Their daughter announced her engagement later.

2. The surgeon washed his hands.

3. The pianist was diligent.

4. The young boy gritted his teeth.

5. Her assistant is always late.

More practice (answers on the website)

6. The mayor explained his position.

7. The train came early.

8. Three other customers placed orders that day.

9. Her friend was helpful.

10. That hot meal tastes great.

Lesson 10: Transitive and intransitive verbs

Take a look at the following questions, each with an action verb.

1. What did you <u>write</u>?
2. Who did you <u>annoy</u>?
3. What did you <u>throw</u>?

These are all perfectly fine questions and easy to answer, e.g. *I wrote a letter, I annoyed my neighbor, I threw a ball*.

Now compare the first group of questions to the next group, each of which also has an action verb.

4. *What did you *sleep*?
5. *What did you *die*?
6. *Who did you *arrive*?

These questions are all strange and can't really be answered. That's because the verbs in this second group are verbs that do not act on anything.

Thus, you can see that there are two kinds of verbs. One kind, such as *write, annoy*, and *throw*, acts upon something. The noun (or noun phrase; see Lesson 28) that the verb acts upon is called the **direct object** of the sentence. (You'll learn more about direct objects in Lesson 39.) Those verbs that act on something are called **transitive** verbs. Typically, in statements, a transitive verb is followed by the noun (or noun phrase) that it is acting upon.

Other verbs, such as *sleep, die*, and *arrive*, do not act upon something. In fact, these verbs can't have a direct object. Notice that you can't say, for example: *I usually sleep the dog*, *They'll arrive the book*. Those verbs that do not act on something and appear in sentences that do not have a direct object are called **intransitive** verbs.

> ### Quick tip 10.1
>
> Action verbs that act upon something are called transitive verbs. Action verbs that do not act upon something are called intransitive verbs.

> ### Quick tip 10.2
>
> If a verb (in any of its forms) can be put in one of the following slots, it is transitive: (a) What did you _____? (b) Who did you _____? If a verb cannot be put in one of these slots, it is intransitive.

So, which of the following verbs are transitive and which intransitive?

7. What did you <u>discover</u>?
8. *What did you <u>struggle</u>?
9. Who did you <u>meet</u>?
10. *What did you <u>laugh</u>?

Since sentences 7 and 9 are fine questions, *discover* and *meet* are transitive verbs. Since sentences 8 and 10 are not acceptable questions, *struggle* and *laugh* are intransitive verbs. Note that although you can say something like, *What did you struggle with?* or, *What did you laugh at?*, you can't ask the questions as they are stated above, and so the verbs are intransitive.

There's also another way to decide if a verb is transitive or intransitive:

> **Quick tip 10.3**
>
> If a verb (in one of its forms) can be put in one of the following slots, it is transitive: (a) He _____ something. (b) He _____ someone.

> **Quick tip 10.4**
>
> If a verb (in one of its forms) can be put in the following slot, it is intransitive: He _____.

Let's use these *Quick tips* to decide which of the following verbs are transitive and which are intransitive:

      11. He discovered something.
      12. He met someone.
      13. He struggled.
      14. He laughed.

Quick tip 10.3 helps identify the verb *discovered* in sentence 11 and the verb *met* in sentence 12 as transitive. *Quick tip* 10.4 helps identify the verb *struggled* in sentence 13 and the verb *laughed* in sentence 14 as intransitive.

Test yourself 10.1

Decide if each of the verbs below is transitive or intransitive. Use *Quick tips* 9.2, 9.3 and 9.4 to help you decide.

	Transitive	Intransitive
Sample: mention	✗	

Getting started (answers on p. 44)   **More practice** (answers on the website)

	Transitive	Intransitive			Transitive	Intransitive
1. tell				6. proclaim		
2. rise				7. vanish		
3. raise				8. omit		
4. fall				9. cry		
5. publish				10. remove		

Now take a look at a few more sentences:

      15a. I ate.
      15b. I ate dinner.
      16a. She dances well.
      16b. She dances the tango well.
      17a. The audience left.
      17b. The audience left the theater.

You can see that there are verbs, such as *eat*, *dance*, and *leave*, that can be used as either transitive or intransitive verbs.

> **Quick tip 10.5**
>
> Some verbs can be either transitive or transitive. These can occur in both of the following slots: (a) He _____ something / someone. (b) He _____.

Test yourself 10.2

Decide if each of the verbs below is transitive, intransitive, or either. Use *Quick tips* 10.2, 10.3, 10.4, and 10.5 to help you decide.

	Transitive	*Intransitive*	*Either*
Sample: play			✗

Getting started (answers on p. 44)

1. beat
2. cough
3. relax
4. drive
5. entertain

More practice (answers on the website)

6. seek
7. fight
8. profit
9. mention
10. paint

Test yourself 10.3

In the sentences below, decide if the underlined verb is being used as a transitive or intransitive verb. Use *Quick tips* 9.2 and 9.3 to help you decide.

	Transitive	*Intransitive*
Sample: They <u>played</u> in the park.		✗

Getting started (answers on p. 44)

1. Greg <u>opened</u> the newspaper.
2. I can <u>read</u> it later.
3. Don't <u>worry</u>!
4. On Sundays, I usually <u>stay</u> at home.
5. It's advisable to <u>wash</u> your hands before eating.

More practice (answers on the website)

6. Samantha can <u>bake</u> at any time of the day.
7. When I'm tired, I <u>complain</u>.
8. She <u>ended</u> the conversation.
9. The athlete <u>hit</u> the ball.
10. My dog <u>licked</u> my face playfully.

Lesson 11: Phrasal verbs

While most verbs are single words, some are **phrasal**: they contain two words. In phrasal verbs, the first word is a verb and the second word is called a **particle**. Here are some examples, with the phrasal verbs underlined:

1. She looked up the answer.
2. We will just drop off the files.
3. The professor pointed out the correct answer.

Notice that the meaning of a phrasal verb is often similar to the meaning of a single verb:

4. She looked up the answer.
   She researched the answer.
5. We will just drop off the files.
   We will just deliver the files.
6. The professor pointed out the correct answer.
   The professor identified the correct answer.

> **Quick tip 11.1**
>
> If you can substitute a single verb for a verb and the word following it, you probably have a phrasal verb. For example, you can say, *She pointed out the truth to us* or *She showed the truth to us. Point out is a* phrasal verb.

We can also still identify phrasal verbs using our *to* _____ or *should* _____ *Quick tips*:

to look up	should look up
to warm up	should warm up
to point out	should point out

Test yourself 11.1

Each of the sentences below contains a phrasal verb. Underline the phrasal verb, using the verb substitution tip and the *to* _____ and *should* _____ tips to help you.

Sample: The lecturer summed up his main points.

Getting started (answers on p. 44)

1. He fixed up the lighting in the hall.

2. They read over the document many times.

3. You dream up the most amazing things.

4. Ron takes out the garbage every Monday night.

5. I will pay off my mortgage in fifteen years.

More practice (answers on the website)

6. Yesterday, the company's president handed in her resignation.

7. She took over the entire operation.

8. Unfortunately, the buyer of my property blew off the deal.

9. It is obvious that she cooked up the whole story.

10. You bring up an interesting point.

In many cases, the two parts of a phrasal verb, the verb and its particle, can be separated:

    7. She <u>looked</u> the answer <u>up</u>.

    8. We will just <u>drop</u> the files <u>off</u>.

    9. The professor <u>pointed</u> the correct answer <u>out</u>.

Even when the two parts are separated, it's still a phrasal, or multi-word, verb. When you can separate the two parts in this way, you know that you've got a phrasal verb.

> **Quick tip 11.2**
>
> If you can move a particle away from its verb, you have a phrasal verb. For example, since you can say both *She looked up the answer* and *She looked the answer up*, *look up* is a phrasal verb.

Test yourself 11.2

Underline the phrasal verbs in each of the sentences below. The particle will not necessarily be next to its verb.

Sample: The students will <u>hand</u> their assignment <u>in</u> tomorrow.

Getting started (answers on p. 44)

1. Mr. Parker helped out his neighbors.

2. You should call the agency up.

3. Those children put on a show.

4. What brought this reaction about?

5. The hurricane tore the roofs of many houses off.

More practice (answers on the website)

6. The first member of the relay team passed off the baton successfully.

7. The herdsman gathered all his sheep in.

8. Debbie kept up her grades in graduate school.

9. I took my glasses off quickly.

10. Last month the bank signed the deed over to me.

In some cases, a particle cannot be separated from its verb:

    10. She <u>asked for</u> the receptionist.

    11. The lawyer <u>objected to</u> the defendant's statement.

    12. He will <u>look into</u> the judge's decision.

In these cases, you cannot say:

13. *She <u>asked</u> the receptionist <u>for</u>.
14. *The lawyer <u>objected</u> the defendant's statement <u>to</u>.
15. *He will <u>look</u> the judge's decision <u>into</u>.

So *Quick tip* 11.2 is not useful in these cases; you have to rely on the verb substitution test and the *to* and *should* tests.

Test yourself 11.3

Some of the sentences below contain a one word verb and some contain a phrasal verb. Underline the one word verb or phrasal verb in each sentence.

Sample: They <u>owed</u> her a lot of money.

Getting started (answers on p. 44)

1. Eat up your dinner!

2. The girls will put the puzzles away.

3. I understand that concept.

4. Birds fly south for the winter.

5. The elderly woman got off the bus with great difficulty.

More practice (answers on the website)

6. We ate out last night.

7. The show ran far too long.

8. They checked out the scenery around their hotel.

9. The pitcher threw the batter out in the eighth inning.

10. The butcher opened his store up at 7 A.M.

To enhance your understanding

Take a look at these groups of sentences:

16. She <u>looked up</u> the answer.   She <u>looked</u> the answer <u>up</u>.
    *She <u>looked up</u> it.   She <u>looked</u> it <u>up</u>.
17. We will just <u>drop off</u> the children. We will just <u>drop</u> the children <u>off</u>.
    *We will just <u>drop off</u> them.   We will just <u>drop</u> them <u>off</u>.
18. He <u>pointed out</u> the other girl.   He <u>pointed</u> the other girl <u>out</u>.
    *He <u>pointed out</u> her.   He <u>pointed</u> her <u>out</u>.

As you can see, in some cases (those with an asterisk), a particle cannot be next to its verb; the two parts must be separated. As a matter of fact, this is true in all of those cases where the direct object of the verb (what the verb is acting upon) is one of the following words: *me, you, him, her, it, us, them*. You might recognize these words as pronouns. You'll learn about these pronouns in Lesson 21, about direct objects in Lesson 39, and more about verbs and their particles in Lesson 30.

Answer keys: *Test yourself, Getting started* questions – Unit 2

Test yourself 7.1

	Verb	Not a verb
1. defend	✘	
2. include	✘	
3. largest		✘
4. how		✘
5. learn	✘	

Test yourself 7.2

1. must not <u>worry</u>
2. might <u>keep</u>
3. <u>wish</u> for peace
4. may sometimes <u>cook</u>
5. will <u>travel</u>

Test yourself 8.1

1. wrote: <u>write</u>
2. talking: <u>talk</u>
3. thought: <u>think</u>
4. considered: <u>consider</u>
5. seen: <u>see</u>

Test yourself 8.2

	Verb	Not a verb
1. danced	✘	
2. sofa		✘
3. large		✘
4. gave	✘	
5. stares	✘	

Test yourself 8.3

1. The host <u>greeted</u> us cordially.
2. She should <u>say</u> that again.
3. Jonathan <u>walked</u> over to the car.
4. He <u>washes</u> dishes every evening.
5. You can't <u>speak</u> Vietnamese.

Test yourself 9.1

	Verb	Not a verb
1. tasted	✗	
2. friendly		✗
3. shady		✗
4. be	✗	
5. got	✗	

Test yourself 9.2

1. Barry will <u>feel</u> awful about it.
2. Melissa <u>resembles</u> her mother.
3. Zack <u>sounded</u> extremely angry.
4. The fish <u>tasted</u> undercooked.
5. You <u>were</u> not home early.

Test yourself 9.3

1. Paul <u>was</u> in power at that moment.
2. They <u>are</u> absolutely correct in their thinking.
3. Your suitcases <u>were</u> in the overhead compartment during the flight.
4. Christina has <u>been</u> wanting to go to Europe for a long time.
5. What <u>is</u> wrong with <u>being</u> a good student?

Test yourself 9.4

1. They<u>'re</u> usually home by now.
2. <u>Are</u> you worried about anything?
3. I heard that the flight <u>was</u> late.
4. We<u>'re</u> honored by your presence.
5. It<u>'s</u> too bad that the Yankees lost last night.

Test yourself 9.5

	Verb	Not a verb
1. resemble	✗	
2. become	✗	
3. this		✗
4. be	✗	
5. new		✗

Test yourself 9.6

	Verb	Not a verb
1. appeared	✗	
2. attends	✗	
3. whenever		✗
4. was	✗	
5. heard	✗	

Test yourself 9.7

1. The car spun out of control.
2. Don't talk during the movie.
3. The doctor tied a strip of gauze around her hand.
4. Maxine spent too much money.
5. They saw the play last Sunday.

Test yourself 9.8

1. That was the best meal in the world.
2. I understand your point.
3. Maybe they know each other well.
4. She is from Wisconsin.
5. Those flowers smell heavenly.

Test yourself 9.9

	Action	*Linking*
1. The Czar was a person of high rank.		✗
2. That dog barks a lot.	✗	
3. Mr. Kelly watched the traffic below his window.	✗	
4. You have been a terrific friend to me over the years.		✗
5. I love the way the pillows feel so cozy in this hotel.		✗

Test yourself 9.10

	Action	*Linking*
1. They became best friends.		✗
2. It is not nearly the same as mine.		✗
3. Unfortunately, I forgot your birthday this year.	✗	
4. I went to the corner bakery.	✗	
5. Mark remains a legend to this day.		✗

Test yourself 9.11

	Action	*Linking*
1. He grew potatoes on his farm.	✗	
2. I looked at the mess all around me.	✗	
3. Stephen looks happy today.		✗
4. In reality, exceptions rarely prove the rule.	✗	
5. Learning the rule proved difficult.		✗

Test yourself 9.12

1. Their daughter announced her engagement later.
2. The surgeon washed his hands.
3. The pianist was diligent.
4. The young boy gritted his teeth.
5. Her assistant is always late.

Test yourself 10.1

	Transitive	Intransitive
1. tell	✗	
2. rise		✗
3. raise	✗	
4. fall		✗
5. publish	✗	

Test yourself 10.2

	Transitive	Intransitive	Either
1. beat	✗		
2. cough		✗	
3. relax		✗	
4. drive			✗
5. entertain			✗

Test yourself 10.3

	Transitive	Intransitive
1. Greg opened the newspaper.	✗	
2. I can read it later.	✗	
3. Don't worry!		✗
4. On Sundays, I usually stay at home.		✗
5. It's advisable to wash your hands before eating.	✗	

Test yourself 11.1

1. He fixed up the lighting in the hall.
2. They read over the document many times.
3. You dream up the most amazing things.
4. Ron takes out the garbage every Monday night.
5. I will pay off my mortgage in fifteen years.

Test yourself 11.2

1. Mr. Parker helped out his neighbors.
2. You should call the agency up.
3. Those children put on a show.
4. What brought this reaction about?
5. The hurricane tore the roofs of many houses off.

Test yourself 11.3

1. Eat up your dinner!
2. The girls will put the puzzles away.
3. I understand that concept.
4. Birds fly south for the winter.
5. The elderly woman got off the bus with great difficulty.

☞ **FOR A REVIEW EXERCISE OF THIS UNIT, SEE THE WEBSITE.**

UNIT 3: DETERMINERS

Determiners are words that can occur directly before a noun, tell us a bit more about that noun, and introduce it. The determiners are underlined in the sentences below, with the following noun in bold:

1. I milked the **cow**.
2. It is Harry's **turn**.
3. They bought that **house**.
4. John has more **money**.

These sentences have examples of the four major types of determiners: articles, possessives, demonstratives, and quantifiers. Generally, a noun will have only one of these determiner types in front of it. We'll be discussing each of these four types in this unit, starting with articles, the easiest and most common.

Lesson 12: Articles

How can you identify an **article**?
It doesn't get any easier than this!

> **Quick tip 12.1**
>
> There are only three articles in English: *the, a* and *an*.

Articles give us information about a noun; they indicate whether or not the noun is a specific one known to both the speaker and listener. Take a look at these examples to see what we mean:

1. I bought a red car. (The listener doesn't know anything about the red car.)
2. The red car was on sale. (The listener knows which car the speaker is talking about.)

The is commonly called the **definite article**; *a* and *an* are called **indefinite articles**. The definite article may be used with both singular and plural nouns, but the indefinite articles only with singular nouns, as we can see in the following examples:

the idea	the ideas
an apple	* an apples
a revolution	* a revolutions

Test yourself 12.1

Underline the articles in each of the sentences below. A sentence may have more than one article.
Sample: We watched a video last night.

Getting started (answers on p. 55)

1. The last week of the month was a busy one in the store.

2. Summer was a special time for Melissa.

3. There's an unusual idea floating around.

4. I turned a corner in the long hall.

5. A dirty spoon had fallen to the floor.

More practice (answers on the website)

6. In the middle of the night, I heard a strange noise.

7. Jackie turned off the road too soon.

8. Your mother's favorite actor appeared in the show we saw last night.

9. A pear is just as tasty as an apple, as far as I am concerned.

10. The guys bought two cans of paint: an orange one and a beige one.

What's the difference between *a* and *an*? See if you notice a pattern when you look at these examples:

a red tablecloth	an ancient right
a situation	an interesting message
a boring lecture	an intruder

The articles *a* and *an* have the same meaning and use. The only difference between them is that *a* is used when the next word begins with a consonant sound, while *an* is used when the next word begins with a vowel sound.

To enhance your understanding

What about *a uniform* and *an hour*? Do these contradict what we've said about when to use *a* and *an*? It certainly looks like *a* is being used before a vowel, and *an* is being used before a consonant. But in fact, that's not the case. These phrases follow the rule perfectly. Remember that *a* is used when the next word begins with a consonant <u>sound</u>. The first <u>letter</u> of the next word doesn't matter; only its first sound matters.

So what's the first sound of the word *uniform*? Say it out loud and listen carefully. You will hear that the first <u>sound</u> of the word is the sound [y], as in *yes*. We really say "y-uniform" (and also "y-unicorn," "y-usual," etc.). Since "y," a consonant, is the first sound, we use *a* before *uniform*.

What's the first <u>sound</u> of the word *hour*? Say the word out loud, and you will notice that in fact we don't pronounce the letter "h." Rather, *hour* begins with a vowel sound, as in the word *our*, and so we say *an hour*.

Thus, apparent exceptions, like *a uniform* and *an hour*, are not exceptions at all.

Test yourself 12.2

For each sentence, underline each article with a <u>solid line</u>, each noun with a <u>double underline</u>, and each verb with a <u>squiggly line</u>. Some sentences have more than one article and noun; some have no article. If you can answer these questions, you have achieved a solid understanding of how to identify articles, nouns, and verbs, three of the most common parts of speech!

Sample: <u>A</u> <u>pilot</u> spoke to the <u>crew</u>.

Getting started (answers on p. 55)

1. A waiter walked to the table.

2. The trainer calmed the dog down.

3. He argued about the bill for hours.

4. I usually eat a sandwich and a cookie for lunch.

5. She watches TV every night.

More practice (answers on the website)

6. The train appeared suddenly.

7. Diane put the chicken in the salad.

8. The repairman did not finish his job.

9. Children like cake.

10. Nowadays Elena takes skiing lessons at least once a week.

Lesson 13: Demonstratives

Here's another easy category. There are only four **demonstratives**: *this*, *that*, *these*, and *those*.

> **Quick tip 13.1**
>
> There are only four demonstratives in English: *this*, *that*, *these*, and *those*.

Notice again that, just like articles, each of these can occur directly before a noun: *this table*, *these tables*, *that idea*, *those ideas*. Demonstratives are words that "point" to something or someone.

Test yourself 13.1

Underline the demonstrative in each of the sentences below.
Sample: <u>Those</u> performers were all also composers.

Getting started (answers on p. 55)

1. You can use this book.
2. Those speeches he gave were impressive.
3. They don't speak that language.
4. Kirsten sold all these items.
5. This side of the Atlantic Ocean is more familiar to me.

More practice (answers on the website)

6. She likes to listen to that song.
7. Those mistakes will catch up with Andrew one day.
8. I don't like these pictures.
9. That man is a technician.
10. Lots of people like to patronize this restaurant.

Test yourself 13.2

Underline the determiners in the sentences below. They will be either articles or demonstratives.
Sample: There were shops selling <u>a</u> variety of <u>those</u> handmade items.

Getting started (answers on p. 55)

1. On top of the pile of fabrics was a sleeping cat.
2. That leader met with the residents of the village.
3. This taxi is heading toward a large shopping mall.
4. The instructor chose a very informative textbook.
5. These pants won't fit in those drawers.

More practice (answers on the website)

6. The audience is tired of all those lame jokes.
7. Once in a while I think of my childhood friends.
8. Those pedestrians better keep to the right of the main road.
9. This work is the brainchild of a madman.
10. We found this piece of paper on the top shelf of a dusty bookcase.

Test yourself 13.3

Identify each determiner in the sentences below by underlining it with a solid line if it is a demonstrative and with a squiggly line if it is an article.

Sample: Larry is holding <u>this</u> meeting at <u>the</u> hotel.

Getting started (answers on p. 55)

1. Are you looking for a better job?

2. That movie follows a young family after they immigrate to this country.

3. Jane met an Englishman there whom she later married.

4. The weather was so wonderful at the beach.

5. All those cups of coffee won't help you get a good night's rest.

More practice (answers on the website)

6. I recognize this soccer player as a big star from Italy.

7. Playing a game of chess in this park always interests me.

8. Those students who did the exercises in the text will likely pass the final.

9. The garbage is piling up on the sidewalk.

10. This lesson is a piece of cake, isn't it?

Lesson 14: Possessives

Possessives are words that indicate ownership or belonging. The possessives are under-lined in the sentences below.

    1. I sold <u>my</u> car.

    2. <u>Betty's</u> neighbor is an architect.

The possessive in sentence 1 is called a **possessive pronoun**; the possessive in sentence 2 is called a **possessive proper noun**. Notice that, just like articles and demonstratives, possessive pronouns and possessive proper nouns can appear directly before a noun. We'll discuss each of these separately.

Possessive pronouns

There are just a few possessive pronouns that function as determiners. These are com-monly referred to as **possessive pronouns with determiner function** or **possessive adjectives**. We will call them simply **determiner possessive pronouns**. (For another function of possessive pronouns, see Lesson 24.)

> **Quick tip 14.1**
>
> The determiner possessive pronouns are: *my, your, his, her, its, our, their.*

Test yourself 14.1

Underline the determiner possessive pronoun in each of the sentences below.
Sample: <u>My</u> school won the state championship last year.

Getting started (answers on p. 55)

1. His face always shows what he's thinking.

2. They go to their house in the mountains every summer.

3. It took three days for your letter to get here.

4. We liked her mother.

5. Our product is superior to what you have to offer.

More practice (answers on the website)

6. The price of the stock I am considering buying does not reflect its true worth.

7. Would you like to take a ride in your new car?

8. Friends, I will be counting on your votes.

9. The children went to the movies together with their father.

10. Matt does not share his feelings easily.

Possessive proper nouns

The possessive proper nouns are underlined in this next sentence:

    3. I saw <u>Mary's</u> cat chase <u>Mrs. Smith's</u> dog, which ran across <u>Jim's</u> yard.

Remember, names do not have to be names of just people. For example, *London's*, *America's*, and *IBM's* are each possessive proper nouns: *London's bridges*, *America's highways*, *IBM's products*. (See Lesson 6 to remind yourself about proper nouns.)

To enhance your understanding

While possessive proper nouns can function as determiners, possessive common nouns (see Lesson 6), for example *the girl's hat*, are considered to be adjectives. (See Lesson 16 for more about adjectives.) This is because possessive common nouns, but not possessive proper nouns, can have a determiner in front of them – keeping in mind that a noun will generally have just one determiner introducing it. See the following examples:

4. The girl's hat is new. (girl's = possessive common noun)
5. *The Mary's hat is new. (Mary's = possessive proper noun)

Test yourself 14.2

Underline the possessive proper noun in each of the sentences below.
Sample: *Gone With the Wind*'s cast was amazing.

Getting started (answers on p. 56)

1. Leah's eyes met those of the man at the counter.
2. It was Harry's turn to say something.
3. They were impressed by Rome's restaurants.
4. Mickey Mouse's picture is hanging on my wall.
5. John always wanted to visit Harvard's campus.

More practice (answers on the website)

6. France's soccer team lost to another team.
7. Macy's women's department is on the third floor.
8. Mrs. Johnson's office is located directly above mine.
9. After dinner, we went up to Beth's apartment.
10. I never get tired of The Beatles' songs.

Test yourself 14.3

Underline the possessive determiner in each of the sentences below. The determiner will either be a possessive pronoun or a possessive proper noun.
Sample: Your committee is meeting tomorrow.

Getting started (answers on p. 56)

1. She suggested that it was all Martin's fault.
2. Why don't you give it to your daughter?
3. That was a breathtaking view of New York's skyline.
4. He bought a souvenir for his son.
5. The Adamses did not care for their new neighbors.

More practice (answers on the website)

6. The public was eagerly awaiting Congress's new energy policy.
7. My apartment is either too hot or too cold.
8. Abraham Lincoln's life was interesting.
9. Our crew prepared to dock.
10. On Thursday afternoon, the actor was practicing his lines.

Test yourself 14.4

For each determiner below, indicate if it is an article (e.g. *the*, *an*), demonstrative (e.g. *this*, *those*), possessive pronoun (e.g. *your*, *our*), or possessive proper noun (e.g. *Mary's*, *London's*).

Sample: Law and Order's   <u>possessive proper noun</u>

Getting started (answers on p. 56)

1. their   ....

2. an   ....

3. George's   ....

4. those   ....

5. its   ....

More practice (answers on the website)

6. the   ....

7. San Francisco's   ....

8. this   ....

9. my   ....

10. a   ....

Test yourself 14.5

Underline the determiner in each of the sentences below. It will either be an article, demonstrative, possessive pronoun, or possessive proper noun. Some sentences may contain more than one determiner.

Sample: The room contained <u>a</u> sofa, <u>a</u> chair, and, on <u>the</u> wall, <u>Melinda's</u> portrait.

Getting started (answers on p. 56)

1. She knew what her mother had done for the family.

2. There wasn't much information in his letters.

3. These books are clearly the best.

4. Rosa's husband put a surprise in her lunch box.

5. Jerry's uncle likes to drink a glass of wine with his dinner.

More practice (answers on the website)

6. This actress should get an Oscar for her performance in that movie.

7. The doctor's secretary usually walks a mile on her lunch break.

8. Those children love to take a dip in their new pool in the backyard.

9. On her way to work, Maggie's car broke down.

10. Jet Blue's crew served dinner while I was sleeping.

Lesson 15: Quantifiers

There are words, such as *every* and *several*, that indicate amount, or quantity, and these are called **quantifiers**. Quantifiers can act as determiners; that is, they can come before and introduce a noun. The determiners are underlined in the following sentences:

1. All businesses need to have a budget.
2. Some people like eating eel.
3. She enjoyed few things as much as food.

Some common quantifiers are listed below:

all	enough	much
any	every	neither
both	few	no
each	little	several
either	most	some

Quick tip 15.1

Words of quantity, quantifiers, can act as determiners and precede a noun. Some examples are: *all, some, several,* and *much*.

Test yourself 15.1

Underline the quantifier in each of the sentences below. The quantifiers will all be from the list above.
Sample: I met several chefs at that school.

Getting started (answers on p. 56)

1. There is no writer who is as famous as Shakespeare.

2. Enough money was raised to build a new wing on the hospital.

3. I don't take much sugar in my coffee.

4. With little effort, I solved the crossword puzzle.

5. All experiments test hypotheses.

More practice (answers on the website)

6. Most professors have earned a doctorate.

7. Every noun that is human is also animate.

8. Neither option is particularly good.

9. Any man who drinks and drives puts his life in danger.

10. You leave me with few alternatives.

Test yourself 15.2

For each determiner below, indicate if it is an article (e.g. *the, an*), demonstrative (e.g. *this, those*), possessive pronoun (e.g. *your, our*), possessive proper noun (e.g. *Mary's, London's*), or quantifier (e.g. *every, some*).
Sample: that   demonstrative

Getting started (answers on p. 56)

1. Main Street's   ....
2. your   ....
3. few   ....
4. those   ....
5. the   ....

More practice (answers on the website)

6. its   ....
7. both   ....
8. Madrid's   ....
9. several   ....
10. an   ....

Test yourself 15.3

Underline the determiner in each of the sentences below. It will either be an <u>article</u> (e.g. *the, an*), <u>demonstrative</u> (e.g. *this*, *those*), <u>possessive pronoun</u> (e.g. *your, our*), <u>possessive proper noun</u> (e.g. *Mary's, London's*), or <u>quantifier</u> (e.g. *few, most*). Some sentences may contain more than one determiner.

Sample: <u>Joan's</u> mother valued <u>her</u> efforts.

Getting started (answers on p. 57)

1. Chicago's architecture is diverse.
2. I know that man and his wife.
3. She packed several dresses into her suitcase.
4. He had traveled to few places over the years.
5. Each child at the party brought a gift.

More practice (answers on the website)

6. Let's not forget those messages.
7. Every time we eat out, you order several appetizers.
8. Any man who is my friend's enemy is no friend of mine.
9. I bought these strawberries at her uncle's grocery store.
10. This event wasn't much fun.

Answer keys: *Test yourself, Getting started* questions – Unit 3

Test yourself 12.1

1. The last week of the month was a busy one in the store.
2. Summer was a special time for Melissa.
3. There's an unusual idea floating around.
4. I turned a corner in the long hall.
5. A dirty spoon had fallen to the floor.

Test yourself 12.2

1. A waiter walked to the table.
2. The trainer calmed the dog down.
3. He argued about the bill for hours.
4. I usually eat a sandwich and a cookie for lunch.
5. She watches TV every night.

Test yourself 13.1

1. You can use this book.
2. Those speeches he gave were impressive.
3. They don't speak that language.
4. Kirsten sold all these items.
5. This side of the Atlantic Ocean is more familiar to me.

Test yourself 13.2

1. On top of the pile of fabrics was a sleeping cat.
2. That leader met with the residents of the village.
3. This taxi is heading toward a large shopping mall.
4. The instructor chose a very informative textbook.
5. These pants won't fit in those drawers.

Test yourself 13.3

1. Are you looking for a better job?
2. That movie follows a young family after they immigrate to this country.
3. Jane met an Englishman there whom she later married.
4. The weather was so wonderful at the beach.
5. All those cups of coffee won't help you get a good night's rest.

Test yourself 14.1

1. His face always shows what he's thinking.
2. They go to their house in the mountains every summer.

3. It took three days for <u>your</u> letter to get here.
4. We liked <u>her</u> mother.
5. <u>Our</u> product is superior to what you have to offer.

Test yourself 14.2

1. <u>Leah's</u> eyes met those of the man at the counter.
2. It was <u>Harry's</u> turn to say something.
3. They were impressed by <u>Rome's</u> restaurants.
4. <u>Mickey Mouse's</u> picture is hanging on my wall.
5. John always wanted to visit <u>Harvard's</u> campus.

Test yourself 14.3

1. She suggested that it was all <u>Martin's</u> fault.
2. Why don't you give it to <u>your</u> daughter?
3. That was a breathtaking view of <u>New York's</u> skyline.
4. He bought a souvenir for <u>his</u> son.
5. The Adamses did not care for <u>their</u> new neighbors.

Test yourself 14.4

1. their   <u>possessive pronoun</u>
2. an   <u>article</u>
3. George's   <u>possessive proper noun</u>
4. those   <u>demonstrative</u>
5. its   <u>possessive pronoun</u>

Test yourself 14.5

1. She knew what <u>her</u> mother had done for <u>the</u> family.
2. There wasn't much information in <u>his</u> letters.
3. <u>These</u> books are clearly <u>the</u> best.
4. <u>Rosa's</u> husband put <u>a</u> surprise in <u>her</u> lunch box.
5. <u>Jerry's</u> uncle likes to drink <u>a</u> glass of wine with <u>his</u> dinner.

Test yourself 15.1

1. There is <u>no</u> writer who is as famous as Shakespeare.
2. <u>Enough</u> money was raised to build a new wing on the hospital.
3. I don't take <u>much</u> sugar in my coffee.
4. With <u>little</u> effort, I solved the crossword puzzle.
5. <u>All</u> experiments test hypotheses.

Test yourself 15.2

1. Main Street's   <u>possessive proper noun</u>
2. your   <u>possessive pronoun</u>
3. few   <u>quantifier</u>
4. those   <u>demonstrative</u>
5. the   <u>article</u>

Test yourself 15.3

1. <u>Chicago's</u> architecture is diverse.
2. I know <u>that</u> man and <u>his</u> wife.
3. She packed <u>several</u> dresses into <u>her</u> suitcase.
4. He had traveled to <u>few</u> places over <u>the</u> years.
5. <u>Each</u> child at <u>the</u> party brought <u>a</u> gift.

☞ **FOR A REVIEW EXERCISE OF THIS UNIT, SEE THE WEBSITE.**

Lesson 16: Identifying adjectives

An **adjective** is a word that refers to a characteristic of a noun. How can you identify an adjective?

If you can put a word between *the* and a noun (like *boy*, or *idea*), then that word is an adjective.

> **Quick tip 16.1**
>
> If you can put a word between *the* and a noun (for example, *the* _____ *boy)*, then that word is an adjective.

For example, since we can say *the tall boy, tall* is an adjective. Similarly, we can say *the silly boy, the interesting boy,* and *the young boy.* Therefore, *silly, interesting,* and *young* are all adjectives.

A number of adjectives, all used in the phrase *the* _____ *boy* are listed below. The adjectives are underlined:

1. the <u>brilliant</u> boy
2. the <u>embarrassed</u> boy
3. the <u>blonde</u> boy
4. the <u>hungry</u> boy
5. the <u>delightful</u> boy

Compare these phrases to *the very boy, the a boy,* and *the talk boy. Very, a,* and *talk* are not adjectives.

What do adjectives actually do? Adjectives always tell us something about a noun. Another way of saying this is that they modify a noun. In the phrases we've just looked at, the underlined adjectives tell us something about, or modify, the noun *boy.*

Test yourself 16.1

Which of the following words are adjectives? See if they sound right when you put them here: *the* _____ *thing.* Check the appropriate column.

	Adjective	Not an adjective
Sample: have		**✗**

Getting started (answers on p. 63)

	Adjective	Not an adjective
1. yellow	....	....
2. wonderful	....	....
3. these	....	....
4. quickly	....	....
5. unreliable	....	....

More practice (answers on the website)

	Adjective	Not an adjective
6. is	....	....
7. pure	....	....
8. on	....	....
9. creative	....	....
10. almost	....	....

Test yourself 16.2

Underline the adjectives in the sentences below. In each case, the adjective will be between *the* and a noun. A sentence may have more than one adjective.

Sample: She has been the <u>strong</u> leader of this company for years.

Getting started (answers on p. 63)

1. The strange robots marched towards the city.

2. It was the last day of school.

3. We tugged at the enormous gate.

4. The billowing smoke alerted us to the fire.

5. The sudden sandstorm forced the surprised bathers to flee the beach.

More practice (answers on the website)

6. She received the exciting news in the noisy restaurant.

7. The blind beggar was sitting at the busy corner.

8. Jeremy did not get the subtle humor of the play.

9. The poor people of the world outnumber the rich ones.

10. Keep your hands off the hot stove!

As we've said, a good way to decide if a word is an adjective is to see if it can be placed between *the* and a noun. But that doesn't mean that that's the only place where an adjective can occur; it's just a way to test a word to see if it's an adjective.

Here are some sentences where the adjective is in a different place. In each case, the adjective is underlined.

6. He is a <u>tall</u> boy.
7. My <u>best</u> friend loves <u>chocolate</u> cake.
8. The house had a <u>low</u> roof.
9. <u>Large</u> cars are harder to drive than <u>small</u> cars.

Let's make sure that each of the underlined words above passes the adjective test, that is, that it can appear between *the* and a noun.

10. tall: the tall boy
11. best: the best movie
12. chocolate: the chocolate bar
13. low: the low ceiling
14. large: the large window
15. small: the small window.

As you can see, each of these words passes the adjective test. Notice also that each of these words describes a characteristic of a noun.

Test yourself 16.3

Use the adjective test to find the adjectives in each of the sentences below. A sentence may have more than one adjective.

Sample: It took a <u>long</u> time to arrive at our <u>next</u> destination.

Getting started (answers on p. 63)

1. Evenings were a special time for the family.

2. The next week was a busy one in the store.

3. There's an unusual idea floating around.

4. I turned a corner in the long hall.

5. A dirty fork had fallen to the floor.

More practice (answers on the website)

6. I wrote a boring letter.

7. Mary's younger brother was already there.

8. The American flag was behind Edward's desk.

9. I could see his face in the red light from the exit sign.

10. We gathered the important facts from those dusty books.

What do you notice about the underlined adjectives in the phrases below?

    16. the delicious rich cake

    17. my tall, red-haired, entertaining friend

    18. a bright, colorful, blue, striped pattern

As you can see, a noun can have more than one adjective modifying it. In fact, there is no limit to the number of adjectives that can modify a noun (except the patience and tolerance of the listener!).

Test yourself 16.4

Underline the adjectives in each of the sentences below. Some of the nouns will be modified by more than one adjective.

Sample: She ate all the crisp, crunchy chips.

Getting started (answers on p. 63)

1. They went off to see an old, gloomy, historic mansion in southern England.

2. She had anticipated his sudden arrival.

3. Angela ignored his annoying, persistent questions.

4. I must get rid of my decrepit, banged-up little old car.

5. We wouldn't want to cross this wide, busy street, would we?

More practice (answers on the website)

6. You should heed the advice of wise men and women.

7. Wild animals can be dangerous.

8. The lovely young lady read one of her favorite novels on her comfortable sofa.

9. Why did you buy this outdated computer in the first place?

10. The Dodgers' frustrated manager benched his brash young pitcher.

Remember that sometimes a word can function as one word category, or part of speech, in one sentence, and as another word category in another sentence (see Lesson 2). For example, let's look at the word *cream*. In the sentence *I brought the cream*, *cream* is a noun. But in the sentence *That's a cream cake*, *cream* is an adjective, telling us more about the noun *cake*.

Test yourself 16.5

In each of the sentences below, decide if the underlined words are functioning as nouns or adjectives.

Sample: That copy isn't legible.   adjective

Getting started (answers on p. 63)

1. The window ledge is too narrow for a plant. ....

2. That window is stuck shut. ....

3. This has been a chilly spring. ....

4. I'm enjoying this spring weather. ....

5. The morning hours are not my best. ....

More practice (answers on the website)

6. I drink two cups of coffee each morning. ....

7. In most public restaurants, it is forbidden to smoke a cigarette. ....

8. Cigarette smokers must go for X-ray tests regularly. ....

9. My nephew was looking for travel companions. ....

10. Foreign travel can be both exhausting and exhilarating. ....

Test yourself 16.6

In each of the sentences below, decide if the underlined words are functioning as nouns, verbs, or adjectives.

Sample: That's a jail cell.   adjective

Getting started (answers on p. 63)

1. He goes to a day school. ....

2. I work during the day. ....

3. The defendant will shock them when they hear his response. ....

4. It was a terrible shock. ....

5. I will voice my opinion if I want to. ....

More practice (answers on the website)

6. The singer had a wonderful voice. ....

7. Some people call the larynx a voice box. ....

8. Some languages have both formal and informal terms of address. ....

9. I don't wish to address this question at this time. ....

10. Did you put my information in your address book? ....

Test yourself 16.7

In each of the sentences below, identify the word category of each word in each sentence.

Sample: The instructor answered her unspoken question.

determiner – noun – verb – determiner – adjective – noun

Getting started (answers on p. 64)

1. A light rain fell.

....

2. Ernie's friend likes a good argument.

....

3. His employee received that small bonus.

....

4. Some big cars take premium gasoline.

....

5. This question deserves a serious answer.

....

More practice (answers on the website)

6. The policeman's warning scared my passengers.

....

7. Most guests enjoyed the lavish party.

....

8. Your best friend had a soda.

....

9. Good marriages have many joyous moments.

....

10. His daughter bought a stunning Italian dress.

....

Answer keys: *Test yourself, Getting started questions* – Unit 4

Test yourself 16.1

	Adjective	Not an adjective
1. yellow	✗	
2. wonderful	✗	
3. these		✗
4. quickly		✗
5. unreliable	✗	

Test yourself 16.2

1. The <u>strange</u> robots marched towards the city.
2. It was the <u>last</u> day of school.
3. We tugged at the <u>enormous</u> gate.
4. The <u>billowing</u> smoke alerted us to the fire.
5. The <u>sudden</u> sandstorm forced the <u>surprised</u> bathers to flee the beach.

Test yourself 16.3

1. Evenings were a <u>special</u> time for the family.
2. The <u>next</u> week was a <u>busy</u> one in the store.
3. There's an <u>unusual</u> idea floating around.
4. I turned a corner in the <u>long</u> hall.
5. A <u>dirty</u> fork had fallen to the floor.

Test yourself 16.4

1. They went off to see an <u>old</u>, <u>gloomy</u>, <u>historic</u> mansion in <u>southern</u> England.
2. She had anticipated his <u>sudden</u> arrival.
3. Angela ignored his <u>annoying</u>, <u>persistent</u> questions.
4. I must get rid of my <u>decrepit</u>, <u>banged-up</u> <u>little</u> <u>old</u> car.
5. We wouldn't want to cross this <u>wide</u>, <u>busy</u> street, would we?

Test yourself 16.5

1. The <u>window</u> ledge is too narrow for a plant.   adjective
2. That <u>window</u> is stuck shut.   noun
3. This has been a chilly <u>spring</u>.   noun
4. I'm enjoying this <u>spring</u> weather.   adjective
5. The <u>morning</u> hours are not my best.   adjective

Test yourself 16.6

1. He goes to a <u>day</u> school.   adjective
2. I work during the <u>day</u>.   noun

3. The defendant will <u>shock</u> them when they hear his response. <u>verb</u>
4. It was a terrible <u>shock</u>. <u>noun</u>
5. I will <u>voice</u> my opinion if I want to. <u>verb</u>

Test yourself 16.7

1. A light rain fell.
   <u>determiner – adjective – noun – verb</u>
2. Ernie's friend likes a good argument.
   <u>determiner – noun – verb – determiner – adjective – noun</u>
3. His employee received that small bonus.
   <u>determiner – noun – verb – determiner – adjective – noun</u>
4. Some big cars take premium gasoline.
   <u>determiner – adjective – noun – verb – adjective – noun</u>
5. This question deserves a serious answer.
   <u>determiner – noun – verb – determiner – adjective – noun</u>

☞ **FOR A REVIEW EXERCISE OF THIS UNIT, SEE THE WEBSITE.**

Lesson 17: Identifying prepositions

What is a **preposition**? The prepositions are underlined in the following sentences.

1. She made notes on the paper.
2. My office is between the post office and the laundromat.
3. I'll meet you after work.

Quick tip 17.1

Prepositions are words, usually small, that typically indicate information about direction, location, or time. There is only a small number of prepositions in English. Some commonly used examples are *at, from, in, on,* and *to.*

The following are common prepositions:

about	beneath	into	throughout
above	beside	like	till
across	between	near	to
after	beyond	of	toward(s)
against	by	off	under
along	despite	on	until
among	down	onto	up
around	during	out	upon
at	for	over	with
before	from	since	within
behind	in	through	without
below			

Quick tip 17.2

If you can put a word in one of the empty slots in one of the following sentences, the word is a preposition: *I walked _____ the table. It happened _____ that time.*

This tip will help you identify many, though not all, prepositions.

Test yourself 17.1

Underline the prepositions in the sentences below. There may be more than one. Use the *Quick tips* and the list of prepositions to help you.

Sample: My friends are going with me.

Getting started (answers on p. 68)

1. Let's go into the dining room.

2. It was the dumbest thing he did in his entire life.

3. Felice was having dinner on the patio.

4. She ran to the candy store.

5. I looked for you during the intermission.

More practice (answers on the website)

6. We were flying over Europe.

7. Lenore looked beneath the rock.

8. She found the pot of gold.

9. Is it over the rainbow?

10. He appeared at the right place at the right time.

Test yourself 17.2

Underline the prepositions with a solid line and the nouns with a squiggly line in each of the sentences below.

Sample: There's a small house near the field.

Getting started (answers on p. 68)

1. A uniformed guard stood near the massive entryway.

2. She leaned out the window and waved to the large crowd.

3. The older woman from Chicago had already left.

4. She staggered into the store.

5. Carissa sat at the computer in a large room.

More practice (answers on the website)

6. Are you going to the prom with Stan?

7. Mike always gives a nice present to his wife on her birthday.

8. Please don't ask how my day at the office was!

9. I couldn't open the door of my car without my key.

10. Let's meet at or near midnight.

To enhance your understanding

Don't confuse the two types of *to*:

    4. I want to go home. (infinitive: *to* + verb)

    5. I went to Chicago. (preposition: *to* + noun)

Test yourself 17.3

Underline the prepositions with a solid line, the verbs with a double underline, and the adjectives with a squiggly line in the sentences below.

Sample: I'll buy us a large bucket of chicken.

Getting started (answers on p. 68)

1. Jean walked around the grounds of the magnificent estate.

2. His friend pounded him on the back.

3. The puppy gazed at him expectantly.

4. The loud music in that store bothered Jamie.

5. He has hot coffee before class.

More practice (answers on the website)

6. José buys fresh bread for his family every week.

7. Do you want tickets to the new play?

8. The young bride's mother seemed happy among her friends.

9. The tireless teenager ran across the park with his new running shoes.

10. I placed some small apples near the sink.

To further enhance your understanding

Take a look at the following sentences.

6. I'm standing in front of my house.
7. That man was ahead of her.
8. Please get out of his way.

Each of these sentences contains a multiword preposition, that is, a preposition consisting of more than one word. Below is a list of common multiword prepositions, commonly called **compound** or **phrasal prepositions**.

across from	inside of
ahead of	in spite of
along with	instead of
because of	on account of
by means of	on top of
due to	out of
for the sake of	over to
in addition to	together with
in front of	up to

For more about prepositions, see Lesson 29.

Answer keys: *Test yourself, Getting started* questions – Unit 5

Test yourself 17.1

1. Let's go <u>into</u> the dining room.
2. It was the dumbest thing he did <u>in</u> his entire life.
3. Felice was having dinner <u>on</u> the patio.
4. She ran <u>to</u> the candy store.
5. I looked <u>for</u> you <u>during</u> the intermission.

Test yourself 17.2

1. A uniformed <u>guard</u> stood <u>near</u> the massive <u>entryway</u>.
2. She leaned <u>out</u> the <u>window</u> and waved <u>to</u> the large <u>crowd</u>.
3. The older <u>woman</u> <u>from</u> Chicago had already left.
4. She staggered <u>into</u> the <u>store</u>.
5. <u>Carissa</u> sat <u>at</u> the <u>computer</u> <u>in</u> a large <u>room</u>.

Test yourself 17.3

1. Jean <u>walked</u> <u>around</u> the grounds <u>of</u> the <u>magnificient</u> state.
2. His friend <u>pounded</u> him <u>on</u> the back.
3. The puppy <u>gazed</u> <u>at</u> him expectantly.
4. The <u>loud</u> music <u>in</u> that store <u>bothered</u> Jamie.
5. He <u>has</u> <u>hot</u> coffee <u>before</u> class.

☞ **FOR A REVIEW EXERCISE OF THIS UNIT, SEE THE WEBSITE.**

1. I saw Mary at the store.
2. I saw Mary and John at the store.
3. I saw Mary and John and Harry at the store.
4. I saw Mary and John and Harry and Melissa at the store.
5. I saw Mary and John and Harry and Melissa and ten other people at the store.
6. I saw ...

Well, you get the idea.

What are conjunctions? Conjunctions are connectors. They are words, such as and, that join words, phrases and sentences together. Some other conjunctions are underlined in the sentences below.

7. He didn't respond much, just occasionally said "yes" or "no."
8. They take life seriously but are still fun to be around.
9. I thought that he was crazy.
10. Adam left the room before Tabitha could say another thing.
11. Just turn right when you get to the corner.

There are different kinds of conjunctions. We'll look at coordinating conjunctions first.

Lesson 18: Coordinating conjunctions

Coordinating conjunctions connect any two units that are the same type. For example, they can connect two sentences, two nouns, two verbs, two determiners, two prepositions, or two adjectives.

> ### Quick tip 18.1
>
> There are three common coordinating conjunctions in English. They are: *and*, *or*, and *but*. Four less common ones are *for*, *so*, *yet*, and *nor*.

> ### Quick tip 18.2
>
> A commonly used way to remember the coordinating conjunctions is to think of FANBOYS: F (*for*), A (*and*), N (*nor*), B (*but*), O (*or*), Y (*yet*), S (*so*).

But given that *and*, *or*, and *but* are the most common, you'll be in good shape if you just remember those.

The coordinating conjunctions in the sentences below are underlined.

1. **You asked my friend**, <u>and</u> **then the other two came as well**.
2. **I go** <u>or</u> **he goes**.
3. **It wasn't dark** <u>but</u> **the moon was out**.

In these sentences, you can see that the coordinating conjunction has a complete sentence on either side of it. (The sentences on either side are in bold.) Thus, the conjunction in these examples is connecting two sentences.

In the next group of sentences, you can see that the coordinating conjunction has a noun on either side of it. Thus, the conjunction is joining two nouns. The nouns are in bold.

4. The children had **milk** <u>and</u> **cookies**.
5. People study **medicine** <u>or</u> **dentistry** when they enroll at that institution.

In the next sentences, the coordinating conjunction is joining two adjectives. The adjectives are in bold.

6. That restaurant is known for **healthy** <u>and</u> **nutritious** food.
7. I'm buying either the **striped** <u>or</u> **paisley** wallpaper.

Test yourself 18.1

Underline the coordinating conjunction in each sentence below. Remember that the coordinating conjunctions are: *and, or, but, for, so, yet, nor*.

Sample: The old carpet was worn out <u>but</u> the furniture looked relatively new.

Getting started (answers on p. 79)

1. You can hide between trips and make believe you're innocent.

2. Was it near here or over there?

3. Roger looked around but he didn't see anything.

4. They'll eat chicken or turkey for dinner.

5. Mr. Joseph pulled out three letters and handed one to each of the men.

More practice (answers on the website)

6. He wants to work through the night but I don't.

7. The general sent the dispatch to the army and the navy.

8. He went to the cloister or to the small chapel nearby.

9. Maud is not hungry, nor is her sister thirsty.

10. He'll come over or he'll call.

Test yourself 18.2

Underline the coordinating conjunction in each sentence below. Then decide if the conjunction is joining two sentences or two nouns. In this exercise, if there is not a complete sentence on either side of the conjunction, it is joining two nouns.

Sample: Mary decided to have either soup or salad.   nouns

Getting started (answers on p. 79)

1. Mr. Eagle was called away on business, so Mrs. Broxton took his place at the meeting. ....

2. He'd heard of it, but he didn't like the idea. ....

3. Erin felt real excitement and enthusiasm. ....

4. It was raining hard, yet we went to the ball game. ....

5. The airline attendant asked, "Would you like coffee or tea?" ....

More practice (answers on the website)

6. The color TV was too expensive, so Nancy didn't buy it. ....

7. Do you swear to tell the truth, nothing but the truth? ....

8. At one time my favorite band was *Katrina and the Waves*. ....

9. Sammy wanted to go skydiving, but his parents didn't let him. ....

10. For me, going to Paris is always a treat, for I love its architecture. ....

Test yourself 18.3

Underline the coordinating conjunction in each sentence below. Then decide if the conjunction is joining two verbs, two adjectives, or two prepositions.

Sample: That is a difficult but worthwhile lesson.   adjectives

Getting started (answers on p. 79)

1. I'll be near or between the stacks.

2. He came up with a quick and effective remedy.

3. I hope you won't worry or brood too much about it.

4. This trip will be expensive but worthwhile.

5. I am at or near a breakthrough.

More practice (answers on the website)

6. Don't you hate to eat and run?   ....

7. What size shirt are you looking for: small or large?   ....

8. They came and went in a hurry.   ....

9. At seven in the morning Tamara is sluggish yet efficient. ....

10. It is not advisable to drink and drive at the same time.   ....

Test yourself 18.4

Write down the seven coordinating conjunctions. (Remember FANBOYS.) Answers on p. 79.

1. ....   5. ....

2. ....   6. ....

3. ....   7. ....

4. ....

Lesson 19: Subordinating conjunctions

Another kind of conjunction is called a **subordinating conjunction**. Here are some examples of sentences with subordinating conjunctions. The subordinating conjunctions are underlined.

1. She continued arguing <u>until</u> everyone finally agreed with her.
2. They live down south <u>when</u> the weather gets cold.
3. Jack will buy a house <u>once</u> he gets a job.
4. She listened to his comments politely, <u>even though</u> they sounded silly.
5. They stopped talking <u>when</u> it was Eleanor's turn.

Subordinating conjunctions connect sentences; however, the two parts that are connected are not of equal value in terms of the meaning of the whole sentence. There is a main sentence with a subpart; the subordinating conjunction connects the subpart to the main sentence. Here are sentences 1 through 5 again, but this time with the main sentences in bold.

6. **She continued arguing** <u>until</u> everyone finally agreed with her.
7. **They live down south** <u>when</u> the weather gets cold.
8. **Jack will buy a house** <u>once</u> he gets a job.
9. **She listened to his comments politely**, <u>even though</u> they sounded silly.
10. **They stopped talking** <u>when</u> it was Eleanor's turn.

> **Quick tip 19.1**
>
> Subordinating conjunctions connect a sentence with another sentence, which is a subpart of it. The subpart sentence is called a **dependent clause** (or **subordinate clause**). In the following sentence, the subordinating conjunction is underlined and the dependent clause is in italics: Nick decided to try to escape, <u>*although*</u> *he knew his chances were slim*.

The common subordinating conjunctions are listed below.

after	even though	than	whenever
although	how	that	where
as	if	though	wherever
as if	in order that	till	whether
as though	once	unless	which
because	rather than	until	while
before	since	what	who
even if	so (that)	when	why

You can see that sometimes a subordinating conjunction consists of more than one word.

Test yourself 19.1

Underline the subordinating conjunctions in the sentences below. Use the list above to help you.

Sample: She was so tired _that_ she didn't bother brushing her teeth.

Getting started (answers on p. 79)

1. I'll leave the note here because I'm in a hurry.
2. Nick had coached him thoroughly, even though they hadn't had much time.
3. He could see the faint glow of a pipe that Dr. Walters had lit.
4. You should stay here since they obviously need you.
5. She hasn't called here although she'd said she would.

More practice (answers on the website)

6. Jake would be free once he reached the fence.
7. You were behaving as if you were the boss.
8. They were determined to go for a walk, unless it was going to rain.
9. Kevin should think twice before he speaks.
10. I am going to finish this job even if it takes hours.

Here are the same sentences we saw earlier, but this time with the dependent clauses in italics; the subordinating conjunctions are still underlined.

11. She continued arguing _until everyone finally agreed with her_.
12. They live down south _when the weather gets cold_.
13. Jack will buy a house _once he gets a job_.
14. She listened to his comments politely, _even though they sounded silly_.
15. They stopped talking _when it was Eleanor's turn_.

Notice that the subordinating conjunction is always the first word of the dependent clause.

Quick tip 19.2

The subordinating conjunction is always the first word of the dependent clause.

In all of the examples we've looked at so far, the dependent clause has come after the main sentence. But sometimes the dependent clause comes before the main sentence. In the following examples, the subordinating conjunctions are underlined, and the main sentences are in bold:

16. <u>If</u> he knew the truth, **her father would throw the doll away**.
17. <u>When</u> I brought my first paycheck home, **I wanted to frame it**.
18. <u>Once</u> he gets a job, **Jack will buy a house**.
19. <u>When</u> it was Eleanor's turn, **they stopped talking**.

Notice that sentences 18 and 19 are the same as sentences 13 and 15, except that in sentences 18 and 19 the subordinating conjunction and the rest of the dependent clause come before the main sentence rather than after it.

Test yourself 19.2

Underline the subordinating conjunction in each of the sentences below. In each of these sentences, the dependent clause comes before the main sentence.

Sample: <u>Although</u> he was not happily married, he remained faithful to his wife.

Getting started (answers on p. 80)

1. Even though he calmed down, he did not go back to the table immediately.

2. While I enjoy being in the yard, I hate mowing the lawn.

3. Unless there's a heavy downpour, I'm going on that trip.

4. Why anyone would swim in ice cold water, I just don't understand.

5. Whether you are right or wrong, I will support you.

More practice (answers on the website)

6. Wherever we travel, we always have fun together.

7. As I was looking for my keys, I noticed a package in front of the door.

8. Just after they crossed the river, the drawbridge opened up.

9. Before anyone could shout a warning, the tree fell.

10. Since you think you are so smart, tell me the capital of Ghana!

Test yourself 19.3

Underline the subordinating conjunction in each of the sentences below. In some of them, the dependent clause will be after the main sentence; in others, it will come before the main sentence. Again, use the list of subordinating conjunctions to help you.
Sample: <u>Even if</u> you get angry, I will still be there for you.

Getting started (answers on p. 80)

1. Sally spent a lot of time with the babysitter, because her mother had to work.

2. Since you're always busy, I decided to go to the movies without you.

3. After he read the article, he decided not to argue any further.

4. We will move to Seattle, unless you can convince me not to.

5. As if speaking Igbo wasn't enough, this professor speaks Yoruba as well.

More practice (answers on the website)

6. I always get anxious when I am in the doctor's office.

7. Though Tatiana passed the bar exam, she won't be practicing law until next year.

8. Did you ever wonder how children learn language?

9. Once he finishes college, he will look for a job.

10. I took the express train so that I could arrive on time.

Test yourself 19.4 – Grand finale

In each of the sentences below, underline the coordinating or subordinating conjunction. Also, write C if it's a coordinating conjunction and S if it's a subordinating conjunction.
Sample: I work at the mall <u>when</u> I'm home for the holidays. (S)

Getting started (answers on p. 80)

1. I'm the owner and editor of the local newspaper.

2. Before Megan helped him, George would have to prove his loyalty.

3. There's more than one career that he's interested in.

4. They painted her house while she was at work.

5. I arrived early but I still wasn't the first in line.

More practice (answers on the website)

6. If you can understand this, you are a genius!

7. Because you are a dear friend, I will share this with you.

8. Some people are aggressive yet polite.

9. Her administrative assistant will work on that project until it is completed.

10. I rely on Joe to fix my computer, for he is an electronics expert.

To enhance your understanding

Don't confuse conjunctions with prepositions. Some words may function as either:

20a. I've been working hard, for I hope to be promoted. (Coordinating conjunction: connects two sentences.)

20b. I've been working hard for IBM. (Preposition: introduces a noun.)

21a. John left before they served dinner. (Subordinating conjunction: connects two sentences.)

21b. John left before dinner. (Preposition: introduces a noun.)

Lesson 20: Correlative conjunctions

1. <u>Both</u> the windows <u>and</u> the doors need to be replaced.
2. <u>Either</u> I cook <u>or</u> we order take-out.
3. <u>Neither</u> the French <u>nor</u> the British were willing to surrender.
4. <u>If</u> that's a problem, <u>then</u> let me know.

You can see that the underlined conjunctions in these sentences come in pairs, for example *both/and*. The two parts "go together" in these sentences, even though they're not next to each other. These conjunction pairs are called **correlative conjunctions**.

> **Quick tip 20.1**
>
> Correlative conjunctions are two-part conjunctions. Common correlative conjunctions are: *both/and, either/or, if/then, neither/nor.*

Test yourself 20.1

Underline the correlative conjunctions in the sentences below. Don't forget to underline both parts.
Sample: <u>Either</u> the Democratic <u>or</u> the Republican candidate will win.

Getting started (answers on p. 80)

1. Neither you nor your friends are likely to win that raffle.

2. Both Laurette and Denise have been working towards that goal.

3. If my neighbor decides to plant bushes there, then I'll do some landscaping on my side of the fence as well.

4. Neither Don's comments nor his actions surprised me.

5. This athlete is likely to win either a gold or a silver medal.

More practice (answers on the website)

6. If the train runs on Sunday, then I won't drive.

7. Both the director and the playwright attended the rehearsal.

8. Neither Iowa nor Tennessee lies on the shore of the Atlantic Ocean.

9. If they're as nice as they seem, then we'll all get along well.

10. You must call either heads or tails.

Test yourself 20.2 – Grand finale

In each of the sentences below, underline the coordinating, subordinating, or correlative conjunction. Also, write C if it's a coordinating conjunction, S if it's a subordinating conjunction, and CORR if it's a correlative conjunction.
Sample: 1. <u>Neither</u> the brown <u>nor</u> the black shoes look good with that outfit.   (CORR)

Getting started (answers on p. 80)

1. They were pleased with the plan and happy about the decision.

2. I'll see you when you get here.

3. They're worried because she hasn't been feeling well lately.

4. Our encounter was short but sweet.

5. If you tell the truth, then I won't get upset.

More practice (answers on the website)

6. I will be on this case till it is resolved.

7. Once she settles down in her apartment, Jane does not plan to move for a while.

8. You and I make a good team.

9. Either you or I will get to the bottom of this.

10. They dressed as though they were members of the aristocracy.

Answer keys: *Test yourself, Getting started* questions – Unit 6

Test yourself 18.1

1. You can hide between trips <u>and</u> make believe you're innocent.
2. Was it near here <u>or</u> over there?
3. Roger looked around <u>but</u> he didn't see anything.
4. They'll eat chicken <u>or</u> turkey for dinner.
5. Mr. Joseph pulled out three letters <u>and</u> handed one to each of the men.

Test yourself 18.2

1. Mr. Eagle was called away on business, <u>so</u> Mrs. Broxton took his place at the meeting.   <u>sentences</u>
2. He'd heard of it, <u>but</u> he didn't like the idea.   <u>sentences</u>
3. Erin felt real excitement <u>and</u> enthusiasm.   <u>nouns</u>
4. It was raining hard, <u>yet</u> we went to the ball game.   <u>sentences</u>
5. The airline attendant asked, "Would you like coffee <u>or</u> tea?"   <u>nouns</u>

Test yourself 18.3

1. I'll be near <u>or</u> between the stacks.   <u>prepositions</u>
2. He came up with a quick <u>and</u> effective remedy.   <u>adjectives</u>
3. I hope you won't worry <u>or</u> brood too much about it.   <u>verbs</u>
4. This trip will be expensive <u>but</u> worthwhile.   <u>adjectives</u>
5. I am at <u>or</u> near a breakthrough.   <u>prepositions</u>

Test yourself 18.4

1. **For**
2. **And**
3. **Nor**
4. **But**
5. **Or**
6. **Yet**
7. **So**

Test yourself 19.1

1. I'll leave the note here <u>because</u> I'm in a hurry.
2. Nick had coached him thoroughly, <u>even though</u> they hadn't had much time.
3. He could see the faint glow of a pipe <u>that</u> Dr. Walters had lit.
4. You should stay here <u>since</u> they obviously need you.
5. She hasn't called here <u>although</u> she'd said she would.

Test yourself 19.2

1. Even though he calmed down, he did not go back to the table immediately.
2. While I enjoy being in the yard, I hate mowing the lawn.
3. Unless there's a heavy downpour, I'm going on that trip.
4. Why anyone would swim in ice cold water, I just don't understand.
5. Whether you are right or wrong, I will support you.

Test yourself 19.3

1. Sally spent a lot of time with the babysitter, because her mother had to work.
2. Since you're always busy, I decided to go to the movies without you.
3. After he read the article, he decided not to argue any further.
4. We will move to Seattle, unless you can convince me not to.
5. As if speaking Igbo wasn't enough, this professor speaks Yoruba as well.

Test yourself 19.4

1. I'm the owner and editor of the local newspaper. (C)
2. Before Megan helped him, George would have to prove his loyalty. (S)
3. There's more than one career that he's interested in. (S)
4. They painted her house while she was at work. (S)
5. I arrived early but I still wasn't the first in line. (C)

Test yourself 20.1

1. Neither you nor your friends are likely to win that raffle.
2. Both Laurette and Denise have been working towards that goal.
3. If my neighbor decides to plant bushes there, then I'll do some landscaping on my side of the fence as well.
4. Neither Don's comments nor his actions surprised me.
5. This athlete is likely to win either a gold or a silver medal.

Test yourself 20.2

1. They were pleased with the plan and happy about the decision. (C)
2. I'll see you when you get here. (S)
3. They're worried because she hasn't been feeling well lately. (S)
4. Our encounter was short but sweet. (C)
5. If you tell the truth, then I won't get upset. (CORR)

☞ **FOR A REVIEW EXERCISE OF THIS UNIT, SEE THE WEBSITE.**

As Melissa entered the door of the dimly lit Cathedral, Melissa held tightly to Melissa's backpack. Suddenly, Melissa thought that Melissa saw a shadow moving. "This is scary," whispered Melissa to Melissa.

What's strange about the sentences in the above text? What is strange is that they're missing **pronouns**, words that replace nouns in a sentence. You'll probably agree that these next sentences are a vast improvement on the first version:

As Melissa entered the door of the dimly lit Cathedral, she held tightly to her backpack. Suddenly, she thought that she saw a shadow moving. "This is scary," whispered Melissa to herself.

We may never find out what happens to Melissa, but replacing *Melissa* with pronouns like *she* and *her* makes her far more palatable.

As far as pronouns go, there's bad news and there's good news. The bad news is that there are a number of different kinds of pronouns. The good news is that there are only a few pronouns of each type. Look at the pronouns themselves and get a feel for the kinds of words they are. Some of the types may have long labels, but the pronouns themselves are usually short words.

Lesson 21: Subject and object pronouns

Subject pronouns

Let's look at the following sentences:

     1a. <u>Diplomats</u> travel extensively.
     1b. <u>They</u> travel extensively.
     2a. <u>Professor Susan Fields</u> chaired the meeting.
     2b. <u>She</u> chaired the meeting.
     3a. <u>Ben</u> plays cards every week.
     3b. <u>He</u> plays cards every week.

Notice that in each sentence pair, the underlined pronoun replaces the underlined noun. The underlined noun is doing the action in the sentence and comes before the verb. This kind of noun is called the **subject** of the sentence and the pronoun that replaces it is called a **subject pronoun**.

Now let's examine these sentences:

     4a. <u>Biology</u> is her favorite subject.
     4b. <u>It</u> is her favorite subject.
     5a. <u>Bob</u> seems happy.
     5b. <u>He</u> seems happy.
     6a. <u>Mrs. Peters</u> becomes agitated easily.
     6b. <u>She</u> becomes agitated easily.

Notice again that in each sentence pair, the underlined pronoun replaces the underlined noun. Here, the underlined nouns come before linking verbs (see Lesson 9); although they are not performing an action, they are still considered to be subjects. Again, the pronoun that replaces the subject is a subject pronoun.

There are only seven subject pronouns; they are listed in *Quick tip* 21.1.

Quick tip 21.1

The subject pronouns are: *I, you, he, she, it, we, they.*

Test yourself 21.1

Underline the subject pronouns in the sentences below.

Sample: <u>We</u> wandered around town, looking for a place to have lunch.

Getting started (answers on p. 99)

1. I crossed the piazza and headed towards the church.

2. Unfortunately, it was closed.

3. They simply stood there, waiting for me.

4. Yesterday, she went shopping.

5. We should get together sometime.

More practice (answers on the website)

6. He is the grandson of an immigrant from Italy.

7. We often dream about important things.

8. You have been to their house for dinner.

9. They often have interesting discussions.

10. Last night they drove to San Francisco.

Object pronouns

7a. Karen bought <u>the red car</u>.
7b. Karen bought <u>it</u>.
8a. The prize was given to <u>Steve and Bill</u>.
8b. The prize was given to <u>them</u>.
9a. I'm watching <u>the baby</u>.
9b. I'm watching <u>her</u>.

The underlined nouns in the sentences above are **not** subjects. Rather, they are **objects**: they either follow the main verb or they follow a preposition. (For more on objects, see Unit 13.) Pronouns that replace objects, like those underlined in sentences 7b, 8b, and 9b above, are called **object pronouns**.

There are only seven object pronouns; they are listed in *Quick tip* 21.2.

> **Quick tip 21.2**
>
> The object pronouns are: me, *you, her, him, it, us, them*.

You can see that two pronouns, *you* and *it*, are particularly hardworking: they can function as either subject or object pronouns.

Test yourself 21.2

Underline the object pronouns in each of the sentences below. There may be more than one pronoun in a sentence.
Sample: Churchill called <u>them</u> to a meeting.

Getting started (answers on p. 99)

1. Mary heard him.

2. The detective watched us suspiciously.

3. Stop bothering me!

4. Steven sat down between him and her.

5. Do the students understand it?

More practice (answers on the website)

6. My friends have never heard of them.

7. Barry gave her a present.

8. Harry's cousin lives near them.

9. Most competitors were envious of him.

10. A strange man is standing next to you and me.

Test yourself 21.3

Decide if each pronoun below is a subject or object pronoun.
Sample: we <u>subject</u>

Getting started (answers on p. 99)

1. them ....
2. he ....
3. I ....
4. us ....
5. her ....

More practice (answers on the website)

6. they ....
7. she ....
8. me ....
9. him ....
10. we ....

Test yourself 21.4

Underline the pronouns in each of the sentences below. Identify each either as a subject pronoun or an object pronoun. Keep in mind that the pronouns _you_ and _it_ can be either subject or object pronouns, depending on how they are being used. There may be more than one pronoun in a sentence. Sample: You really did it right. (subject; object)

Getting started (answers on p. 99)

1. The clerk had been sent to work with him.
2. The research required them to work closely together.
3. It is brighter than that other lamp.
4. If you know the answer, please tell me.
5. We will be moving near you.

More practice (answers on the website)

6. They were hiding in the bushes.
7. I am giving it to you.
8. He went too far this time.
9. Theresa's parents worried about her.
10. She hears from him often.

You know that when you're talking about yourself, you use the pronouns _I_ or _me_, and when you're talking about a group of people, you use the pronouns _they_ or _them_. That is, we choose different pronouns depending on the person or thing the pronouns refer to. Pronouns that vary in this way are called **personal pronouns**. Subject and object pronouns are types of personal pronouns; see Lessons 22 and 24 for two other kinds.

Personal pronouns that refer to the speaker in a conversation, like _I_ and _we_, are called **first person pronouns**. Those that refer to the listener, like _you_, are called **second person pronouns**. And those that refer to anyone or anything else, like _he_ or _they_, are called **third person pronouns**.

In addition, pronouns that refer to only one person or thing, like _I_ and _he_, are called **singular pronouns**; those that refer to more than one person or thing, like _we_ and _they_, are called **plural pronouns**.

Here's a complete breakdown of the subject and object pronouns:

	Subject	_Object_
First person singular	I	me
Second person singular	you	you
Third person singular	he, she, it	him, her, it
First person plural	we	us
Second person plural	you	you
Third person plural	they	them

Lesson 22: Reflexive pronouns

Do the following sentences seem strange to you?

1. John Smith saw John Smith in the mirror.
2. My friends were talking among my friends.
3. Sam's only cat was grooming Sam's only cat.

These sentences are strange because they're missing **reflexive pronouns**, those pronouns that end in *-self* or *-selves*. As you can see from the sentences below, we use reflexive pronouns whenever we refer to the same person or thing more than once in the same basic sentence. Sentences 1–3 should be stated like this:

4. John Smith saw himself in the mirror.
5. My best friends were talking among themselves.
6. Sam's only cat was grooming herself.

Here are some more examples, first without and then with a reflexive pronoun.

7a. The boy washed the boy.
7b. The boy washed himself.
8a. Tom and Harry watched Tom and Harry on the video.
8b. Tom and Harry watched themselves on the video.
9a. You can see you doing that.
9b. You can see yourself doing that.

Notice that if we hear, for example, *The boy washed the boy*, without a reflexive pronoun, then we assume that someone's talking about two different boys. Similarly, the sentence *He shaved him* suggests that the person (a male) who did the shaving and the person (a male) who received the shaving are not the same. The reflexive pronoun lets the listener know that the speaker is referring to the same person or thing.

Quick tip 22.1 lists the reflexive pronouns. They're easy to identify because they all end in *-self* or *-selves* (*Quick tip* 22.2).

Quick tip 22.1

The reflexive pronouns are: *myself, yourself, himself, herself, itself, ourselves, yourselves, themselves*.

Quick tip 22.2

All the reflexive pronouns end in *-self* (singular) or *-selves* (plural).

Test yourself 22.1

Underline the reflexive pronouns in each of the sentences below.
Sample: That computer is so smart it can repair itself.

Getting started (answers on p. 99)

1. John was a person who always pushed himself to the limit.

2. Watch yourself!

3. We prided ourselves on being silly.

4. The directors of that company can blame no one but themselves.

5. I see myself as a successful writer someday.

More practice (answers on the website)

6. All of you should be ashamed of yourselves!

7. Rosanna treated herself to a lavish vacation.

8. I wish my car started itself in the dead of winter.

9. Would everyone in the room please identify himself?

10. You should take better care of yourself!

Test yourself 22.2

Underline the reflexive, subject, and object pronouns in each of the sentences below. Label each as reflexive, subject, or object. Some sentences will have more than one pronoun.
Sample: Greta's perseverance benefitted both <u>herself</u> and the rest of the staff.   (reflexive)

Getting started (answers on p. 99)

1. I have found that I can do it when the room is quiet.

2. He noticed that she often immersed herself in a book.

3. We have known her for years.

4. Some guests told us that they forced themselves to get up at 6 A.M.

5. You don't need to explain yourself to me.

More practice (answers on the website)

6. Mr. Ballantine said that he appreciated us.

7. If you want to leave, please let me know.

8. Who among us wants to commit himself to another year of service?

9. Jay's wife promised herself never to do it again.

10. Reflexive pronouns are easy to identify, don't you agree?

Lesson 23: Demonstrative pronouns

Do you remember the underlined words in the sentences below?
1. Are you sure you want <u>this</u>?
2. We agreed about <u>that</u>.
3. I'm not sure I like <u>these</u>.
4. <u>Those</u> look delicious.

In Lesson 13 we talked about the use of demonstratives before a noun, for example: *this dog*, *that idea*, *these songs*, *those curtains*. That is, we talked about demonstratives used as determiners. But demonstratives can also be used without a noun following them, as you can see from sentences 1–4. In these cases, because the demonstrative replaces a noun (or noun phrase), it is called a **demonstrative pronoun**. For example, in sentence 1, the demonstrative pronoun *this* can be replacing a noun such as *spaghetti* or *magazines*.

It's easy to remember demonstrative pronouns, because there are only four of them; they are listed in *Quick tip* 23.1.

Quick tip 23.1

There are only four demonstrative pronouns: *this, that, these,* and *those*.

It might help you remember the word "demonstrative" if you think of these words as "demonstrating" something, in a way, pointing to something.

Test yourself 23.1

Underline the demonstrative pronoun in each of the sentences below.
Sample: Lenny wasn't sure he really wanted <u>those</u>.

Getting started (answers on p. 100)

1. That wasn't really Hannah's job, but I appreciate her doing it anyway.

2. Natasha really likes these.

3. He wasn't good at riddles but managed to solve those.

4. I never thought it would come to this.

5. These are very difficult times.

More practice (answers on the website)

6. Those were the good old days.

7. Sean thought he would never see that.

8. This is absolutely unacceptable.

9. Mrs. Wallace would rather buy these.

10. That is the funniest thing I've ever seen.

Test yourself 23.2

Decide if each pronoun below is a subject, object, reflexive, or demonstrative pronoun.
Sample: she subject

Getting started (answers on p. 100)   *More practice* (answers on the website)

1. yourselves ....   6. them ....

2. those ....   7. that ....

3. me ....   8. us ....

4. we ....   9. herself ....

5. itself ....   10. these ....

Test yourself 23.3

Underline the pronouns in each of the sentences below. Label each as demonstrative, subject, object, or reflexive. Some sentences will have more than one pronoun.

Sample: Did <u>you</u> spill <u>that</u> on <u>yourself</u>?   (subject; demonstrative; reflexive)

Getting started (answers on p. 100)

1. We were angry at ourselves. _____

2. He asked us to explain this. _____

3. It works just as well at home. _____

4. They sent these to us. _____

5. The baseball player dusted himself off. _____

More practice (answers on the website)

6. You should do this for yourself. _____

7. This reminds me of why I should respect myself. _____

8. That is the way they should behave themselves. _____

9. We excused ourselves right after dinner. _____

10. It could bother them. _____

Lesson 24: Possessive pronouns

You won't be surprised to learn that possessive pronouns are pronouns that indicate possession, or ownership. Some possessive pronouns are underlined here:

1. Mr. Smith explained his ideas to the audience.
2. I wish I could accept their invitation.
3. That suitcase isn't mine.
4. Yours was the best essay in the class.

If you look closely, you'll notice that the possessive pronouns in sentences 1–4 fall into two groups. The ones in sentences 1 and 2 are followed by a noun: *his ideas*, *their invitation*. The ones in sentences 3 and 4 are not followed by a noun; rather, they stand on their own in the sentence. We'll talk about each kind separately.

The possessive pronouns in sentences 1 and 2 may look familiar to you. That's because they were described in Lesson 14, as part of our discussion of determiners. Like articles (*a*, *an*, *the*), possessive pronouns which function as determiners can occur in the slot _____ *house* (for example, *his house*, *our house*, *your house*). Since they function as determiners, you can understand why they are followed by a noun. In *Quick tip* 14.1 we called these determiner possessive pronouns and provided the full list. We repeat them here: *my, your, his, her, its, our, their*.

Test yourself 24.1

Underline the determiner possessive pronoun in each of the sentences below. Remember: determiner possessive pronouns are followed by nouns.
Sample: Many of our ideas back then were equally absurd.

Getting started (answers on p. 100)

1. The woman hid her feelings well.
2. He was younger than his wife.
3. Mr. and Mrs. Bradford adored their son.
4. Thomas and Natalie were the best students in my class.
5. Your eyes look very tired.

More practice (answers on the website)

6. The salesman's car does not show its age.
7. We should just pack up our things and get out of here.
8. I took a look at your face and I knew immediately that you were honest.
9. My daughter is very good about brushing her teeth regularly.
10. Gamblers are secretive about their losses.

Now on to the possessive pronouns in sentences 3 and 4, the kind that can stand alone in a sentence. Here are some more examples:

5. The Greens' tent came loose in the storm but ours remained secure.
6. Yours was the first card I noticed.
7. The scientist hurried from that laboratory to mine.

These possessive pronouns replace a whole noun (actually, a whole noun phrase, but we haven't gotten to that yet; see Lesson 28). And since the word *nominal* means "noun-like," these pronouns are sometimes called **possessive pronouns with nominal function**. We will simply call them **nominal possessive pronouns**.

> **Quick tip 24.1**
>
> Nominal possessive pronouns replace a whole noun (or noun phrase). For example, instead of saying *That book is Sally's book* we can simply say, *That book is hers*. The nominal possessive pronouns are: *mine, yours, his, hers, its, ours, theirs*.

Notice that the pronouns *his* and *its* can function either as determiner possessive pronouns (see *Quick tip* 14.1) or as nominal possessive pronouns (see *Quick tip* 24.1).

> **To enhance your understanding**
> Don't confuse possessive pronouns with contracted pronouns:
>
> 8a. It's (= it is) a wonderful day. (contracted pronoun)
> 8b. Its positives outweigh its negatives. (determiner possessive pronoun)
> 9a. You're (= you are) absolutely right. (contracted pronoun)
> 9b. Your shoelaces are untied. (determiner possessive pronoun)
> 10a. They're (= they are) leaving. (contracted pronoun)
> 10b. Their leaving early was unexpected. (determiner possessive pronoun)
> As you can see, the contracted pronoun is always written with an apostrophe.

Test yourself 24.2

Underline the nominal possessive pronoun in each of the sentences below.
Sample: Pete and Cathy are convinced the idea was theirs.

Getting started (answers on p. 100)

1. The rattlesnake is his.

2. The mother needs her nourishment and the baby needs hers also.

3. Yours is the room on the left.

4. The computer on the table is mine.

5. Ours is the next house on the block.

More practice (answers on the website)

6. Theirs will probably be the best dog in the show.

7. Hiring the band is not Dave's responsibility – it is yours.

8. Whatever the neighbors want to haul away is theirs for the taking.

9. Most people's experience is probably similar to hers.

10. His is not the only opinion that matters.

Test yourself 24.3

Decide if each possessive pronoun below is a determiner or a nominal possessive pronoun.
Sample: yours nominal

Getting started (answers on p. 100)

1. my ....
2. theirs ....
3. mine ....
4. your ....
5. her ....

More practice (answers on the website)

6. our ....
7. their ....
8. ours ....
9. hers ....
10. his ....

Test yourself 24.4

Underline the possessive pronoun in each of the sentences below. Then indicate if it functions as a determiner or a nominal possessive pronoun.

Sample: Jack's trip was good, but not nearly as exciting as <u>theirs</u>.   (determiner)

Getting started (answers on p. 101)

1. Listening to music might interfere with your ability to concentrate.   ....

2. Some of the CDs are ours.   ....

3. The prisoner was ordered to hand over his things.   ....

4. In my opinion, you should apologize.   ....

5. Hers is the only dissenting voice in the room.   ....

More practice (answers on the website)

6. The big suitcase over there is mine.   ....

7. Someone wants to buy our company.   ....

8. Some day this will all be yours.   ....

9. The suspects had their day in court.   ....

10. The bank is going to need her signature.   ....

Test yourself 24.5

Decide if each pronoun below is a determiner possessive pronoun (*my, our*, etc.), nominal possessive pronoun (*mine, ours*, etc.), subject pronoun (*I, we*, etc.), object pronoun (*me, us*, etc.), reflexive pronoun (*myself, ourselves*, etc.), or demonstrative pronoun (*this, these*, etc.).

Sample: that <u>demonstrative</u>

Getting started (answers on p. 101)

1. their ....
2. them ....
3. yourselves ....
4. we ....
5. hers ....

More practice (answers on the website)

6. us ....
7. itself ....
8. those ....
9. me ....
10. yours ....

Test yourself 24.6 – Grand finale

Underline the pronouns in each of the sentences below. Label each as determiner possessive, nominal possessive, subject, object, demonstrative, or reflexive. Some sentences will have more than one pronoun.

Sample: <u>They</u> were convinced that <u>she</u> would do a great job for <u>them</u>.   (subject; subject; object)

Getting started (answers on p. 101)

1. Their employees were working during lunch. ....

2. He asked us for the answer. ....

3. It made a huge difference to her and to her friends. ....

4. She looked at herself in the rearview mirror of my car. ....

5. Some guy introduced himself and gave me his business card. ....

More practice (answers on the website)

6. You shouldn't compare your accomplishments to theirs. ....

7. The candidates presented themselves and their positions to us. ....

8. Are all these hers or mine? ....

9. You should thank him for bringing that to your attention. ....

10. We saved this for last because of its complexity and because the opportunity
    presented itself to include all pronoun types in it – but the final judgment is yours!

....

Lesson 25: Interrogative pronouns

What do you notice about the underlined words in the following sentences?

1. Who went first?
2. What was the man carrying?
3. Which did you buy?

You undoubtedly recognize them as question words. They are called **interrogative pronouns**; we list them in *Quick tip* 25.1.

Quick tip 25.1

Interrogative pronouns are question words. The interrogative pronouns are: *how, what, when, where, which, who, whom, whose, why*. Look for the question mark to help find them.

You may be wondering why these are considered to be pronouns. Like other pronouns, interrogative pronouns represent something else, often a noun. They represent missing information, information that's in the answer to a question:

4a. Who went first?
4b. Harry went first.
5a. What was the man carrying?
5b. The man was carrying a camera.
6a. Which did you buy?
6b. I bought the red car.

Since, when we ask a question, we don't yet know what the answer will be, we have no choice but to use a question word, or interrogative pronoun, to represent the information we are asking about.

To enhance your understanding

Don't confuse the following – they sound the same:

7a. Who's (= who is) there?
7b. Whose party are we going to?

Test yourself 25.1

Underline the interrogative pronoun in each of the sentences below.
Sample: Why is his approach so exciting?

Getting started (answers on p. 101)

1. To whom did you send the package?

2. Whose is it?

3. What can the producer do about it?

4. How can I believe you are telling the truth?

5. Where have you been?

More practice (answers on the website)

6. When did you come home last night?

7. Why is it so dark in this room?

8. Which do you prefer?

9. Who gave you permission to open that box?

10. From whom did you get this call?

Test yourself 25.2

Decide if each pronoun below is an interrogative pronoun (*who*, *what*), demonstrative pronoun (*this*, *these*, etc.), object pronoun (*me*, *us*, etc.), or reflexive pronoun (*myself*, *ourselves*, etc.).
Sample: myself   reflexive

Getting started (answers on p. 101)

1. herself ....

2. which ....

3. who ....

4. those ....

5. him ....

More practice (answers on the website)

6. itself ....

7. how ....

8. what ....

9. us ....

10. whom ....

Test yourself 25.3

Underline the interrogative, possessive, and subject pronouns in each of the sentences below. Label each as interrogative (*what*, *who*, etc.), determiner possessive (*my*, *our*, etc.), nominal possessive (*mine*, *ours*, etc.), or subject (*I*, *we*, etc.). Some sentences will have more than one pronoun. (Remember that interrogative pronouns are used in questions, so look for that question mark to help you.)
Sample: What are you looking for?   (interrogative; subject)

Getting started (answers on p. 101)

1. Where did your friend hide the ball? ....

2. Which does Jack like: coffee or tea? ....

3. Ours was the only entry in the contest. ....

4. We kept our promise. ....

5. Your business is yours alone. ....

More practice (answers on the website)

6. Why didn't you wash your car? ....

7. He thought that the brown coat was his. ....

8. The bicycle is mine, not hers. ....

9. I mailed my package to Korea. ....

10. When will he arrive? ....

Test yourself 25.4

Underline the pronouns in each of the sentences below. Don't worry about what kind of pronoun each is. Some sentences will have more than one pronoun.
Sample: <u>What</u> will <u>they</u> buy at <u>his</u> store?

Getting started (answers on p. 102)

1. You keep hurting yourself when you go skiing.

2. We should get it to them as soon as possible.

3. Who was Bill thinking of sending them to?

4. She has a great opportunity to advance herself in her company.

5. When will your great novel be finished?

More practice (answers on the website)

6. Our hope is that one day we will find ourselves living it up in style.

7. That will never happen under his watch.

8. Her determination gave her the impetus to improve herself.

9. Where are those new shirts you bought yourself yesterday?

10. Our ball club prides itself on its ability to win most of our games.

To further enhance your understanding

As we discussed at the beginning of this Lesson, interrogatives function as pronouns – they replace nouns. Note, however, that some interrogatives can also function as determiners – they can precede a noun. You can see this in the examples below:

8. <u>Which book</u> did you read last?

9. <u>Whose purse</u> is on the table?

10. <u>What name</u> did they choose for their baby?

Lesson 26: Relative pronouns

Here are some sentences with interrogative pronouns, like the ones you've already seen in Lesson 25. The interrogative pronouns are underlined.

    1. <u>Who</u> was laughing?

    2. <u>Whose</u> is this?

Now look at the following sentences, which contain the same underlined words. How are these sentences different from sentences 1 and 2?

    3. I like the woman <u>who</u> lives next door.

    4. He's the engineer <u>whose</u> life was disrupted by a messy divorce.

You've probably noticed that, unlike sentences 1 and 2 above, sentences 3 and 4 are not questions. The same pronouns are being used, but not to ask a question. Instead, these pronouns are used in sentences 3 and 4 to replace a noun that's already mentioned earlier in the sentence. When used this way, these pronouns are called **relative pronouns**. They are listed in *Quick tip* 26.1

Quick tip 26.1

The common relative pronouns are: *that, which, who, whom, whose*. They refer back to a noun in the sentence.

Test yourself 26.1

Underline the relative pronoun in each of the sentences below.

Sample: The prominent oil man <u>who</u> bought that house is not a generous man.

Getting started (answers on p. 102)

1. John's is the essay that was the most well-written.

2. His wife was the woman whom he loved the most.

3. There is no one who can make me laugh more than you.

4. Danny bought a gift which appealed to him.

5. Last week I met the man whose cousin married my friend.

More practice (answers on the website)

6. In general, Sharon is nice to people whom she meets.

7. I will stand on the line which is shorter.

8. The person who leaves last should turn the lights off.

9. She saw the journey which she had undertaken stretch out before her.

10. Anna leaves a good impression on employers who interview her.

Let's look at sentences 3 and 4 more closely.

    3. I like the woman <u>who</u> lives next door.

In this sentence, who lives next door? Answer: *the woman*. So instead of saying something like *I like the woman. The woman lives next door*, we replace the second occurrence of *the woman* with the pronoun who, giving us the sentence *I like the woman who lives next door*. In fact, the word *who* is doing two things: it's representing *the woman* and it's joining *lives next door* to the main part of the sentence.

    4. He's the engineer whose life was disrupted by a messy divorce.

In this sentence, whose life was disrupted by a messy divorce? Answer: *the engineer's*. So instead of saying something like *He's the engineer. The engineer's life was disrupted by a messy divorce*, we replace the second occurrence of *the engineer* (actually, in this case, *the engineer's*) with the pronoun *whose*, giving us the sentence *He's the engineer whose life was disrupted by a messy divorce*. Again, the word *whose* is doing two things: it's representing *the engineer* and it's joining *life was disrupted by a messy divorce* to the main part of the sentence.

In the following sentence, what broke?

    5. Sam fixed the computer that broke.

Answer: *the computer*. So instead of saying something like *Sam fixed the computer. The computer broke*, we replace the second occurrence of *the computer* with the pronoun that, giving us the sentence *Sam fixed the computer that broke*. Again, the word *that* is doing two things: it's representing *the computer* and it's joining *broke* to the main part of the sentence.

You may remember that in Lesson 19 we talked about subordinating conjunctions, which are words that connect a sentence (the main sentence) with another sentence which is a subpart of it. The relative pronouns here are doing the same thing and in fact, relative pronouns are one kind of subordinating conjunction (and appear on the list in Lesson 19).

Quick tip 26.2

Relative pronouns are a type of subordinating conjunction. A relative pronoun typically occurs soon after the noun it refers to. Example: *He liked the teacher who gave easy tests.*

Test yourself 26.2

The relative pronoun is underlined in each of the sentences below. Your job is to find the noun that the relative pronoun is referring to.

Sample: I watched a few movies that were really bad.   (movies)

Getting started (answers on p. 102)

1. They are men who are ambitious.

2. The salesman noticed the potatoes that he planted.

3. It is worth buying stocks which increase in value.

4. The guests whom we invited a week ago just arrived.

5 The flight that was supposed to leave at 5 is still delayed.

More practice (answers on the website)

6. The patients whose lives are in danger need those drugs.

7. The bus which has just arrived is scheduled to leave for Phoenix.

8. Rebecca noticed the tourists who were gathered around the statue.

9. The milk that Jane bought seems to be fresh.

10. The contractor whom we hired did not show up today.

Test yourself 26.3

Underline and identify the interrogative or relative pronoun in each of the sentences below. (Remember that the interrogative pronouns will always be in a question.) In this exercise, the sentences will only have either an interrogative or a relative pronoun, but not both.
Sample: Why are you going?   (interrogative)

Getting started (answers on p. 102)

1. What can I do about it?

2. Adam is the person whom you need to talk to.

3. I fixed the clock that was broken.

4. The police will find the person who committed this crime.

5. When will the show start?

More practice (answers on the website)

6. Which do you want us to choose?

7. The restaurant in which we ate was awful.

8. I don't care for the earrings which this actress is wearing.

9. Several of the boys who attended the party became rowdy.

10. He's happy with the solution that I'm proposing.

To enhance your understanding

Notice that the word *that* has lots of uses. These are demonstrated here:

6. I think that man is intriguing.   (demonstrative determiner)
7. I think that is the way to go.   (demonstrative pronoun)
8. I think that the sun will shine tomorrow.   (subordinating conjunction: introducing a clause)
9. I think the car that you want was sold yesterday.   (relative pronoun: introducing a clause and referring back to a noun)

You can have more than one *that* within the same sentence:

10. I think that that is the cat that belongs to you.

And that's that!

To further enhance your understanding

There are also some less commonly used relative pronouns with the suffix *-ever*. Some examples:

11. I'll be happy with whatever you decide to do.
12. My mother always told me to marry whoever I wanted to.
13. They can travel with whomever they choose.

There is an important difference between the relative pronouns ending in *-ever* and those we looked at earlier and listed in *Quick tip* 26.1. As you can see in sentences 11–13, the *-ever* relative pronouns do not refer back to a noun that comes before. Rather, they represent a noun all by themselves.

Answer keys: *Test yourself, Getting started* questions – Unit 7

Test yourself 21.1

1. I crossed the piazza and headed towards the church.
2. Unfortunately, it was closed.
3. They simply stood there, waiting for me.
4. Yesterday, she went shopping.
5. We should get together sometime.

Test yourself 21.2

1. Mary heard him.
2. The detectives watched us suspiciously.
3. Stop bothering me!
4. Steven sat down between him and her.
5. Do the students understand it?

Test yourself 21.3

1. them   object
2. he   subject
3. I   subject
4. us   object
5. her   object

Test yourself 21.4

1. The clerk had been sent to work with him. (object)
2. The research required them to work closely together. (object)
3. It is brighter than that other lamp. (subject)
4. If you know the answer, please tell me. (subject; object)
5. We will be moving near you. (subject; object)

Test yourself 22.1

1. John was a person who always pushed himself to the limit.
2. Watch yourself!
3. We prided ourselves on being sillly.
4. The directors of that company can blame no one but themselves.
5. I see myself as a successful writer someday.

Test yourself 22.2

1. I have found that I can do it when the room is quiet.
   (subject; subject; object)

2. He noticed that <u>she</u> often immersed <u>herself</u> in a book.
   (subject; subject; reflexive)

3. <u>We</u> have known <u>her</u> for years.   (subject; object)

4. Some guests told <u>us</u> that <u>they</u> forced <u>themselves</u> to get up at 6 A.M.
   (object; subject; reflexive)

5. <u>You</u> don't need to explain <u>yourself</u> to <u>me</u>.   (subject; reflexive; object)

Test yourself 23.1

1. <u>That</u> wasn't really Hannah's job, but I appreciate her doing it anyway.
2. Natasha really likes <u>these</u>.
3. He wasn't good at riddles but managed to solve <u>those</u>.
4. I never thought it would come to <u>this</u>.
5. <u>These</u> are very difficult times.

Test yourself 23.2

1. yourselves   <u>reflexive</u>
2. those   <u>demonstrative</u>
3. me   <u>object</u>
4. we   <u>subject</u>
5. itself   <u>reflexive</u>

Test yourself 23.3

1. <u>We</u> were angry at <u>ourselves</u>.   (subject; reflexive)
2. <u>He</u> asked <u>us</u> to explain <u>this</u>.   (subject; object; demonstrative)
3. <u>It</u> works just as well at home.   (subject)
4. <u>They</u> sent <u>these</u> to <u>us</u>.   (subject; demonstrative; object)
5. The baseball player dusted <u>himself</u> off.   (reflexive)

Test yourself 24.1

1. The woman hid <u>her</u> feelings well.
2. He was younger than <u>his</u> wife.
3. Mr. and Mrs. Bradford adored <u>their</u> son.
4. Thomas and Natalie were the best students in <u>my</u> class.
5. <u>Your</u> eyes look very tired.

Test yourself 24.2

1. The rattlesnake is <u>his</u>.
2. The mother needs her nourishment and the baby needs <u>hers</u> also.
3. <u>Yours</u> is the room on the left.
4. The computer on the table is <u>mine</u>.
5. <u>Ours</u> is the next house on the block.

Test yourself 24.3

1. my   <u>determiner</u>
2. theirs   <u>nominal</u>
3. mine   <u>nominal</u>
4. your   <u>determiner</u>
5. her   <u>determiner</u>

Test yourself 24.4

1. Listening to music might interfere with <u>your</u> ability to concentrate.   (determiner)
2. Some of those CDs are <u>ours</u>.   (nominal)
3. The prisoner was ordered to hand over <u>his</u> things.   (determiner)
4. In <u>my</u> opinion, you should apologize.   (determiner)
5. <u>Hers</u> is the only dissenting voice in the room.   (nominal)

Test yourself 24.5

1. their   <u>determiner possessive</u>
2. them   <u>object</u>
3. yourselves   <u>reflexive</u>
4. we   <u>subject</u>
5. hers nominal <u>possessive</u>

Test yourself 24.6

1. <u>Their</u> employees were working during lunch.
   (determiner possessive)
2. <u>He</u> asked <u>us</u> for the answer.
   (subject; object)
3. It made a huge difference to <u>her</u> and to <u>her</u> friends.
   (subject; object; determiner possessive)
4. <u>She</u> looked at <u>herself</u> in the rearview mirror of <u>my</u> car.
   (subject; reflexive; determiner possessive)
5. Some guy introduced <u>himself</u> and gave <u>me</u> <u>his</u> business card.
   (reflexive; object; determiner possessive)

Test yourself 25.1

1. To <u>whom</u> did you send the package?
2. <u>Whose</u> is it?
3. <u>What</u> can the producer do about it?
4. <u>How</u> can I believe you are telling the truth?
5. <u>Where</u> have you been?

Test yourself 25.2

1. herself   <u>reflexive</u>
2. which   <u>interrogative</u>
3. who   <u>interrogative</u>
4. those   <u>demonstrative</u>
5. him   <u>object</u>

Test yourself 25.3

1. <u>Where</u> did <u>your</u> friend hide the ball?   (interrogative; determiner possessive)
2. <u>Which</u> does Jack like: coffee or tea?   (interrogative)
3. <u>Ours</u> was the only entry in the contest.   (nominal possessive)
4. <u>We</u> kept <u>our</u> promise.   (subject; determiner possessive)
5. <u>Your</u> business is <u>yours</u> alone.   (determiner possessive; nominal possessive)

Test yourself 25.4

1. <u>You</u> keep hurting <u>yourself</u> when <u>you</u> go skiing.
2. <u>We</u> should get <u>it</u> to <u>them</u> as soon as possible.
3. <u>Who</u> was Bill thinking of sending <u>them</u> to?
4. <u>She</u> has a great opportunity to advance <u>herself</u> in <u>her</u> company.
5. <u>When</u> will <u>your</u> great novel be finished?

Test yourself 26.1

1. John's is the essay <u>that</u> was the most well written.
2. His wife was the woman <u>whom</u> he loved the most.
3. There is no one <u>who</u> can make me laugh more than you.
4. Danny bought a gift <u>which</u> appealed to him.
5. Last week I met the man <u>whose</u> cousin married my friend.

Test yourself 26.2

1. They are men <u>who</u> are ambitious.   (men)
2. The salesman noticed the potatoes <u>that</u> he planted.   (potatoes)
3. It is worth buying stocks <u>which</u> increase in value.   (stocks)
4. The guests <u>whom</u> we invited a week ago just arrived.   (guests)
5. The flight <u>that</u> was supposed to leave at 5 is still delayed.   (flight)

Test yourself 26.3

1. <u>What</u> can I do about it?   (interrogative)
2. Adam is the person <u>whom</u> you need to talk to.   (relative)
3. I fixed the clock <u>that</u> was broken.   (relative)
4. The police will find the person <u>who</u> committed this crime.   (relative)
5. <u>When</u> will the show start?   (interrogative)

☞ **FOR A REVIEW EXERCISE OF THIS UNIT, SEE THE WEBSITE.**

Lesson 27: Identifying adverbs

We've saved adverbs for last because they can be a bit tricky. Adverbs do lots of different things and can be in lots of different places in a sentence. In fact, the chances are, if you don't know what else a word is, it's probably an adverb.

The adverbs are underlined in the sentences below:

1. I live <u>here</u>.   (information about location)
2. My brother is arriving <u>today</u>.   (information about time)
3. She dances <u>gracefully</u>.   (information about manner)
4. That child is <u>very</u> sweet.   (degree information about an adjective, in this case, about *sweet*)
5. She works <u>extremely</u> efficiently.   (degree information about another adverb, in this case, about *efficiently*)

Quick tip 27.1

Adverbs generally indicate information about location, time, degree, and manner. They provide extra information about the action in a sentence, about adjectives and about other adverbs.

Quick tip 27.2

If you don't know what else a word is (and you've eliminated the other parts of speech), it's probably an adverb.

While unfortunately, we can't give you a simple rule that will help you identify adverbs 100 percent of the time, the tips below will help you correctly identify adverbs in many cases.

Quick tip 27.3

Can the word go in the following slot? *Mary slept* _____. If so, it's probably an adverb. For example, *Mary slept <u>peacefully</u>. Peacefully* is an adverb.

Quick tip 27.4

Can the word go in the following slot? _____, *I gave / will give my speech.* If so, it's probably an adverb. For example, *<u>Yesterday</u>, I gave my speech. Yesterday* is an adverb. *Or: <u>Tomorrow</u>, I will give my speech. Tomorrow* is an adverb.

> **Quick tip 27.5**
>
> Can the word go in the following slot? *He is _____ happy.* If so, it's probably an adverb. For example, *He is <u>very</u> happy. Very* is an adverb.

> **Quick tip 27.6**
>
> Does the word end in the suffix *-ly*? Is it an adjective? If it ends in *-ly* and it's <u>not</u> an adjective, it's probably an adverb (e.g. *hopefully, happily, unusually*).

Test yourself 27.1

Underline the adverbs in each of the sentences below.
Sample: They had <u>deliberately</u> been silent when they entered the room.

Getting started (answers on p. 107)

1. She returned the book and quietly left.

2. I'm leaving for Europe tomorrow.

3. That horse is an unusually calm animal.

4. The train came to a stop suddenly.

5. That remark was too shocking.

More practice (answers on the website)

6. Why don't you call her sometimes?

7. We were told to handle the merchandise carefully.

8. The doctor informed his patient that his prognosis was very good.

9. The Morgans are not leaving today.

10. Unexpectedly, the principal ordered everyone into the auditorium.

Many, though not all, adverbs end in -ly (*rapidly, innocently, sweetly*, etc.). However, some adjectives also end in *-ly*, for example *lovely, friendly*. It's easy to distinguish them. Just remember that the adjectives can go in the slot *the _____ boy: the <u>lovely</u> boy, the <u>friendly</u> boy*.

While adverbs can go before the adjective, for example *the <u>extremely</u> friendly boy* (*extremely* is an adverb), adverbs cannot occupy the slot directly before the noun. That is, one cannot say, **the extremely boy* or **the innocently boy*, so *extremely* and *innocently* are not adjectives; they must be adverbs.

Note that some nouns, for example the flower *lily*, end in *-ly* as well. And just to add a little more spice to the recipe, there are some words that can be used either as adverbs or as adjectives:

    6a. That is a <u>pretty</u> easy book. (*Pretty* is similar to the word *very* here, and is an adverb of degree.)

    6b. That is a <u>pretty</u> child. (*Pretty* is an adjective.)

    7a. You drive too <u>fast</u>. (*Fast* tells us more about the verb *drive*, so it is an adverb.)

    7b. This actor's delivery was too <u>fast</u>. (*Fast* tells us more about the noun *delivery*, so it is an adjective.)

Test yourself 27.2

For each word below, decide if it is an adverb or an adjective. Use the test for adjectives to help you decide: *the _____ boy.*
Sample: rarely   adverb

Getting started (answers on p. 107)

1. happily   ....
2. ugly   ....
3. clearly   ....
4. gently   ....
5. manly   ....

More practice (answers on the website)

6. predictably   ....
7. nearly   ....
8. proudly   ....
9. barely   ....
10. silly   ....

Test yourself 27.3

Decide whether the underlined word in each sentence is being used as an adjective or an adverb.

	Adjective	*Adverb*
Sample: He recently increased his <u>yearly</u> salary.	✗	....

Getting started (answers on p. 107)

	Adjective	Adverb
1. He was <u>busily</u> writing a letter when the doorbell rang.	....	....
2. That is a very <u>hilly</u> road.	....	....
3. They fell <u>hopelessly</u> in love at first sight.	....	....
4. I never realized that you have such <u>curly</u> hair.	....	....
5. The soprano gave a <u>masterly</u> performance.	....	....

More practice (answers on the website)

	Adjective	Adverb
6. Mr. Sawyer is paid <u>weekly</u>.	....	....
7. She <u>undoubtedly</u> deserves top honors.	....	....
8. This lady <u>eerily</u> resembles my grandmother.	....	....
9. Janet <u>fully</u> concurs with her husband's decision.	....	....
10. Your new house is very <u>lovely</u>.	....	....

Test yourself 27.4

Underline the adverbs with a solid line and the adjectives with a squiggly line in the sentences below.
Sample: He was <u>clearly</u> working on a <u>difficult</u> report.

Getting started (answers on p. 107)

1. Excitedly, the men dragged the heavy sack to the clearing.
2. I've checked on the situation very thoroughly.
3. Adam waited inside.
4. The old fellow left town yesterday.
5. Afterwards, he regretted his actions.

More practice (answers on the website)

6. Your generous gift was completely unnecessary.

7. Let's agree on this beforehand.

8. This offer is too good to pass up.

9. I often think of you fondly.

10. The mailman left an unopened package at the door.

Test yourself 27.5 – Grand Finale

For each sentence below, write ADV above each adverb, ADJ above each adjective, N above each noun, and V above each verb.

               N   V   ADV

Sample: The teacher looked at him coldly.

Getting started (answers on p. 107)

1. My roommate usually sleeps very late.

2. Yesterday, the girl accompanied her older sister to the mall.

3. He walked slowly toward the foggy station.

4. The experienced senator quickly evaded their probing questions.

5. Later, we took a leisurely walk down by the beach.

More practice (answers on the website)

6. The once popular guitarist appeared on TV regularly.

7. Successful brokers will surely receive sizeable commissions.

8. We recently had a wonderful time in Spain.

9. I will take a quick dip in the inviting blue waters of the ocean.

10. Obviously, you are not the same person now that you were when I first met you.

Answer keys: *Test yourself, Getting started* questions – Unit 8

Test yourself 27.1

1. She returned the book and <u>quietly</u> left.
2. I'm leaving for Europe <u>tomorrow</u>.
3. That horse is an <u>unusually</u> calm animal.
4. The train came to a stop <u>suddenly</u>.
5. That remark was <u>too</u> shocking.

Test yourself 27.2

1. happily   <u>adverb</u>
2. ugly   <u>adjective</u>
3. clearly   <u>adverb</u>
4. gently   <u>adverb</u>
5. manly   <u>adjective</u>

Test yourself 27.3

	Adjective	Adverb
1. He was <u>busily</u> writing a letter when the doorbell rang.		✗
2. That is a very <u>hilly</u> road.	✗	
3. They fell <u>hopelessly</u> in love at first sight.		✗
4. I never realized that you have such <u>curly</u> hair.	✗	
5. The soprano gave a <u>masterly</u> performance.	✗	

Test yourself 27.4

1. <u>Excitedly</u>, the men dragged the <u>heavy</u> sack to the clearing.
2. I've checked on the situation <u>very</u> <u>thoroughly</u>.
3. Adam waited <u>inside</u>.
4. The <u>old</u> fellow left town <u>yesterday</u>.
5. <u>Afterwards</u>, he regretted his actions.

Test yourself 27.5

1.   N   ADV   V · ADV ADJ
   My roommate usually sleeps very late.
2.   ADV   N   V   ADJ   N   N
   Yesterday, the girl accompanied her older sister to the mall.
3.   V   ADV   ADJ   N
   He walked slowly toward the foggy station.

4. ADJ N ADV V ADJ N

The experienced senator quickly evaded their probing questions.

5. ADV V ADJ N ADV   N

Later, we took a leisurely walk down by the beach.

☞ **FOR A REVIEW EXERCISE OF THIS UNIT, SEE THE WEBSITE.**

Review matching exercise and answer key – Part I

Review matching exercise

Match the underlined word or words to the appropriate term in each set. Use each term only once.

Sample: <u>Merlin's</u> assistant was an apprentice magician.   possessive proper noun

Set A

article	particle	singular noun
coordinating conjunction	phrasal verb	transitive verb
determiner possessive pronoun	preposition	

1. Michael dipped his foot in the <u>pool</u>.   ....

2. He had made <u>his</u> fortune overnight.   ....

3. Don't <u>pick up</u> a thing!   ....

4. Her gardener <u>watered</u> the lawn.   ....

5. The authorities were investigating the possibility of <u>an</u> illegal smuggling ring.   ....

6. She always figures <u>out</u> the answer eventually.   ....

7. We've installed a generator <u>but</u> not a back-up system.   ....

8. They need these tools <u>for</u> their project.   ....

Set B

base form of verb	irregular plural noun	subordinating
correlative conjunction	linking verb	conjunction
demonstrative determiner	quantifier	

1. You can <u>visit</u> more often.   ....

2. The dentist took x-rays of her <u>teeth</u>.   ....

3. I <u>became</u> better and better at Monopoly.   ....

4. <u>If</u> Bob makes breakfast, it will save us a lot of time.   ....

5. He believes that <u>both</u> people want to come to an agreement.   ....

6. <u>Neither</u> his accountant <u>nor</u> his stockbroker was able to help.   ....

7. She never got tired of watching <u>those</u> movies.   ....

Answer key: Review matching exercise – Part I

Set A

1. Michael dipped his foot in the <u>pool</u>.   singular noun

2. He had made <u>his</u> fortune overnight.   determiner possessive pronoun

3. Don't <u>pick up</u> a thing!   phrasal verb

4. Her gardener <u>watered</u> the lawn.   transitive verb

5. The authorities were investigating the possibility
   of <u>an</u> illegal smuggling ring.   article

6. She always figures <u>out</u> the answer eventually.   particle

7. We've installed a generator <u>but</u> not a back-up system.   coordinating conjunction

8. They need these tools <u>for</u> their project.   preposition

Set B

1. You can <u>visit</u> more often.   base form of verb

2. The dentist took x-rays of her <u>teeth</u>.   irregular plural noun

3. I <u>became</u> better and better at Monopoly.   linking verb

4. <u>If</u> Bob makes breakfast, it will save us a lot of time.   subordinating conjunction

5. He believes that <u>both</u> people want to come to
   an agreement.   quantifier

6. <u>Neither</u> his accountant <u>nor</u> his stockbroker was
   able to help.   correlative conjunction

7. She never got tired of watching <u>those</u> movies.   demonstrative determiner

PART II: KINDS OF PHRASES

Just as you know a lot about word categories without necessarily realizing that you do, you know a lot about combining words into phrases and phrases into sentences. As we talk about phrases and sentences, we'll be referring to many of the word categories you learned about in Part I, so check back there if you need to.

Let's start by taking a look at the following sentence:

     1. The little boy laughed.

If you were asked to divide the sentence into two parts, what would the parts be? Speakers of English typically separate the sentence after the word *boy*:

     2. The little boy + laughed.

Other groupings, like the ones below, generally seem unnatural to native speakers of English:

     3. The + little boy laughed.

     4. The little + boy laughed.

That is, we all sense that *the little boy* forms a unit and that *laughed* forms another unit. Units like these are called phrases.

So we can start off our discussion by suggesting that there are two parts to sentence 1. We could call them Part A and Part B, or Harry and George, but we'll use the terminology of modern linguistics and refer to them as the **noun phrase** and the **verb phrase**. The noun phrase in our sentence is *the little boy*; the verb phrase is *laughed*. Of course, there are other phrases as well. We'll look at the most common ones in the units of Part II.

Lesson 28: The basic structure of noun phrases

There are all kinds of noun phrases and we can discover them by seeing some of the things we can substitute for the noun phrase, *the little boy*. The underlined portions of the sentences below are all noun phrases and any one of them can replace *the little boy* in the sentence *The little boy laughed*.

1. <u>Audiences</u> laughed.
2. <u>Younger audiences</u> laughed.
3. <u>The girl</u> laughed.
4. <u>The little girl</u> laughed.
5. <u>The cute little girl</u> laughed.
6. <u>John</u> laughed.
7. <u>They</u> laughed.

Of course, there are lots of things that <u>cannot</u> replace *the little boy*, for example:

8. *My very quickly laughed.
9. *Near his laughed.
10. *Went away laughed.

You're probably not surprised to learn that *My very quickly*, *Near his*, and *Went away* are <u>not</u> noun phrases.

So what can be a noun phrase?

In sentences 1–6, the noun phrases all have something in common: each consists of at least a noun. (See Unit 1 to refresh your memory about nouns.)

Here are the noun phrases again, with the nouns underlined:

<u>audiences</u>
younger <u>audiences</u>
the <u>girl</u>
the little <u>girl</u>
the cute little <u>girl</u>
<u>John</u>

In sentence 1, *Audiences laughed*, and in sentence 6, *John laughed*, the noun phrase consists of just a noun: *audiences* in sentence 1 and *John* in sentence 6.

Quick tip 28.1

A noun phrase can consist of a noun alone, for example, *audiences, John*.

Test yourself 28.1

Underline the noun phrase in each of the sentences below. In this exercise, the noun phrase will always consist of a noun alone. Some sentences may have more than one noun phrase.
Sample: <u>Sugar</u> is not very healthy.

Getting started (answers on p. 119)

1. Pirates were looking for treasure.

2. Furniture can be expensive.

3. Boys often want to be policemen.

4. People think money is useful.

5. Jeremy was eating rice.

More practice (answers on the website)

6. Sometimes juries make mistakes.

7. Jenny visited friends yesterday.

8. Oil is thicker than water.

9. Joel hates bananas.

10. Writers often like to work alone.

You can also see, in sentences 2–5, that a noun phrase can have other words in addition to just a noun. Let's see what those other words can be:

younger audiences:	adjective + noun
the girl:	determiner + noun
the little girl:	determiner + adjective + noun
the cute little girl:	determiner + adjectives + noun

(See Units 3 and 4 to remind yourself about determiners and adjectives.)

Quick tip 28.2

A noun phrase can consist of a determiner, one or more adjectives, and a noun. The determiner and adjective(s) are optional.

Test yourself 28.2

Underline the noun phrases in each of the sentences below. In this exercise, the noun phrase will always consist of a determiner + noun; the determiner will always be an article, that is, *the*, *a*, or *an*. Some sentences may have more than one noun phrase.
Sample: A man stole the car.

Getting started (answers on p. 119)

1. The winner was overjoyed.

2. The crowd dispersed peacefully.

3. A minute can seem like an eternity.

4. The dentist gave the patient a toothbrush.

5. The couple forgot to tip the waiter.

More practice (answers on the website)

6. A Mercedes costs more than a Chevy.

7. The Andersons bought a house.

8. The children are sleeping.

9. The lake is near the village.

10. The professor paid the student a compliment.

Here are some more examples with different determiners and nouns. (You may recall from Unit 3 that the determiner always comes before the noun.) The whole noun phrase is underlined.

11. <u>A man</u> laughed.
12. <u>Her friend</u> laughed.
13. <u>That lady</u> laughed.
14. <u>Many people</u> laughed.

Notice that these noun phrases don't have to appear only at the beginning of the sentence:

15. The criminal is <u>a man</u>.
16. I looked at <u>her friend</u>.
17. Do you know <u>that lady</u>?
18. The clown made <u>many people</u> laugh.

Test yourself 28.3

Underline the noun phrases in each of the sentences below. In this exercise, the noun phrase will always consist of a determiner (any kind) + noun. Some sentences may have more than one noun phrase.
Sample: <u>My hat</u> blew off in <u>the wind</u>.

Getting started (answers on p. 119)

1. His doorman hailed a taxi.

2. As the doctor toured the ward, a group of her interns went along.

3. Your daughter looks great in this picture.

4. Some people keep their jewelry in a safe deposit box.

5. Jack's friend is an artist.

More practice (answers on the website)

6. While driving in a snowstorm, Alex's car veered off the road.

7. Several spectators wanted that ballplayer thrown out of the game.

8. The train pulled into the station.

9. Most people are proud of their country.

10. Andrea's grandmother used to bake a pie in her kitchen for her grandchildren.

Here are examples of noun phrases consisting of a determiner plus an adjective plus a noun (the whole noun phrase is underlined):

19. <u>The best fruit</u> is grown on <u>the west coast</u>.
20. <u>Our new shoes</u> got completely soaked.
21. <u>That old dog</u> is <u>my favorite one</u>.
22. <u>Every new task</u> is challenging.

Test yourself 28.4

Underline the noun phrases in each of the sentences below. In this exercise, the noun phrase will always consist of determiner + adjective + noun. Some sentences may have more than one noun phrase.
Sample: <u>My young cousin</u> got on <u>that scary roller-coaster</u>.

Getting started (answers on p. 119)

1. That adorable baby was born in a rundown house in a small town.

2. The elderly woman wrote a short novel.

3. His crazy adventure began with those strange letters.

4. *Some Enchanted Evening* is a beautiful song from a classic show.

5. Jackie's famous father is a talented immigrant from a South American country.

More practice (answers on the website)

6. These old cookies are stale.

7. A little attention often helps a bruised ego.

8. Each passing moment is a terrible waste.

9. Our new house sits on the outermost edge of this secluded island.

10. Many submitted manuscripts are piled up on the cluttered desk of the finicky editor.

Test yourself 28.5

For each of the underlined noun phrases below, decide if it is: determiner + noun or determiner + adjective + noun.

Sample: He was not in <u>a reasonable mood</u>.   determiner + adjective + noun

Getting started (answers on p. 119)

1. <u>The pleasure</u> in his voice was real.

   ....

2. <u>That annoying customer</u> still got a good deal.

   ....

3. Count <u>your blessings</u>!

   ....

4. <u>Jonathan's jacket</u> is brand new.

   ....

5. He plays with <u>his new gadget</u> every day.

   ....

More practice (answers on the website)

6. His divorce received <u>much publicity</u>.

   ....

7. I want <u>the latest model</u> for my office.

   ....

8. Let's hope <u>this terrible weather</u> changes soon.

   ....

9. I don't care for <u>her new attitude</u>.

   ....

10. <u>The motorcade</u> passed by quickly.

    ....

> Here are some examples where the noun phrase consists of a determiner, more than one adjective, and a noun (the whole noun phrase is underlined):
>
> 23. <u>The dull brown liquid</u> spilled onto <u>his priceless antique carpet</u>.
> 24. <u>Elderly, infirm individuals</u> really need <u>that important health benefit</u>.
> 25. <u>A worn checkered apron</u> hung by <u>the sagging, unpainted kitchen door</u>.

Test yourself 28.6

Underline the noun phrases in each of the sentences below. In this exercise, the noun phrase will always consist of determiner + adjective(s) + noun. Some sentences may have more than one noun phrase.

Sample: <u>The pushy, aggressive salesman</u> at <u>the automobile dealership</u> was not helpful.

Getting started (answers on p. 119)

1. The small white dog ran away.

2. The close friends loved watching the old, classic movies.

3. Some Japanese cars are rated very highly.

4. My lovely niece arrived in a brand new convertible.

5. Those pesky flies ruined my Australian vacation.

More practice (answers on the website)

6. Your beautiful shiny hair is enviable.

7. The crazy idea of your nutty sister turned out to be not so crazy after all.

8. The Siamese cat was extremely sociable.

9. My reliable old friend made a terrible mistake.

10. This poor, hungry man is craving a hearty hot meat sandwich.

Don't forget that a noun phrase doesn't have to have a determiner. Here are some examples in which the noun phrases (underlined) consist only of adjective(s) and a noun:

26. Cold drinks are delicious.

27. Talented, creative actors don't always become big stars.

28. Individual rights are important to preserve.

Proper nouns generally don't have adjectives or determiners in front of them. *creative Nicole*, for example, is ungrammatical.

Sentence 7, *They laughed*, is yet another kind of noun phrase. In this case, the noun phrase consists of just a pronoun, *they*. (See Unit 7 to remind yourself about pronouns.)

> **Quick tip 28.3**
>
> A noun phrase can consist of just a pronoun, for example *he* or *them*.

Notice that you can have a determiner before a noun, for example, *the monkey*, but you'd never put one before a pronoun: *the he*, for example, is ungrammatical. We also do not usually put an adjective before a pronoun:*pretty she*, for example, is ungrammatical.

Test yourself 28.7

Underline the noun phrase in each of the sentences below. In this exercise, the noun phrase will always consist of a pronoun. Some sentences may have more than one noun phrase.
Sample: You are always good to her.

Getting started (answers on p. 120)

1. He ran away.

2. I love watching them.

3. They were extremely sociable.

4. We want to invite you over.

5. He did it and didn't even tell us about it.

More practice (answers on the website)

6. It made me curious.

7. She left us confused.

8. I am better for it.

9. You will help me, won't you?

10. They left yesterday.

To sum up, the kinds of noun phrases we've discussed are listed below. While there are more kinds of noun phrases, what we've done here is to show you some basic ones.

noun	(example: *water*)
adjective + noun	(example: *cold water*)
determiner + noun	(example: *a teacher*)
determiner + adjective(s) + noun	(example: *a smart teacher*)
pronoun	(example: *she*)

Test yourself 28.8

Identify the part of speech of each word in each of the underlined noun phrases below. It will be either: noun (alone), determiner + noun, adjective(s) + noun, determiner + adjective(s) + noun, or pronoun (alone).

Sample: He spoke in <u>a friendly, cooperative manner</u>.   determiner + adjectives + noun

Getting started (answers on p. 120)

1. The pleasure in <u>your voice</u> was real. ....
2. I still have <u>that infamous necklace</u>. ....
3. I forgot to mention <u>it</u> to you. ....
4. <u>Mr. Bentley</u> is a successful businessman. ....
5. Cobras are <u>dangerous snakes</u>. ....

More practice (answers on the website)

6. Don't forget to buy <u>a low-fat turkey sandwich</u>! ....
7. <u>The coffee</u> is too hot to drink. ....
8. She buys a pair of <u>new shoes</u> every year. ....
9. He took a cruise with <u>his rich, generous uncle</u>. ....
10. You may not know that <u>whales</u> are mammals. ....

Test yourself 28.9 – Grand finale

Underline the noun phrases in the sentences below. There may be more than one in a sentence.

Sample: <u>I</u> am sharing <u>the relevant information</u> with <u>you</u>.

Getting started (answers on p. 120)

1. Joe traveled often.

2. The blazing sun can cause damage to your skin.

3. The unlucky scientist walked back.

4. We turned and left.

5. Those calculating politicians responded evasively.

More practice (answers on the website)

6. The beaches of Tahiti are high on my list of places to visit.

7. Cigarettes are not good for your health, don't you agree?

8. I think you should recommend this book to them.

9. Disneyland is a popular destination for European tourists.

10. Arnold hurried in.

Answer keys: *Test yourself, Getting started questions* – Unit 9

Test yourself 28.1

1. Pirates were looking for treasure.
2. Furniture can be expensive.
3. Boys often want to be policemen.
4. People think money is useful.
5. Jeremy was eating rice.

Test yourself 28.2

1. The winner was overjoyed.
2. The crowd dispersed peacefully.
3. A minute can seem like an eternity.
4. The dentist gave the patient a toothbrush.
5. The couple forgot to tip the waiter.

Test yourself 28.3

1. His doorman hailed a taxi.
2. As the doctor toured the ward, a group of her interns went along.
3. Your daughter looks great in this picture.
4. Some people keep their jewelry in a safe deposit box.
5. Jack's friend is an artist.

Test yourself 28.4

1. That adorable baby was born in a rundown house in a small town.
2. The elderly woman wrote a short novel.
3. His crazy adventure began with those strange letters.
4. *Some Enchanted Evening* is a beautiful song from a classic show.
5. Jackie's famous father is a talented immigrant from a South American country.

Test yourself 28.5

1. The pleasure in his voice was real.	determiner + noun
2. That annoying customer still got a good deal.	determiner + adjective + noun
3. Count your blessings!	determiner + noun
4. Jonathan's jacket is brand new.	determiner + noun
5. He plays with his new gadget every day.	determiner + adjective + noun

Test yourself 28.6

1. The small white dog ran away.
2. The close friends loved watching the old, classic movies.

3. Some Japanese cars are rated very highly.
4. My lovely niece arrived in a brand new convertible.
5. Those pesky flies ruined my Australian vacation.

Test yourself 28.7

1. He ran away.
2. I love watching them.
3. They were extremely sociable.
4. We want to invite you over.
5. He did it and didn't even tell us about it.

Test yourself 28.8

1. The pleasure in your voice was real.   determiner + noun
2. I still have that infamous necklace.   determiner + adjective + noun
3. I forgot to mention it to you.   pronoun
4. Mr. Bentley is a successful businessman.   noun
5. Cobras are dangerous snakes.   adjective + noun

Test yourself 28.9

1. Joe traveled often.
2. The blazing sun can cause damage to your skin.
3. The unlucky scientist walked back.
4. We turned and left.
5. Those calculating politicians responded evasively.

☞ **FOR A REVIEW EXERCISE OF THIS UNIT, SEE THE WEBSITE.**

Lesson 29: The basic structure of prepositional phrases

What do you notice about the following sentences?

1. The toy is <u>on</u> the red table.
2. We live <u>near</u> him.
3. The cute guy walked Mary <u>to</u> the corner.
4. The Jones family traveled <u>around</u> Arizona.

Each of these sentences contains a preposition, which is underlined. Here again are the common prepositions which we listed in Lesson 17:

about	beneath	into	throughout
above	beside	like	till
across	between	near	to
after	beyond	of	toward(s)
against	by	off	under
along	despite	on	until
among	down	onto	up
around	during	out	upon
at	for	over	with
before	from	since	within
behind	in	through	without
below			

What follows a preposition? In sentences 1–4, the prepositions are followed by:

5. the red table (determiner + adjective + noun)
6. him   (pronoun)
7. the corner   (determiner + noun)
8. Arizona   (proper noun)

As you may remember from Lesson 28, each of these is a kind of noun phrase. In fact, a preposition is always followed by a noun phrase, called the **object of the preposition**, and the preposition and its noun phrase form a unit which is called a **prepositional phrase**.

> **Quick tip 29.1**
>
> A prepositional phrase consists of a preposition plus a noun phrase, for example *in the closet*.

We don't have to list the different kinds of noun phrases in *Quick tip* 29.1, because we've already identified them in Lesson 28; we can just refer to noun phrases in general. So it's really useful to have this concept of a noun phrase, and it's a concept that you'll see come up again in other lessons.

Here are some more examples of sentences with prepositional phrases (underlined):

9. Let's carry the sofa <u>into the house</u>.
10. That makes sense <u>to us</u>.
11. There was a small lamp <u>on her dresser</u>.
12. Jeanie was living <u>in New York</u>.
13. The boss had no love <u>for his employees</u>.

You can see that each prepositional phrase consists of a preposition and a noun phrase.

Test yourself 29.1

Underline the prepositional phrases in the sentences below. Look for the preposition that begins the prepositional phrase.

Sample: He knew a lot <u>about that subject</u>.

Getting started (answers on p. 125)

1. The fabric was between the boxes.

2. She always eats her lunch with a methodical thoroughness.

3. There was a temple near the hotel.

4. The gift was for a close friend.

5. The congressman is speaking to the press.

More practice (answers on the website)

6. My son had lunch at McDonald's.

7. She was sitting by the open window.

8. I never heard from him again.

9. The little boy was hiding under the round table.

10. She traveled without her husband.

Test yourself 29.2

Here are the same sentences as in *Test yourself* 29.1. This time, underline the preposition with a solid line and the noun phrase with a squiggly line <u>within</u> each of the prepositional phrases in the sentences below.

Sample: He knew a lot <u>about</u> that subject.

Getting started (answers on p. 125)

1. The fabric was between the boxes.

2. She always eats her lunch with a methodical thoroughness.

3. There was a temple near the hotel.

4. The gift was for a close friend.

5. The congressman is speaking to the press.

More practice (answers on the website)

6. My son had lunch at McDonald's.

7. She was sitting by the open window.

8. I never heard from him again.

9. The little boy was hiding under the round table.

10. She traveled without her husband.

To enhance your understanding

Let's compare two sentences with the word *up*:

14. I looked <u>up</u> your phone number.
15. I walked <u>up</u> the steep hill.

These sentences certainly look very similar. Each has the word *up* followed by a noun phrase. But in fact, the sentences are different. For one thing, in sentence 14, *up* can be moved to the other side of the noun phrase without changing its meaning:

16. I looked your phone number <u>up</u>.

In sentence 15, *up* cannot be moved:

17. *I walked the steep hill <u>up</u>.

Also, in sentence 14, *look up* is a unit; *up* feels closely connected to *look*. In fact, *look up* can be replaced by a single verb and still have more or less the same meaning, for example, *I <u>researched</u> your phone number*. In sentence 14, *up* is part of the verb and is called a verb particle. You may recall that we talked about these verb plus particle combinations in Lesson 11, where we said they were called phrasal verbs. In sentence 15, *up* is not connected to the verb, so it is not a particle; rather, it is a preposition.

Here are some more examples of sentences with verb particles. Notice that in each of these cases, the verb plus particle can be replaced by a single verb and the particle can be moved.

18a. Her husband <u>carried out</u> the garbage. (Her husband <u>removed</u> the garbage.)

18b. Her husband <u>carried</u> the garbage <u>out</u>.

19a. The criminal <u>covered up</u> the crime. (The criminal <u>hid</u> the crime.)

19b. The criminal <u>covered</u> the crime <u>up</u>.

20a. Don't just <u>brush off</u> her objections. (Don't just <u>dismiss</u> her objections.)

20b. Don't just <u>brush</u> her objections <u>off</u>.

In contrast, here are some more examples of sentences with prepositions. Notice that in each case, the preposition cannot be moved to the other side of its noun phrase.

21a. He looked <u>out</u> the door.

21b. *He looked the door <u>out</u>.

22a. The hiker slowly walked <u>up</u> the hill.

22a. *The hiker slowly walked the hill <u>up</u>.

23a. Take the pot <u>off</u> the stove.

23b. *Take the pot the stove <u>off</u>.

As we discussed above, the preposition is tied to the noun phrase following it, forming a prepositional phrase.

Can a sentence contain more than one prepositional phrase? We started our discussion of prepositional phrases with the following sentences, each of which had only one prepositional phrase (underlined):

24. The toy is <u>on the red table</u>.

25. We live <u>near him</u>.

26. The cute guy walked Mary <u>to the corner</u>.

27. The Jones family traveled <u>around Arizona</u>.

We can expand these sentences, adding another propositional phrase (underlined) to each:

28. The toy is on the red table <u>in the living room</u>.

29. We live near him <u>in Manhattan</u>.

30. The cute guy <u>from Argentina</u> walked Mary to the corner.

31. The Jones family traveled around Arizona <u>in a rented minivan</u>.

In theory, there's no limit to the number of prepositional phrases that a sentence can have. Take a look at one with quite a few prepositional phrases:

32. They landed the plane <u>in a grassy field</u> <u>near the park</u> <u>by the river</u> <u>in San Francisco</u>.

In reality, however, each sentence we say has a finite length – we have to stop talking at some point!

Test yourself 29.3

Underline the prepositional phrases in the sentences below. A sentence may contain more than one prepositional phrase. Look for the preposition that begins each prepositional phrase.
Sample: She could see the light of the fire in the darkness beyond her tent.

Getting started (answers on p. 125)

1. Andy ran into the field across the road.

2. That first winter had been spent in New Hampshire.

3. She told the story of the night she first arrived at the house.

4. The lady in the red dress bought a bottle of perfume with her credit card.

5. I met my long lost friend at the airport.

More practice (answers on the website)

6. Sally arrived in New Orleans around midnight.

7. My uncle walked into the office and breathed a sigh of relief.

8. We went to see the levee along the Mississippi River.

9. I saw this big ship on the Mediterranean Sea disappear beyond the horizon.

10. To some people, that is one of the greatest movies ever made.

Answer keys: *Test yourself, Getting started* questions – Unit 10

Test yourself 29.1

1. The fabric was <u>between the boxes</u>.
2. She always eats her lunch <u>with a methodical thoroughness</u>.
3. There was a temple <u>near the hotel</u>.
4. The gift was <u>for a close friend</u>.
5. The congressman is speaking <u>to the press</u>.

Test yourself 29.2

1. The fabric was <u>between the boxes</u>.
2. She always eats her lunch with a <u>methodical thoroughness</u>.
3. There was a temple <u>near the hotel</u>.
4. The gift was <u>for a close friend</u>.
5. The congressman is speaking <u>to the press</u>.

Test yourself 29.3

1. Andy ran <u>into the field</u> <u>across the road</u>.
2. That first winter had been spent <u>in New Hampshire</u>.
3. She told the story <u>of the night</u> she first arrived <u>at the house</u>.
4. The lady <u>in the red dress</u> bought a bottle <u>of perfume</u> <u>with her credit card</u>.
5. I met my long lost friend <u>at the airport</u>.

☞ **FOR A REVIEW EXERCISE OF THIS UNIT, SEE THE WEBSITE.**

Lesson 30: The basic structure of verb phrases

Remember the sentence, *The little boy laughed*? As we talked about earlier, *The little boy* is a noun phrase (see Lesson 28) and *laughed* is a verb phrase. There are different kinds of verb phrases, and we can begin to discover them by seeing what we can substitute for the verb phrase, *laughed*, in this sentence. The underlined portions of the sentences below are all verb phrases, and any one of them can replace *laughed* in the sentence, *The little boy laughed*.

1. The little boy left.
2. The little boy chased the ball.
3. The little boy chased the red ball.
4. The little boy chased it.
5. The little boy chased Henry.

Of course, there are lots of things that cannot replace *laughed* in this sentence, for example:

6. *The little boy his extremely.
7. *The little boy near from.
8. *The little boy they.

You're probably not surprised to learn that *his extremely*, *near from*, and *they* are not verb phrases.

Have you noticed anything that all the underlined verb phrases in sentences 1–5 have in common? Each verb phrase has a verb. In fact, in sentence 1, the verb phrase has nothing in it but a verb, *left*. A verb phrase may also have other words, as you can see in sentences 2–5, but the least that every verb phrase has to have is a verb. (See Unit 2 to remind yourself about verbs.)

> **Quick tip 30.1**
>
> Every verb phrase contains a verb, for example *laughs, left*.

In sentences 1–5, the verb is the first word in the verb phrase and is its most important part.

Test yourself 30.1

Underline the verb phrase in each of the sentences below. In this exercise, the verb phrase will consist of only a verb.
Sample: The family arrived.

Getting started (answers on p. 135)

1. Freddy disappeared.
2. A young woman cried.
3. The soldiers wait.
4. I slept.
5. The little girl smiled.

More practice (answers on the website)

6. The music stopped.

7. We agree.

8. Last night the guests left.

9. Time flies.

10. A problem arose.

If we look at sentences 2–5, we see that a verb phrase can have more in it than just a verb. Let's start with sentence 2, *The little boy chased the ball*. The verb phrase is:

9. chased the ball   (verb + determiner + noun)

You may remember from Lesson 28 that determiner + noun is a kind of noun phrase. Thus, in this sentence, the verb phrase consists of a verb followed by one kind of noun phrase.

Let's look at the verb phrases in sentences 3–5:

10. chased the red ball   (verb + determiner + adjective + noun)
11. chased it   (verb + pronoun)
12. chased Henry   (verb + noun)

You can see that in each case, the verb phrase consists of a verb followed by a noun phrase.

> **Quick tip 30.2**
>
> A verb phrase can consist of a verb plus a noun phrase, for example *chased the ball.*

Again, we don't have to list the different kinds of noun phrases here, because we've already listed them in Lesson 28; we can just refer to noun phrases in general.

Test yourself 30.2

Underline the verb phrase in each of the sentences below. It may help to first find the verb, which is the first word of these verb phrases. In each sentence here, the verb phrase consists of a verb + noun phrase.

Sample: We welcomed them.

Getting started (answers on p. 135)

1. He created a monster.

2. Frank broke the plate.

3. Sherry and I left the house.

4. The detective examined the old broken doorknob.

5. We resent those comments.

More practice (answers on the website)

6. I read an interesting book.

7. Their younger sister crossed the hall.

8. The Australian swimming team defeated the French.

9. The rich wife bought some insurance.

10. Courtney ordered soup.

Test yourself 30.3

Here are the same sentences as in *Test yourself* 30.2. This time, in each sentence underline the verb with a solid line and the noun phrase within each verb phrase with a squiggly line.

Sample: We welcomed them.

Getting started (answers on p. 135)

1. He created a monster.
2. Frank broke the plate.
3. Sherry and I left the house.
4. The detective examined the old broken doorknob.
5. We resent those comments.

More practice (answers on the website)

6. I read an interesting book.
7. Their younger sister crossed the hall.
8. The Australian swimming team defeated the French.
9. The rich wife bought some insurance.
10. Courtney ordered soup.

In Lesson 9, we talked about the fact that some verbs are action verbs, like *run*, *write*, and *discover*, while others are linking verbs, like *be*, *feel*, and *become*. The verb phrases we've looked at so far have all contained action verbs. Verb phrases with linking verbs are different from verb phrases with action verbs. Let's compare two sentences:

11. John saw the teacher.
12. John is the teacher.

In each sentence, the verb phrase is underlined, and each verb phrase consists of a verb + noun phrase. (*Saw* and *is* are the verbs and *the teacher* is the noun phrase.) But can you see how the verb phrases in sentences 11 and 12 differ? You've probably noticed that in sentence 11, *the teacher* is receiving the action, but in sentence 12, there is no action (after all, *is* is a linking verb, not an action verb). So while the structures of sentences 11 and 12 appear to be similar on the surface, the sentences are quite different in meaning.

The following verb phrases with linking verbs are different in structure as well as in meaning from verb phrases with action verbs:

13. John is tall.
14. My sister became anxious.

As you (hopefully!) remember from Lesson 16, *tall* and *anxious* are adjectives. So when the verb is a linking verb, it can be followed by an adjective alone. An action verb cannot be followed by just an adjective, as you can see:

15. *John saw tall.
16. *John saw upset.

Quick tip 30.3

A verb phrase can consist of a linking verb plus an adjective, for example *is tall*.

An adjective which follows a linking verb and is not part of a noun phrase is traditionally called a **predicate adjective**, as in the example *John is tall* (sentence 13). In contrast, an adjective which is part of a noun phrase is traditionally called an **attributive adjective**, as in the example *John has a tall sister*.

Test yourself 30.4

Underline the verb phrase in each of the sentences below. It may help to first find the verb, which is the first word of these verb phrases. In each sentence here, the verb phrase consists of linking verb + adjective.

Sample: We are hungry.

Getting started (answers on p. 135)

1. The argument was silly.
2. The dress felt comfortable.
3. Steven became sick.
4. The point of this exercise seems obvious.
5. The children got excited.

More practice (answers on the website)

6. You look happy.
7. Her voice sounds raspy.
8. She felt embarrassed.
9. The new director proved difficult.
10. Your pie tastes delicious.

Test yourself 30.5

Here are the same sentences as in *Test yourself* 30.4. This time, within each verb phrase, underline the verb with a solid line and the adjective with a squiggly line.
Sample: We are hungry.

Getting started (answers on p. 135)

1. The argument was silly.
2. The dress felt comfortable.
3. Steven became sick.
4. The point of this exercise seems obvious.
5. The children got excited.

More practice (answers on the website)

6. You look happy.
7. Her voice sounds raspy.
8. She felt embarrassed.
9. The new director proved difficult.
10. Your pie tastes delicious.

Test yourself 30.6

Underline the verb phrase in each of the sentences below. In some sentences, the verb will be an action verb alone or it will be followed by a noun phrase (for example, *saw the cat*). In other sentences the verb will be a linking verb and may be followed by a noun phrase or by an adjective alone (for example, *looked hungry*).
Sample: He prepared his speech.

Getting started (answers on p. 135)

1. Brady was a radio engineer.
2. The king sent a clear message.
3. Those flowers look gorgeous.
4. Most able-bodied adults work.
5. I recognized them.

More practice (answers on the website)

6. We adore your lovely little girl.
7. She grew impatient.
8. Your son grew.
9. Chuck became an electrical engineer.
10. The diners wanted more bread.

Test yourself 30.7

Here are the same sentences as in *Test yourself* 30.6. This time, indicate if the verb phrase you've identified is: verb (alone), verb + noun phrase, or verb + adjective.
Sample: He prepared his speech.   verb + noun phrase

Getting started (answers on p. 136)

1. Brady was a radio engineer.   ....
2. The king sent a clear message.   ....

3. Those flowers look gorgeous. ....

4. Most able-bodied adults work. ....

5. I recognized them. ....

More practice (answers on the website)

6. We adore your lovely little girl. ....

7. She grew impatient. ....

8. Your son grew. ....

9. Chuck became an electrical engineer. ....

10. The diners wanted more bread. ....

To enhance your understanding

You may remember, from Lesson 8, that some verbs, for example *smell*, can be used as either action verbs or linking verbs. For example:

17. That dog smells badly. (Meaning, he does a bad job of smelling things.)

18. That dog smells bad. (Meaning, for example, he needs a bath.)

In sentence 17, *smell* is an action verb; it refers to the dog doing the action of smelling. In sentence 18, *smell* is a linking verb; it helps to tell us something about the dog but he's not actually doing anything – he's being something, namely, smelly.

When a verb is used as a linking verb, it can have an adjective, like *bad*, after it. When it's used as an action verb, it can be followed by an adverb, like *badly*, but not by an adjective. In Standard American English, *good* is used only as an adjective. So in Standard American English, it's not considered acceptable to say:

19. You did good.

That's because *did* is an action verb, and an action verb cannot be completed with just an adjective. So why do we often hear people saying sentences like *You did good*? What's happening is that people are starting to use *good* as an adverb, not just as an adjective. Maybe in the future this usage will become more widely accepted, but right now using *good* as an adverb is not considered Standard American English. (In other words, don't say this at a job interview, although it's fine to say with friends.)

Similarly, people sometimes say, *I feel badly*, instead of *I feel bad*, even though they are using *feel* here as a linking verb, not as an action verb. They know that usually an adverb, like *badly*, follows a verb, but adverbs only directly follow action verbs, not linking verbs. (When people incorrectly overapply a rule, it's called **hypercorrection**.)

We can thus explain the difference between *I feel good* ("I'm OK") and *I feel well* ("I have the ability to touch effectively"): in the former sentence *feel* is a linking verb, in the latter it is an action verb.

In Lesson 30, we talked about prepositional phrases. Here are some sentences with their verbs in bold and their prepositional phrases underlined:

20. The Bede family **lives** around the corner.

21. Please **ride** to the stable.

22. He **headed** toward the policeman.

Together, the verb plus prepositional phrase form a verb phrase.

> **Quick tip 30.4**
>
> A verb phrase can consist of a verb plus a prepositional phrase, for example *drove to the mall*.

Test yourself 30.8

Underline the verb phrase in each of the sentences below. It may help to first find the verb, which is the first word of these verb phrases. In each sentence here, the verb phrase consists of a verb + prepositional phrase.
Sample: He frequently <u>came to my office</u>.

Getting started (answers on p. 136)

1. The boat floated in the water.

2. Janice is from Kansas City.

3. Mrs. Miller is at the beach.

4. He looked for me.

5. The sun appeared above the horizon.

More practice (answers on the website)

6. They live near each other.

7. I read between the lines.

8. He learned from his grandfather.

9. She played with her children.

10. Our plane flew over the Atlantic Ocean.

Test yourself 30.9

Underline the verb phrase in each of the sentences below. The verb phrase will either be: verb (alone), verb + noun phrase, or verb + prepositional phrase. Look for the verb to help you get started.
Sample: This <u>is for the whole family</u>.

Getting started (answers on p. 136)

1. Elinor rented a car.

2. The clowns never laugh with the audience.

3. The road trip ended.

4. The band played my favorite song.

5. They left at noon.

More practice (answers on the website)

6. Brandy's three-month-old baby smiled.

7. Our neighbors just returned from their country home.

8. I found the missing piece.

9. We ran through the woods.

10. On holidays, the Watsons entertain.

Test yourself 30.10

Here are the same sentences as in *Test yourself* 30.9. This time, indicate if the verb phrase you've identified is: verb (alone), verb + noun phrase, or verb + prepositional phrase.
Sample: This is for the whole family.   <u>verb + prepositional phrase</u>

Getting started (answers on p. 136)

1. Elinor rented a car.   ....

2. The clowns never laugh with the audience.   ....

3. The road trip ended.   ....

4. The band played my favorite song.   ....

5. They left at noon.   ....

More practice (answers on the website)

6. Brandy's three-month-old baby smiled.

7. Our neighbors just returned from their country home.

8. I found the missing piece.

9. We ran through the woods.

10. On holidays, The Watsons entertain.

Test yourself 30.11

Underline the verb phrase in each of the sentences below. The verb phrase will either be: verb + adjective or verb + prepositional phrase. Look for the verb to help you get started.
Sample: You <u>look pretty</u>.

Getting started (answers on p. 136)

1. Her mother looked under the bed.

2. Jan leaped for the shore.

3. The morning seemed peaceful.

4. The stock market fell hard.

5. She arrived with an empty suitcase.

More practice (answers on the website)

6. A fight arose among the players.

7. The TV host appeared annoyed.

8. The bull ran down the narrow street.

9. It rolled under the bed.

10. The show was disastrous.

Can a verb phrase have a verb followed by both a noun phrase <u>and</u> a prepositional phrase?
23. He walked <u>Mary to the corner</u>.
24. The dog chased <u>the man with the umbrella</u>.
In these sentences, the verb phrase consists of a verb followed by a noun phrase and also a prepositional phrase.

> **Quick tip 30.5**
>
> A verb phrase can consist of a verb plus a noun phrase plus a prepositional phrase, for example *drove her friend to the mall*.

Can we say the following?
25. *He walked <u>to the corner Mary</u>.
26. *The dog chased <u>with the umbrella the man</u>.
These sentences show us that when a verb is followed by a noun phrase and a prepositional phrase, the noun phrase always has to be before the prepositional phrase.

Test yourself 30.12

Underline the verb phrase in each of the sentences below. In each sentence here, the verb phrase consists of a verb + noun phrase + prepositional phrase. It may help to first find the verb, which is the first word of these verb phrases.
Sample: I <u>called my wife during intermission</u>.

Getting started (answers on p. 136)

1. Vivian added calcium to her diet.

2. She knit that blanket from an unusual wool.

3. Her housekeeper rinsed those clothes in warm water.

4. I like my coffee without sugar.

5. Jack and Martha bought a wedding gift at Macy's.

More practice (answers on the website)

6. He put the steak on the grill.

7. A nervous driver pulled her smoking Audi into the repair shop.

8. The young man bought his first computer with his father's credit card.

9. He rescued her from the boring party.

10. Alex met his wife near her office.

Test yourself 30.13

Underline the verb phrase in each of the sentences below. The verb phrases will be either: verb (alone), verb + noun phrase, verb + adjective, verb + prepositional phrase, or verb + noun phrase + prepositional phrase.
Sample: He prepared his speech.

Getting started (answers on p. 137)

1. Your sister is a talented pianist.

2. Their doctor operates at that hospital.

3. Robert threw himself into the battle.

4. The offer sounded unrealistic.

5. His mother went to the drugstore.

More practice (answers on the website)

6. Yesterday we met a few of our friends.

7. Last night I studied.

8. The professor sounded eloquent.

9. We made a deal over dinner.

10. On Tuesdays Sarah paints in her studio.

Test yourself 30.14

Here are the same sentences as in *Test yourself* 30.13. This time, indicate if the verb phrase you've identified is: verb (alone), verb + noun phrase, verb + adjective, verb + prepositional phrase, or verb + noun phrase + prepositional phrase.
Sample: He prepared his speech.   verb + noun phrase

Getting started (answers on p. 137)

1. Your sister is a talented pianist.

2. Their doctor operates at that hospital.

3. Robert threw himself into the battle.

4. The offer sounded unrealistic.

5. His mother went to the drugstore.

More practice (answers on the website)

6. Yesterday we met a few of our friends.

7. Last night I studied.

8. The professor sounded eloquent.

9. We made a deal over dinner.

10. On Tuesdays Sarah paints in her studio.

To sum up, we list below the kinds of verb phrases we've discussed in this lesson:

verb	(example: *laughed*)
verb + adjective	(example: *was happy*)
verb + noun phrase	(example: *left the room*)
verb + preposition phrase	(example: *walked to the corner*)
verb + noun phrase + preposition phrase	(example: *walked Rachel to the corner*)

While there are more kinds of verb phrases, what we've done here is to show you some basic ones.

Answer keys: *Test yourself, Getting started* questions – Unit 11

Test yourself 30.1

1. Freddy <u>disappeared</u>.
2. A young woman <u>cried</u>.
3. The soldiers <u>wait</u>.
4. I <u>slept</u>.
5. The little girl <u>smiled</u>.

Test yourself 30.2

1. He <u>created a monster</u>.
2. Frank <u>broke the plate</u>.
3. Sherry and I <u>left the house</u>.
4. The detective <u>examined the old broken doorknob</u>.
5. We <u>resent those comments</u>.

Test yourself 30.3

1. He created <u>a monster</u>.
2. Frank broke <u>the plate</u>.
3. Sherry and I left <u>the house</u>.
4. The detective examined <u>the old broken doorknob</u>.
5. We resent <u>those comments</u>.

Test yourself 30.4

1. The argument <u>was silly</u>.
2. The dress <u>felt comfortable</u>.
3. Steven <u>became sick</u>.
4. The point of this exercise <u>seems obvious</u>.
5. The children <u>got excited</u>.

Test yourself 30.5

1. The argument was <u>silly</u>.
2. The dress felt <u>comfortable</u>.
3. Steven became <u>sick</u>.
4. The point of this exercise seems <u>obvious</u>.
5. The children got <u>excited</u>.

Test yourself 30.6

1. Brady <u>was a radio engineer</u>.
2. The king <u>sent a clear message</u>.

3. Those flowers <u>look gorgeous</u>.
4. Most able-bodied adults <u>work</u>.
5. I <u>recognized them</u>.

Test yourself 30.7

1. Brady <u>was a radio engineer</u>.	verb + noun phrase
2. The king <u>sent a clear message</u>.	verb + noun phrase
3. Those flowers <u>look gorgeous</u>.	verb +adjective
4. Most able-bodied adults <u>work</u>.	verb
5. I <u>recognized them</u>.	verb + noun phrase

Test yourself 30.8

1. The boat <u>floated in the water</u>.
2. Janice <u>is from Kansas City</u>.
3. Mrs. Miller <u>is at the beach</u>.
4. He <u>looked for me</u>.
5. The sun <u>appeared above the horizon</u>.

Test yourself 30.9

1. Elinor <u>rented a car</u>.
2. The clowns never <u>laugh with the audience</u>.
3. The road trip <u>ended</u>.
4. The band <u>played my favorite song</u>.
5. They <u>left at noon</u>.

Test yourself 30.10

1. Elinor <u>rented a car</u>.	verb + noun phrase
2. The clowns never <u>laugh with the audience</u>.	verb + prepositional phrase
3. The road trip <u>ended</u>.	verb
4. The band <u>played my favorite song</u>.	verb + noun phrase
5. They <u>left at noon</u>.	verb + prepositional phrase

Test yourself 30.11

1. Her mother <u>looked under the bed</u>.
2. Jan <u>leaped for the shore</u>.
3. The morning <u>seemed peaceful</u>.
4. The stock market <u>fell hard</u>.
5. She <u>arrived with an empty suitcase</u>.

Test yourself 30.12

1. Vivian <u>added calcium to her diet</u>.
2. She <u>knit that blanket from an unusual wool</u>.
3. Her housekeeper <u>rinsed those clothes in warm water</u>.
4. I <u>like my coffee without sugar</u>.
5. Jack and Martha <u>bought a wedding gift at Macy's</u>.

Test yourself 30.13

1. Your sister <u>is a talented pianist</u>.
2. Their doctor <u>operates at that hospital</u>.
3. Robert <u>threw himself into the battle</u>.
4. The offer <u>sounded unrealistic</u>.
5. His mother <u>went to the drugstore</u>.

Test yourself 30.14

1. Your sister <u>is a talented pianist</u>.   verb + noun phrase
2. Their doctor <u>operates at that hospital</u>.   verb + prepositional phrase
3. Robert <u>threw himself into the battle</u>.   verb + noun phrase + prepositional phrase
4. The offer <u>sounded unrealistic</u>.   verb + adjective
5. His mother <u>went to the drugstore</u>.   verb + prepositional phrase

☞ **FOR A REVIEW EXERCISE OF THIS UNIT, SEE THE WEBSITE.**

UNIT 12: AUXILIARY PHRASES

So far, each verb we've talked about occurs in a verb phrase. This type of verb is called a **main verb**. Other verbs, called **helping verbs** or **auxiliary verbs**, are found in **auxiliary phrases**. Auxiliary phrases are among the most satisfying to describe. That's because the English auxiliary phrase has a regular pattern, which helps to make it easy to understand. So here's some help with helping verbs.

Lesson 31: The basic structure of auxiliary phrases

What are some sentences with helping (auxiliary) verbs? Here are a few examples, with the helping verb underlined:

1. She <u>should</u> study.
2. She <u>has</u> studied.
3. She <u>is</u> studying.

In these sentences, the main verb is a form of *study*, and the helping verb is helping to give us additional information that we can't get from just the main verb. (See Unit 2 to remind yourself about main verbs.)

There aren't that many helping verbs; the basic ones are listed in *Quick tip* 31.1.

> **Quick tip 31.1**
>
> The basic helping verbs of English are:
> a. can may shall will must
>   could might should would
> b. have has had
> c. am are is
>   was were
>   be been being

Now take another look at sentences 1–3, which have both a helping verb and a main verb. Which comes first? You can see that the main verb always comes after the helping verb.

> **Quick tip 31.2**
>
> If a sentence has both a main verb and a helping verb, the main verb is always last.

Does every sentence of English have a helping verb? Here are examples of sentences that do <u>not</u> have a helping verb. Each only has a main verb, which is underlined.

4. She <u>studies</u> every day.
5. She <u>studied</u> every day.
6. He <u>leaves</u> at 9 in the morning.
7. He <u>left</u> at 9 in the morning.

Test yourself 31.1

Decide whether or not each sentence has a helping verb. Look for the main verb, which is underlined, and see if there's a helping verb before it.

	Helping verb: NO	Helping verb: YES
Sample: He <u>talked</u> about himself.	✗	

Getting started (answers on p. 164)

1. They were <u>arguing</u> loudly.   ....

2. The frog had <u>jumped</u> five feet.   ....

3. You <u>invited</u> everyone.   ....

4. I must <u>buy</u> some milk.   ....

5. Harry <u>lives</u> in Europe.   ....

More practice (answers on the website)

6. Jogging should <u>increase</u> your stamina.   ....

7. I have <u>worked</u> all day.   ....

8. Sam will <u>go</u> fishing tomorrow.   ....

9. Judy <u>left</u> for Dallas at noon.   ....

10. Joey was <u>chasing</u> a rascal all day long.   ....

Test yourself 31.2

Decide whether or not each sentence has a helping verb. This time the main verbs are not underlined.

	Helping verb: NO	*Helping verb: YES*
Sample: Maggie was walking nearby.	....	**✗**

Getting started (answers on p. 164)

1. You might write her a letter.   ....

2. Congress voted on the bill.   ....

3. Beth has survived that ordeal.   ....

4. I could be an actor.   ....

5. The Giants won the Super Bowl.   ....

More practice (answers on the website)

6. You should do that.   ....

7. She could move nearby.   ....

8. My friend wants a two-car garage.   ....

9. Jan must get that report done.   ....

10. The sun rose at 5 A.M. today.   ....

The helping verbs belong to different subgroups, as indicated in *Quick tip* 31.1. We'll take a closer look at each of the three types of helping verbs in the next few lessons.

Lesson 32: Modals

One kind of helping verb is called a **modal**. A modal adds information, such as possibility, necessity, or requests, to the verb that follows. The modals are underlined in the sentences below:

1. Ellen <u>can</u> do the job.
2. I <u>will</u> worry about that later.
3. You <u>should</u> rest before the party.
4. Dennis <u>might</u> change that carpeting.

There are nine basic modals, listed below. (They were group (a) of *Quick tip* 31.1.)

> **Quick tip 32.1**
>
> One kind of helping verb is called a modal. The basic modals of English are:
>
> | | |
> |------|--------|
> | can | could |
> | may | might |
> | shall | should |
> | will | would |
> | must | |

Test yourself 32.1

Underline the modal in each of the sentences below.
Sample: William <u>should</u> tell you the story.

Getting started (answers on p. 164)

1. They must delay the invasion.
2. You will find courage in your heart.
3. Mr. Knight might go with you.
4. You should be proud of yourself.
5. Tomorrow we may go to the movies.

More practice (answers on the website)

6. I could dance up a storm.
7. Lauren can name that tune in 10 seconds.
8. Ashley would win that race.
9. He shall travel to the countryside this weekend.
10. Jerry must renew his passport this month.

Test yourself 32.2

Underline the modal and put a squiggly line under the main verb in each of the sentences below.
Sample: She <u>will</u> b̰ḛ happy.

Getting started (answers on p. 164)

1. The curtains might hide the view.
2. Paul could work on the problem.
3. She can leave this afternoon.
4. You must go to the emergency room immediately.
5. The children will enjoy these gifts.

More practice (answers on the website)

6. We should proceed with caution.

7. You may be right.

8. One would think so.

9. Mrs. Randall will give you an answer tomorrow.

10. His father can postpone his retirement until next year.

To enhance your understanding

Here are the modals again:

can	could
may	might
shall	should
will	would
must	

Historically, those modals on the left have been considered present tense forms while those on the right have been considered past tense forms. (For more on tenses, see Lesson 37.) Note that three of the past tense forms end in the consonant *d*; think of it as a reminder of the past tense suffix *-ed*, as in the verb *stayed*.

To further enhance your understanding

Some expressions are similar to modals but consist of more than one word. They are called **phrasal modals** or **periphrastic modals**. Here are some examples, underlined in the following sentences:

5. I am able to go.
6. I ought to go.
7. I am going to go.
8. I would like to go.
9. I have to go.
10. I need to go.

Notice that many of the phrasal modals have the same meaning as one of the one-word modals; for example:, *am able to = can, ought to = should, am going to = will*.

11. I am able to go = I can go.
12. I ought to go = I should go.
13. I am going to go = I will go.

Note also that phrasal verbs end in *to*, which is followed by the base form of the verb.

Lesson 33: Perfect *have*

In each of the sentences below, the helping verb is a form of *have* – either *have*, *has*, or *had* – and is underlined. (These were listed in group (b) of *Quick tip* 31.1.)

1. She <u>had</u> greeted me happily.
2. They <u>have</u> eaten dinner early today.
3. He <u>has</u> written many articles about the wealthy.

Sentences with the helping verb *have* are said to be expressed in the **perfect aspect**, which adds information to the main verb about real-world time. For example, in sentence 2, using *have* indicates that the action began in the past and is complete.

> **Quick tip 33.1**
>
> One kind of helping verb is the verb *have*. It has three forms: *have*, *has*, and *had*.

Test yourself 33.1

Underline the *have* helping verb in each of the sentences below. It may be in any of the three forms of *have*. In these sentences, it will always be directly before the main verb.
Sample: I <u>have</u> imagined this for years.

Getting started (answers on p. 164)

1. The bridge had collapsed.
2. That cheerful woman has saved the day.
3. My uncles have visited us every summer.
4. Her neighbor has been an attorney for twenty years.
5. Suzie had traveled to Belgium twice before.

More practice (answers on the website)

6. My friend Sal has bought two suits recently.
7. Your remarks have entertained me enormously.
8. Our teacher had sent us an e-mail yesterday.
9. That thought never has crossed my mind.
10. You and I have played chess numerous times.

Test yourself 33.2

Underline the *have* helping verb and put a squiggly line under the main verb in each of the sentences below.
Sample: He <u>had</u> <u>annoyed</u> his boss.

Getting started (answers on p. 165)

1. Joan and Sam have worked for hours.
2. Their mother has spoken of you often.
3. The prime minister had written to him.
4. Your daughter has grown a lot taller.
5. She has seen her friends twice since last Sunday.

More practice (answers on the website)

6. Our dogs have made a mess of the living room.

7. You had warned me not to heed his advice.

8. The chef has prepared this dish perfectly.

9. We have thought about your suggestion seriously.

10. The actors had rehearsed for about an hour.

The verb *have* is not used only as a helping verb in English. It can also be the main verb in a sentence. Here are some examples with *have* used as the main verb. Notice that when *have* is being used as the main verb, it refers to the notion of possession or ownership.

4. I have a comfortable bed.

5. She has a beautiful home.

6. That family had a lot of problems.

Quick tip 33.2

Have can be used as a helping verb or as a main verb. When *have* is used as the main verb, it refers to the idea of possession. When *have* is used as the helping verb, it is always followed by another verb.

Test yourself 33.3

Decide if the forms of *have* in the following sentences are being used as helping verbs or as main verbs.

	Helping verb	Main verb
Sample: Jack had a good time.	....	✗

Getting started (answers on p. 165)

	Helping verb	Main verb
1. Jack has experienced a good time.	....	....
2. He has seen her often.	....	....
3. You have a lot of DVDs.	....	....
4. She had tacos for dinner.	....	....
5. Your professor has the answer to your question.	....	....

More practice (answers on the website)

	Helping verb	Main verb
6. Grandpa has slept on the couch often.	....	....
7. Aisha had trouble with her car this morning.	....	....
8. My aunt has a treadmill in her basement.	....	....
9. Mrs. Stein had called the paramedics.	....	....
10. They have donated that coat to charity.	....	....

You may have noticed that sometimes there are sentences with two occurrences of *have*. Here are some examples.

7. Jack has had a bad time.
8. The mayor had had a close election.
9. We have had a delicious dinner.

How can we account for this? The first occurrence of *have* is a helping verb; the second occurrence of *have* is the main verb (and refers to possession). That is, just as any other main verb can use *have* as a helping verb, the main verb *have* can also use *have* as a helping verb. That results in two forms of *have* in the same sentence.

Lesson 34: Progressive *be*

In each of the sentences below, the helping verb is a form of the verb *be* and is underlined.

1. She <u>is</u> leaving on the train.
2. I <u>was</u> thinking about his behavior.
3. They <u>were</u> managing the restaurant.

(These were listed in group (c) of *Quick tip* 31.1.) In addition to the forms *is*, *was*, and *were*, additional forms of *be* are *am*, *are*, *be*, *been*, and *being*.

Sentences with the helping verb *be* are said to be expressed in the **progressive** or **continuous aspect**, which usually indicates that the action takes place over a period of time.

> **Quick tip 34.1**
>
> One kind of helping verb is *be*. It has the following forms: *am, is, are, was, were, be, been, and being*.

Test yourself 34.1

Underline the form of the *be* helping verb in each of the sentences below.
Sample: He <u>was</u> exercising regularly.

Getting started (answers on p. 165)

1. The reporter was writing her story.
2. He is controlling his temper.
3. You are learning about syntax.
4. They were watching a movie last Sunday.
5. I am doing a lot of things right now.

More practice (answers on the website)

6. The politicians are campaigning in full force.
7. The football teams were finishing the season.
8. Catherine is learning to speak French.
9. Those actors were rehearsing.
10. I was cleaning my closet yesterday.

Test yourself 34.2

Underline the *be* helping verb and put a squiggly line under the main verb in each of the sentences below.
Sample: He <u>is</u> greeting his boss.

Getting started (answers on p. 165)

1. I was talking to Harry.
2. Irving and Annie are studying Latin.
3. He is testing her loyalty.
4. I am taking a walk.
5. You were reading for hours.

More practice (answers on the website)

6. The train is arriving.
7. The wrestlers are getting ready to compete.
8. The manager was closing the store.
9. I am organizing a luncheon for him.
10. The children were playing peacefully.

The verb *be* is not used only as a helping verb in English. It can also be the main verb in a sentence, in which case it's a linking verb. (This was discussed in Lesson 9.) As a reminder, here are some sentences with *be* used as the main verb:

4. I <u>am</u> happy
5. She <u>was</u> an actress.
6. Those Broadway shows <u>are</u> great.

Quick tip 34.2

Be and its forms can be used as a helping verb or as a main verb. When *be* is used as the helping verb, it is always followed by another verb.

Test yourself 34.3

Decide if the forms of *be* in the following sentences are being used as helping verbs or as main verbs.

	Helping verb	*Main verb*
Sample: Joan is a genius.	....	**✗**

Getting started (answers on p. 165)

1. Sam is looking at the mail.	....	....
2. That concept was difficult.	....	....
3. You are helping her a lot.	....	....
4. I am a doctor.	....	....
5. They were watching TV.	....	....

More practice (answers on the website)

6. She was writing her term paper.	....	....
7. David is a famous opera singer.	....	....
8. You are joking, right?	....	....
9. His employees are happy about it.	....	....
10. Jackie and Richard were friends.	....	....

You may have noticed that sometimes there are sentences with two occurrences of *be*. Here are some examples:

7. Andrew is being a nuisance.
8. My friends were being courageous.
9. They are being clowns.

How can we account for this? The first occurrence of *be* is a helping verb; the second occurrence of *be* is the main verb. That is, just as any other main verb can use *be* as a helping verb, the main verb *be* can also use *be* as a helping verb. That results in two forms of *be* in the same sentence.

Lesson 35: Combining auxiliary verbs

All the sentences with helping (auxiliary) verbs that we've looked at so far have had only one helping verb. It's possible, however, for a sentence to have more than one helping verb. Here are some examples of sentences with two helping verbs; the helping verbs are underlined. (Remember that there are three kinds of helping verbs: (a) modals (e.g. *should*, *can*, *might*), (b) *have*, and (c) *be*. See Lessons 32–34.)

    1. She <u>should have</u> studied.   (modal + *have*)

    2. She <u>may be</u> studying.   (modal + *be*)

    3. She <u>has been</u> studying.   (*have* + *be*)

When a sentence has two helping verbs, which helping verb is first? If a sentence has a modal, that will always be the first helping verb, as you can see in sentences 1 and 2. If a sentence has both *have* and *be* as helping verbs, *have* will always be first, as you can see in sentence 3.

Can you think of a sentence with three helping verbs? Sentences 4 and 5 have three helping verbs (underlined):

    4. She <u>should have been</u> studying.

    5. Mary <u>might have been</u> looking at him.

If there are three helping verbs, they are always in the following order: modal + *have* + *be*, as you can see from sentences 4 and 5. And if there are only two helping verbs, they're still in this relative order, with modal first, and *have* before *be*.

> **Quick tip 35.1**
>
> A sentence can have zero, one, or more than one helping verb. If there is more than one, they will always be in the following relative order: modal +*have* +*be*.

Test yourself 35.1

For each sentence below, underline the <u>main</u> verb. Then decide if the sentence has zero, one, two, or three helping verbs before the main verb.

Sample: They may <u>rent</u> a car at the terminal.   <u>1</u>

Getting started (answers on p. 165)

1. She was focusing on the mirror.   ....

2. Andy should have been enjoying his new career.   ....

3. Mrs. Packard's life changed at that point.   ....

4. You can have two scoops of ice cream.   ....

5. I might have committed a serious error.   ....

148

More practice (answers on the website)

6. Tamara has been working for 22 years.　..................
7. He could have been telling the truth.　..................
8. The birds were chirping early in the morning.　..................
9. Gauguin painted in Tahiti.　..................
10. Tomorrow we will go to the movies.　..................

Test yourself 35.2

Underline each helping verb in the sentences below. Each sentence will have at least one helping verb.
Sample: The children <u>have</u> <u>been</u> working hard.

Getting started (answers on p. 165)

1. You should read this book.
2. She had been greeting me happily.
3. Janice might have gotten the flu.
4. My question was bothering him.
5. The prime suspect might have been telling the truth.

More practice (answers on the website)

6. He could have been a hero.
7. The journalists will be traveling throughout Canada.
8. I have written many articles about the wealthy.
9. This has been a difficult time for me.
10. The trial has been going on far too long.

Test yourself 35.3

Underline each helping verb in the sentences below. A sentence will have anywhere from zero to three helping verbs.
Sample: He and Bill shook hands.　(No helping verb.)

Getting started (answers on p. 166)

1. I had been writing to him often.
2. Their mother has spoken of you a lot.
3. Sam will recognize it immediately.
4. We were good friends.
5. You should be studying right now.

More practice (answers on the website)

6. He may have been working on the project.
7. We had a sudden downpour.
8. This storm will pass soon.
9. The attorney may have overstated her case.
10. This relationship is improving rapidly.

Test yourself 35.4

Underline each helping verb in the sentences below and put a squiggly line under the main verb. A sentence will have anywhere from zero to three helping verbs.
Sample: Paul <u>was</u> <u>offering</u> me a drink.

Getting started (answers on p. 166)

1. They can do the research.

2. Suzanne might be leaving sooner.

3. Papa has been teasing him.

4. I might have been being too cautious.

5. The plane was late.

More practice (answers on the website)

6. The student will have completed his assignment by tomorrow.

7. You are being silly.

8. Everyone has had a great time at the party.

9. The show was a great success.

10. It must have been difficult to do that.

Lesson 36: The suffixes of auxiliary verbs

Each helping verb is actually a two-part package. There's the helping verb itself, and then there's the effect that the helping verb has on the verb that follows it.

Look at the sentences below. In each of them, the helping verb is a form of progressive *be* (underlined). What effect does progressive *be* have on the verb that follows it?

1. The children <u>were</u> working hard.
2. I <u>am</u> considering a new job offer.
3. Nothing <u>was</u> limiting his development.
4. Many new advances <u>are</u> emerging.
5. Sam <u>is</u> watching his favorite TV show.

You can see that the verb after the form of *be* always has *-ing* added to its base. This *-ing* form of the verb is referred to as the **present participle** in traditional grammar.

Quick tip 36.1

When the helping verb is progressive *be*, the next verb always has *-ing* added to its base form. Example: *is sleeping*. The *-ing* verb form is called the present participle.

Test yourself 36.1

Each of the following sentences has a form of the helping verb *be*. Underline the *be* verb and the *-ing* ending of the following verb.
Sample: Maggie <u>is</u> sleep<u>ing</u> now.

Getting started (answers on p. 166)

1. She is leaving on the ten o'clock train.
2. The curtains were masking the view.
3. I was wondering about his behavior.
4. Paul is leaning on his wife's chair.
5. They are sounding rather defensive.

More practice (answers on the website)

6. We were attending a graduation ceremony last week.
7. Jim's parents were watching a movie.
8. You are trying too hard.
9. I am dreaming of a gentle snowfall.
10. The President was addressing the nation yesterday.

In each of the following sentences, the helping verb is a form of *have* (underlined). What effect does *have* have on the verb that follows it? (This is a little trickier than the pattern with *be*.)

6. She <u>had</u> greeted me happily.
7. They <u>have</u> eaten dinner early today.
8. That <u>had</u> interested the reporter.
9. Sarah <u>had</u> managed to pry apart the shells.

10. Carla and Raphael <u>have</u> written many books together.
11. He and Bill <u>had</u> shaken hands.

The verb following *have* most frequently has the suffix *-en* or *-ed* added to it. The form of the verb following the helping verb *have* is traditionally called the **past participle**.

> **Quick tip 36.2**
>
> When *have* is the helping verb, the next verb typically has *-ed or -en* added to its base form. Examples: *has eaten, have watched*. The verb form following the helping verb *have* is called the past participle.

Test yourself 36.2

Each of the following sentences has a form of the helping verb *have*. Underline the *have* and the *-ed* or *-en* ending of the following verb.

Sample: You <u>had</u> manag<u>ed</u> the situation very well.

Getting started (answers on p. 166)

1. The women had spoken to each other recently.
2. Unfortunately, the heroine had married the villain.
3. Andy and George have enjoyed themselves enormously.
4. My student has written an interesting essay on technology.
5. The hockey game has ended in a tie.

More practice (answers on the website)

6. The local theater has provided much entertainment over the years.
7. I have seen you somewhere before.
8. Her brother has broken the vase to pieces.
9. They have lied too many times.
10. Mona's boyfriend has surprised her with a wedding proposal.

The *-ed* and *-en* suffixes are the most common endings for past participles. However, for historical reasons, there are actually several ways to form past participles. Note the following patterns of some typical verbs:

Verb base	Perfect	Past participle
be	have been	been
see	have seen	seen
give	have given	given
arrange	have arranged	arranged
walk	have walked	walked
play	have played	played

Another way to form past participles is by changing a vowel of the verb base, sometimes also adding the suffix *-en*. Some examples are:

Verb base	Perfect	Past participle
begin	have begun	begun
sing	have sung	sung
speak	have spoken	spoken
weave	have woven	woven

Sometimes no change at all is made to the verb:

Verb base	Perfect	Past participle
hit	have hit	hit
come	have come	come

There is no magic or hard and fast rule to determine what the past participle of a particular verb is. We simply have to memorize it when we learn English.

In each of the following sentences, the helping verb is a modal (underlined). What effect does a modal have on the verb that follows it?

12. The piano salesman <u>should</u> consider his actions.
13. He <u>will</u> recognize it immediately.
14. Sam <u>could</u> be a star quarterback.
15. The major <u>may</u> speak to you later.

Quick tip 36.3

When the helping verb is a modal, the next verb is always in its base form. Example: can study.

Test yourself 36.3

Each of the following sentences has a modal helping verb. Underline the modal and put a squiggly line under the verb following it, which will be in its base form.
Sample: He <u>should</u> oppose their actions.

Getting started (answers on p. 166)

1. Richard will believe the truth.
2. The waiter might bring it.
3. They may be home late.
4. We shall overcome this obstacle.
5. I would do it in an instant.

More practice (answers on the website)

6. The mail should arrive by noon.
7. Michael can build anything.
8. The waiters must wash their hands often.
9. On a clear day, you could see for miles.
10. The train will make a stop in Atlanta.

What happens to the following verb if there is more than one helping verb in a sentence? Is the pattern the same when a helping verb is followed by another helping verb, rather than the main verb? The patterns we have talked about are the same, whether there is one helping verb or more than one helping verb in a sentence. You can see this in the following sentences:

16. They **have** <u>been</u> see<u>ing</u> the doctor regularly.
17. You **have** <u>been</u> observ<u>ing</u> the situation closely.

Since *have* (in bold) is a helping verb in these sentences, the next verb, *be*, gets the *-en* ending (also in bold). And since *be* (underlined) is also a helping verb, the verb after *be* gets the *-ing* ending (also underlined).

We can also see consistent patterns in the following two sentences:

18. They **should** have seen the doctor regularly.
19. You **might** be observing the situation closely.

In sentence 18 the modal (in bold) causes the next verb, *have*, to be in its base form. The *have* helping verb then affects the form of the next verb, the main verb *see*, which appears in its past participle form, *seen*. Similarly, in sentence 19 the modal, *might*, causes the next verb, *be*, to be in its base form. Then the *be* affects the form of the next verb, the main verb *observe*, which appears in its present participle form, *observing*.

What happens if a sentence has all three kinds of helping verbs? The pattern still remains the same, as you can see in the next set of examples:

20. They **should** have been seeing the doctor regularly.
21. You **might** have been observing the situation more closely.

The modal, which is the first helping verb (in bold), causes *have* to be in its base form. The *have* helping verb (underlined) causes the next verb, *be*, to appear in its past participle form, that is, with the *-en* suffix (also underlined), and *be* (with a squiggly line) causes the next verb, the main verb, to be in its present participle form, that is, ending in *-ing* (also with a squiggly line).

So the overall pattern is completely consistent, whether a sentence has one, two, or three helping verbs.

As we've seen, when progressive *be* is the helping verb, the next verb always has *-ing* added to it. But sometimes verbs ending in the *-ing* suffix have a different use, as we can see in these next sentences:

22. Skiing energizes me.
23. I love cooking.

In these sentences, the *-ing* word does not follow the helping verb *be*. Instead, the *-ing* ending changes the verb into a noun. In fact, notice that the *-ing* word can be replaced with a typical noun in these sentences, for example: *Sugar energizes me*, *I love Mary*. A noun that consists of a verb and the suffix *-ing* is called a **gerund**.

Quick tip 36.4

A noun that consists of a verb and the suffix *-ing* is called a gerund. Example: *Entertain-ing is fun*.

Here are some more examples of sentences with gerunds:

24. Reading is one of life's pleasures.
25. Thinking can be hard work!
26. The criminal admitted lying.
27. They stopped worrying about it.

Test yourself 36.4

Decide if each underlined word ending in *-ing* in the following sentences is being used as a verb, part of the progressive *be* "package," or as a noun, that is, as a gerund. To help you decide, see whether or not the *-ing* word follows the helping verb *be*.

	Verb (progressive)	*Noun (gerund)*
Sample: She likes <u>walking</u> the dog.	....	**✗**

Getting started (answers on p. 166)

1. They are <u>constructing</u> small homes in that part of town.	....	....
2. He was <u>looking</u> for Jonas.	....	....
3. The candidate thought about <u>refusing</u>.	....	....
4. <u>Giving</u> to charity is an old American tradition.	....	....
5. I should have thought of <u>responding</u> earlier.	....	....

More practice (answers on the website)

6. Last night we were <u>having</u> lots of fun.	....	....
7. The employee was <u>being</u> honest with you.	....	....
8. She enjoys <u>listening</u> to her iPod.	....	....
9. Some doctors recommend <u>taking</u> vitamin pills.	....	....
10. I am <u>considering</u> your offer seriously.	....	....

Here is a summary of the three helping verbs we've discussed in this lesson and the form of the verb that follows each:

Helping verb	*Following verb*
modal	base form
perfect *have*	past participle form (typically ending in *-ed* or *-en*)
progressive *be*:	present participle form (always ending in *-ing*)

Two additional helping verbs will be discussed in Lessons 52 and 53.

Lesson 37: Tense

The verb of a sentence gives information about **tense**. Speakers of English generally are aware that, for example, the verb *studies* is a present tense form while the verb *studied* is a past tense form.

Test yourself 37.1

For each verb below, decide if it is in its present tense or past tense form.

	Present tense	*Past tense*
Sample: was		**✗**

Getting started (answers on p. 167)

1. sends		
2. felt		
3. perceived		
4. am		
5. has		

More practice (answers on the website)

6. wrote		
7. sat		
8. walk		
9. arose		
10. sing		

It's important to understand that grammatical tense and real world time are not necessarily the same. Take a look at the following sentences:

1. She studied yesterday.
2. She was studying yesterday.

In sentences 1 and 2, the tense of the underlined verbs, as seen in their forms, is past; the time that is being talked about is also past. So in these cases tense and time are the same.

Now consider the following sentences:

3. I am going to France next summer.
4. She has bought the books for the course.

In sentences 3 and 4, the grammatical tense of the underlined verbs is present. (If these verbs were past tense forms, they would be *was* and *had*, respectively). However, the real-life or actual time that sentence 3 is talking about is in the future; the actual time that sentence 4 is talking about is in the past. So in sentences 3 and 4 we can see that grammatical tense and real-life time are not always the same.

For the rest of this lesson, we'll be focusing on the tense (grammatical form) and not the real-life time of English verbs.

> **Quick tip 37.1**
>
> Time refers to a point in real life at which something occurs. Tense refers to the grammatical form of a verb.

In a simple sentence, tense information is carried by only one verb. If a sentence has helping verbs as well as a main verb, which verb shows tense? In each of the sentences below, the verb that carries the tense information is underlined.

5. John <u>studies</u>.
6. John <u>studied</u>.
7. John <u>has</u> studied.
8. John <u>had</u> studied.
9. John <u>is</u> studying.
10. John <u>was</u> studying.
11. John <u>has</u> been studying.
12. John <u>had</u> been studying.

You can see that in each sentence it is the very first verb that carries the tense information, regardless of whether it's a helping verb or the main verb.

You will notice that we have not included in our list of sentences in 5 through 12 examples of sentences whose first verb is a modal. (Recall from Lesson 34 that modals always come first in sentences with more than one verb.) That is because in general, modals do not carry clear tense information. Look at the following examples:

13. I <u>might</u> do it right now / today.
14. I <u>might</u> do it tomorrow.
15. I <u>might</u> have done it yesterday.

As you can see, the form of the modal is the same (*might*), regardless of whether it refers to time in the present (sentence 13), time in the future (sentence 14), or time in the past (sentence 15). We will consider modals to be tenseless.

Quick tip 37.2

Tense information is always indicated by the first verb in the sentence, excluding modals.

Traditionally, sentences have been grouped into different types, according to the tense of the verb. Let's compare the following two sentences:

16. John studies every day.
17. John studied every day.

You can see that the only difference between sentence 16 and sentence 17 is that in 16, *study* is in its present tense form and in 17 *study* is in its past tense form. On this basis, sentence 16 has **present tense** (or **simple present tense**), while sentence 17 has **past tense** (or **simple past tense**).

Here are some more examples, with the verbs underlined:

18. Ira <u>sighed</u> in relief.   (past)
19. Alice <u>sees</u> her often.   (present)
20. He <u>laughed</u> hysterically.   (past)
21. I often <u>forget</u> the answer. (present)

Quick tip 37.3

Sentences with no helping verb are in either the present or past tense, depending on the form of the verb.

Almost all verbs, like the verbs in sentences 18 and 20, form their past tense by adding the suffix -*ed*. These verbs are called **regular verbs**. Some verbs, however, do not follow this pattern. These verbs are called **irregular verbs**. Some examples of irregular verbs are: *see* (past tense *saw*), *write* (past tense *wrote*), and *hit* (past tense *hit*).

Test yourself 37.2

Decide if each sentence is in the present or past tense. You'll need to find the verb to make this decision.
Sample: Her daughter giggled happily.   past

Getting started (answers on p. 167)

1. They deliver furniture on Tuesdays. ....

2. The senator supports that bill. ....

3. I voted for him. ....

4. I ate a sandwich for lunch. ....

5. The shortstop hit a home run. ....

More practice (answers on the website)

6. Michigan State beat Ohio State. ....

7. Our niece studies anthropology. ....

8. The weather is humid today. ....

9. The repairman arrived at noon. ....

10. My daughter came for a visit. ....

The next two sentences have **future tense** (or **simple future tense**): they have the modal helping verb *will*, followed by the base of the main verb.

22. John <u>will</u> study tomorrow.
23. Jessica <u>will</u> visit her soon.

> **Quick tip 37.4**
>
> Sentences with *will* followed by the main verb are in the future tense.

The future tense can also be expressed with the modal helping verb *shall*: e.g. *John <u>shall</u> study tomorrow*. *Shall* has restricted usage in American English: generally, it's used only in formal speech styles. Consequently, we'll ignore *shall* in our discussion here.

Test yourself 37.3

Decide if each sentence below is in the present, past, or future tense.
Sample: Those Halloween decorations will look scary.   future

Getting started (answers on p. 167)

1. He sleeps late on weekends. ....

2. Zach was proud of his son. ....

3. Bethany will get married soon. ....

4. The show began promptly at 8 P.M. ....

5. My sister will run in the New York City marathon. ....

More practice (answers on the website)

6. The coffee tasted bitter. ....

7. I study in England every summer. ....

8. My younger brother beat me at chess. ....

9. Stu gets up at 7 A.M. every morning. ....

10. We will hold a family reunion in July. ....

As we saw above (in sentences 4, 11, and 12), sentences with the *have* helping verb also change in form to indicate tense:

24. I <u>have</u> bought the books.

25. I <u>had</u> bought the books.

The difference between the two sentences is that sentence 24 is in the present tense, while sentence 25 is in the past tense. Notice that it is only the form of *have* that changes to indicate the tense information. The verb after *have* is always in its past participle form, which does not change to indicate tense. Although sentences with the *have* helping verb are in the perfect aspect, when we talk about a sentence with both tense and aspect, we just use the term "tense." So therefore sentence 24 is in the **present perfect tense** while sentence 25 is in the **past perfect tense**.

> **Quick tip 37.5**
>
> If a sentence has a form of *have* as a helping verb, it will have the word *perfect* as part of the name of its tense.

> **Quick tip 37.6**
>
> The present tense forms of *have* are *have* and *has*. The past tense form of *have* is *had*.

Test yourself 37.4

Decide if each sentence is in the present perfect or past perfect tense. Use the form of *have* to help you make your decision.

Sample: I had believed every word of that broadcast.   <u>past perfect</u>

Getting started (answers on p. 167)

1. She had wanted to do everything her way. ....

2. Martha has known about the surprise. ....

3. Samantha had decided to do that. ....

4. I have written to him about that issue. ....

5. You have been a good friend. ....

More practice (answers on the website)

6. They have purchased a new home. ....

7. On our trip, we had converted $200 to euros. ....

8. Andy has promised to tell the truth. ....

9. The detective had found an important witness. ....

10. The Democrats have won the presidency. ....

What do you think is the tense of the following sentences?

26. John <u>will have</u> studied by then.

27. It <u>will have</u> been an easy test.

Since these sentences have both *will* and a form of *have* as helping verbs, they are in the **future perfect tense**.

> **Quick tip 37.7**
>
> If a sentence has *will* as a helping verb, it will have the word *future* as part of the name of its tense.

Test yourself 37.5

Decide if each sentence below is in the present perfect, past perfect, or future perfect tense. Look at the form of *have* and for the presence or absence of *will* to help you.

Sample: Our friends have dropped by.   <u>present perfect</u>

Getting started (answers on p. 167)

1. They have finished the assignment. ....

2. The alarm clock will have gone off by then. ....

3. Linda had locked the door. ....

4. My friend John has been a great help to me. ....

5. By then, I will have finished studying. ....

More practice (answers on the website)

6. Frank had appeared in a movie once. ....

7. You have encouraged me many times. ....

8. She has written a letter to her sister. ....

9. There had been a flood of inquiries. ....

10. You will have left a great legacy to your children. ....

Last, we come to sentences with a form of *be* as a helping verb. These also change in form to indicate tense:

28. I <u>am</u> buying the book.
29. I <u>was</u> buying the book.

The difference between the two sentences is that sentence 28 is in the present tense, while sentence 29 is in the past tense. Notice that the verb after *be* is in its present participle form (that is, its *-ing* form), which does not change to indicate tense. Remember that although sentences with the *be* helping verb are in the progressive aspect, when we talk about a sentence with both tense and aspect, we just use the term "tense." So therefore sentence 28 is in the **present progressive tense** while sentence 29 is in the **past progressive tense**.

As you might expect, the following sentences are in the **future progressive tense**:

30. I <u>will be</u> leaving at three o'clock.
31. Harry <u>will be</u> running the marathon.

You can see that they have both *will* and *be* as helping verbs.

Quick tip 37.8

If a sentence has a form of *be* as a helping verb, it will have the word *progressive* as part of the name of its tense.

Quick tip 37.9

The present tense forms of *be* are *am, is,* and *are.* The past tense forms of *be* are *was* and *were.*

Test yourself 37.6

Decide if each sentence below is in the present progressive, past progressive, or future progressive tense. Look at the form of *be* and for the presence or absence of *will* to help you.

Sample: He was racing down the steps of the library.   <u>past progressive</u>

Getting started (answers on p. 167)

1. She is packing her bags. ....

2. Tom will be thinking about it all day. ....

3. The computer was working on it. ....

4. It will be snowing tomorrow. ....

5. I am getting tired. ....

More practice (answers on the website)

6. They were buying stamps at the post office. ....

7. Jackie will be starting a new business. ....

8. You surely are kidding. ....

9. The mechanic was washing his car. ....

10. We will be celebrating for hours. ....

Since sentences can have more than one helping verb (see Lesson 35), their tenses can have combinations of the words *present*, *past*, *future*, *perfect*, and *progressive* in their names. Here are examples of each of the possible tenses:

32. Mary speaks to everyone.   (present)
33. Mary spoke to everyone.   (past)
34. Mary will speak to everyone.   (future)
35. Mary has spoken to everyone.   (present perfect)
36. Mary had spoken to everyone.   (past perfect)
37. Mary will have spoken to everyone.   (future perfect)
38. Mary is speaking to everyone.   (present progressive)
39. Mary was speaking to everyone.   (past progressive)
40. Mary will be speaking to everyone.   (future progressive)
41. Mary has been speaking to everyone.   (present perfect progressive)
42. Mary had been speaking to everyone.   (past perfect progressive)
43. Mary will have been speaking to everyone.   (future perfect progressive)

To sum up:

(a) A sentence with *will* always has the word *future* in its tense name.
(b) A sentence with a *have* helping verb always has the word *perfect* in its tense name.
(c) A sentence with a *be* helping verb followed by a verb in its -*ing* form always has the word *progressive* in its tense name.
(d) For sentences without *will*, look at the form of the first helping verb, if there is one, or of the main verb, if there's no helping verb, to decide if the tense is present or past.

Test yourself 37.7

Identify the tense name of each of the verb combinations below.
Sample: had thought   past perfect

Getting started (answers on p. 168)

1. will consider ....
2. experienced ....
3. will have wanted ....
4. had been watching ....
5. will be reading ....

More practice (answers on the website)

6. were acting ....
7. will have been studying ....
8. has had ....
9. have been sleeping ....
10. mention ....

Test yourself 37.8

Identify the tense name of each of the sentences below.
Sample: He will be expecting great things of her.   future progressive

Getting started (answers on p. 168)

1. She was making some progress. ....

2. Marie shrugged her shoulders. ....

3. She will be taking a long walk. ....

4. He has had two serious operations. ....

5. They had been getting numerous phone calls. ....

More practice (answers on the website)

6. Neil is going to Washington tomorrow.

7. Clare has been watching ESPN for years.

8. You will be a champion one day.

9. Luis will have worked for IBM for 40 years.

10. I will have been sleeping for nine hours.

Answer keys: *Test yourself, Getting started* questions – Unit 12

Test yourself 31.1

	Helping verb: NO	Helping verb: YES
1. They were <u>arguing</u> loudly.		✗
2. The frog had <u>jumped</u> five feet.		✗
3. You <u>invited</u> everyone.	✗	
4. I must <u>buy</u> some milk.		✗
5. Harry <u>lives</u> in Europe.	✗	

Test yourself 31.2

	Helping verb: NO	Helping verb: YES
1. You might write her a letter.		✗
2. Congress voted on the bill.	✗	
3. Beth has survived that ordeal.		✗
4. I could be an actor.		✗
5. The Giants won the Super Bowl.	✗	

Test yourself 32.1

1. They <u>must</u> delay the invasion.
2. You <u>will</u> find courage in your heart.
3. Mr. Knight <u>might</u> go with you.
4. You <u>should</u> be proud of yourself.
5. Tomorrow we <u>may</u> go to the movies.

Test yourself 32.2

1. The curtains <u>might hide</u> the view.
2. Paul <u>could work</u> on the problem.
3. She <u>can leave</u> this afternoon.
4. You <u>must go</u> to the emergency room immediately.
5. The children <u>will enjoy</u> these gifts.

Test yourself 33.1

1. The bridge <u>had</u> collapsed.
2. That cheerful woman <u>has</u> saved the day.
3. My uncles <u>have</u> visited us every summer.
4. Her neighbor <u>has</u> been an attorney for twenty years.
5. Suzie <u>had</u> traveled to Belgium twice before.

Test yourself 33.2

1. Joan and Sam <u>have worked</u> for hours.
2. Their mother <u>has spoken</u> of you often.
3. The prime minister <u>had written</u> to him.
4. Your daughter <u>has grown</u> a lot taller.
5. She <u>has seen</u> her friends twice since last Sunday.

Test yourself 33.3

	Helping verb	*Main verb*
1. Jack has experienced a good time.	✗	
2. He has seen her often.	✗	
3. You have a lot of DVDs.		✗
4. She had tacos for dinner.		✗
5. Your professor has the answer to your question.		✗

Test yourself 34.1

1. The reporter <u>was</u> writing her story.
2. He <u>is</u> controlling his temper.
3. You <u>are</u> learning about syntax.
4. They <u>were</u> watching a movie last Sunday.
5. I <u>am</u> doing a lot of things right now.

Test yourself 34.2

1. I <u>was talking</u> to Harry.
2. Irving and Annie <u>are studying</u> Latin.
3. He <u>is testing</u> her loyalty.
4. I <u>am taking</u> a walk.
5. You <u>were reading</u> for hours.

Test yourself 34.3

	Helping verb	*Main verb*
1. Sam is looking at the mail.	✗	
2. That concept was difficult.		✗
3. You are helping her a lot.	✗	
4. I am a doctor.		✗
5. They were watching TV.	✗	

Test yourself 35.1

1. She was <u>focusing</u> on the mirror. ... 1 ...
2. Andy should have been <u>enjoying</u> his new career. ... 3 ...
3. Mrs. Packard's life <u>changed</u> at that point. ... 0 ...
4. You can <u>have</u> two scoops of ice cream. ... 1 ...
5. I might have <u>committed</u> a serious error. ... 2 ...

Test yourself 35.2

1. You <u>should</u> read this book.
2. She <u>had been</u> greeting me happily.

3. Janice <u>might have</u> gotten the flu.

4. My question <u>was</u> bothering him.

5. The prime suspect <u>might have been</u> telling the truth.

Test yourself 35.3

1. I <u>had been</u> writing to him often.

2. Their mother <u>has</u> spoken of you a lot.

3. Sam <u>will</u> recognize it immediately.

4. We were good friends. (No helping verb.)

5. You <u>should be</u> studying right now.

Test yourself 35.4

1. They <u>can do</u> the research.

2. Suzanne <u>might be leaving</u> sooner.

3. Papa <u>has been teasing</u> him.

4. I <u>might have been being</u> too cautious.

5. The plane <u>was</u> late.

Test yourself 36.1

1. She <u>is leaving</u> on the ten o'clock train.

2. The curtains <u>were masking</u> the view.

3. I <u>was wondering</u> about his behavior.

4. Paul <u>is leaning</u> on his wife's chair.

5. They <u>are sounding</u> rather defensive.

Test yourself 36.2

1. The women <u>had spoken</u> to each other recently.

2. Unfortunately, the heroine <u>had married</u> the villain.

3. Andy and George <u>have enjoyed</u> themselves enormously.

4. My student <u>has written</u> an interesting essay on technology.

5. The hockey game <u>has ended</u> in a tie.

Test yourself 36.3

1. Richard <u>will believe</u> the truth.

2. The waiter <u>might bring</u> it.

3. They <u>may be</u> home late.

4. We <u>shall overcome</u> this obstacle.

5. I <u>would do</u> it in an instant.

Test yourself 36.4

	Verb (progressive)	Noun (gerund)
1. They are <u>constructing</u> small homes in that part of town.	✗	
2. He was <u>looking</u> for Jonas.	✗	
3. The candidate thought about <u>refusing</u>.		✗
4. <u>Giving</u> to charity is an old American tradition.		✗
5. I should have thought of <u>responding</u> earlier.		✗

Test yourself 37.1

	Present tense	Past tense
1. sends	✗	
2. felt		✗
3. perceived		✗
4. am	✗	
5. has	✗	

Test yourself 37.2

1. They deliver furniture on Tuesdays. present
2. The senator supports that bill. present
3. I voted for him. past
4. I ate a sandwich for lunch. past
5. The shortstop hit a home run. past

Test yourself 37.3

1. He sleeps late on weekends. present
2. Zach was proud of his son. past
3. Bethany will get married soon. future
4. The show began promptly at 8 P.M. past
5. My sister will run in the New York City marathon. future

Test yourself 37.4

1. She had wanted to do everything her way. past perfect
2. Martha has known about the surprise. present perfect
3. Samantha had decided to do that. past perfect
4. I have written to him about that issue. present perfect
5. You have been a good friend. present perfect

Test yourself 37.5

1. They have finished the assignment. present perfect
2. The alarm clock will have gone off by then. future perfect
3. Linda had locked the door. past perfect
4. My friend John has been a great help to me. present perfect
5. By then, I will have finished studying. future perfect

Test yourself 37.6

1. She is packing her bags. present progressive
2. Tom will be thinking about it all day. future progressive
3. The computer was working on it. past progressive
4. It will be snowing tomorrow. future progressive
5. I am getting tired. present progressive

Test yourself 37.7

1. will consider   <u>future</u>
2. experienced   <u>past</u>
3. will have wanted   <u>future perfect</u>
4. had been watching   <u>past perfect progressive</u>
5. will be reading   <u>future progressive</u>

Test yourself 37.8

1. She was making some progress.   <u>past progressive</u>
2. Marie shrugged her shoulders.   <u>past</u>
3. She will be taking a long walk.   <u>future progressive</u>
4. He has had two serious operations.   <u>present perfect</u>
5. They had been getting numerous phone calls.   <u>past perfect progressive</u>

☞ **FOR A REVIEW EXERCISE OF THIS UNIT, SEE THE WEBSITE.**

UNIT 13: SUBJECTS AND OBJECTS

Sentences may contain several noun phrases. These noun phrases can have different jobs, or functions, within the sentence. Take a look at the following sentence:

On Valentine's Day, <u>my brother</u> bought <u>a bouquet of flowers</u> for <u>his wife</u>.

The underlined noun phrases are doing different things: *my brother* is doing the action, *a bouquet of flowers* is receiving the action, and *his wife* is receiving the flowers. In the lessons of this unit, we discuss in detail these **grammatical functions** (or **grammatical relations**).

Lesson 38: Subjects

We can identify the **subject** of a sentence with an action verb (see Lesson 9) by answering the question: "Who is doing the action?" For example, in the sentence *Confucius spoke many words of wisdom*, the action is *speaking*. Who is, or was, doing the speaking? *Confucius. Confucius* is therefore the subject of the sentence. The subjects are underlined in the following examples:

1. <u>John</u> baked a cake.
2. <u>You</u> are going to grin and bear it.
3. Just then, <u>the children</u> walked in.
4. <u>He</u> delivered a small package.
5. <u>Mr. Bucknose</u>, the carpenter, sleeps in the spare room.
6. Wearily, <u>the group</u> trudged onward.
7. <u>I</u> usually take a nap in the afternoon.

Generally, the subject is at or near the beginning of the sentence. More specifically, the subject is the first noun phrase (see Lesson 28) in the sentence.

> **Quick tip 38.1**
>
> If the main verb of the sentence is an action verb, the subject of the sentence is the doer of the action and generally comes before the verb. It can be found by answering the question: "Who or what is doing the action?"

Test yourself 38.1

Underline the subject in each of the sentences below. In these sentences, it will always be the doer of the action and will be the first noun phrase in the sentence.

Sample: <u>Jeanette</u> demanded an answer to her question.

Getting started (answers on p. 189)

1. The servant accompanied His Lordship.
2. Jean participated in the Tour de France.
3. Such families have often preferred to travel in style.
4. They could do nothing except run.
5. Mr. Tower quietly explained all this to his son.

More practice (answers on the website)

6. The diners are arguing loudly.
7. Your uncle invited me to accompany him on his business trip.
8. The Yankees won the World Series many times.
9. Macy's is holding a huge sale next Sunday.
10. The TV repairman has just arrived.

The subject is underlined in the following sentences:

8. <u>John</u> is tall.
9. <u>That church</u> is impressive.

10. Both brothers became architects.
11. Earlier, she had felt dizzy.

In these sentences, the subject is not performing an action – the verb is not an action verb. Rather, the verb is a linking verb (see Lesson 9). When the verb in the sentence is a linking verb, the subject can be found by asking the question: "Who or what is this sentence about?" In these cases, the subject is found at or near the beginning of the sentence, before the verb.

> **Quick tip 38.2**
>
> If the main verb of the sentence is a linking verb, the subject is who or what the sentence is about; the subject is found before the verb.

Test yourself 38.2

Underline the subject in each of the sentences below. In these sentences, it will always be who or what the sentence is about and will be the first noun phrase in the sentence.
Sample: The professor was imprisoned for his beliefs.

Getting started (answers on p. 189)

1. The Hotel Regina is an attractive place.

2. It became the best-known symbol of Paris.

3. The local merchants were on his side.

4. Charles looked thoughtful.

5. Christine seemed insecure.

More practice (answers on the website)

6. She was determined to meet Dr. Richards again.

7. His older sister resembled her father, unfortunately.

8. Her folks are good people.

9. My son is destined for success as an attorney.

10. Their apology seems genuine.

Test yourself 38.3

Underline the subject in each of the sentences below. In these sentences, it will either be the doer of the action or who or what the sentence is about. The subject will be the first noun phrase in the sentence.
Sample: These proportions are inaccurate.

Getting started (answers on p. 189)

1. The editor looked for new ideas for the magazine.

2. You can rely on the experts at that company.

3. Maggie usually goes berry picking in the summer.

4. Roger is happy with his new computer.

5. The workers went on strike for a couple of weeks.

More practice (answers on the website)

6. Alana's hair smells fresh.

7. I got there on time.

8. They postponed the ball game on account of bad weather.

9. Bowling is a favorite pastime of mine.

10. Some students missed the final exam.

The subject is not always right at the beginning of the sentence:

12. In the afternoon, I usually take a nap.
13. In truth, Don Diego had never really had a career

14. That day, <u>his timing</u> was perfect.

15. When in the country, <u>Jack</u> was up before dawn.

In each of these sentences, the subject is preceded by an adverb (see Lesson 27) or **adverbial clause**, a group of words typically giving information about time, place, or manner.

Test yourself 38.4

Underline the subject in each of the sentences below. The subject will not necessarily be the first noun phrase in the sentence.

Sample: By late afternoon, <u>he</u> is usually exhausted.

Getting started (answers on p. 189)

1. After that, their neighbor came more often to help them.

2. Fortunately, that university program is accredited.

3. In the morning, I'm planting those flowers.

4. Eventually, Mr. Mulligan broke the silence.

5. While running for office, the candidate campaigned vigorously.

More practice (answers on the website)

6. Generally speaking, they don't know many foreign languages.

7. Dr. Wright's chauffeur drove him to the clinic.

8. For many reasons, Michael prefers to live in the suburbs.

9. This movie lasted a long time.

10. Exciting times are much more memorable than boring ones.

Lesson 39: Direct objects

As we saw in Lesson 38, a noun phrase can function as the subject of a sentence. A noun phrase can also have other functions. For example, a noun phrase may be <u>acted upon</u> by the subject and follow the verb. These noun phrases are called **direct objects**. The direct objects in the sentences below are underlined:

1. John baked <u>a cake</u>.
2. Leah had visualized <u>a simple room</u>.
3. She is buying <u>a small studio apartment</u>.
4. My niece rented <u>a movie</u> last night.

How can you tell which noun phrase in a sentence functions as the direct object? In general, the direct object is the answer to the questions: "Who or what is being acted upon? Who or what is receiving the action?" Thus, for example, in the sentence *My niece rented a movie last night*, the direct object is *a movie*, since *a movie* is what is being acted upon (being rented). Typically, direct objects occur immediately after the verb. (We discuss a different pattern in Lesson 40.)

Quick tip 39.1

The direct object of a sentence is receiving the action. It can usually be found by answering the question: "Who or what is being acted upon or receiving the action?" The direct object typically occurs immediately after the verb.

Test yourself 39.1

Underline the direct object in each of the sentences below. Be sure to ask yourself who or what is being acted upon or receiving the action.
Sample: I saw <u>a statue</u> in the museum.

Getting started (answers on p. 189)

1. You must include all relevant facts.
2. Bridget is asking numerous questions.
3. The Spanish ships needed fresh supplies.
4. She will watch the baby.
5. The townspeople have wanted tax relief for years.

More practice (answers on the website)

6. Most people greeted us warmly at the reception.
7. I bought two bottles of Pepsi.
8. Actors must memorize their lines.
9. Last week, Jack renewed his passport.
10. Where did you get that sweater?

Not all sentences have direct objects. Here are examples of sentences with action verbs that do <u>not</u> have direct objects.

5. My friend laughed loudly.

6. Mr. Thomas slept well.

7. You're always worrying.

You may remember, from Lesson 10, that there are transitive and intransitive verbs. Transitive verbs, like *bake* or *rent*, act on something or someone and so they have direct objects. Intransitive verbs, like *laugh*, *sleep*, and *worry*, aren't acting upon something or someone and so don't have direct objects.

What about these next sentences?

8. My friend stopped <u>at the grocery store</u>.

9. Mr. Thomas slept well <u>during the night</u>.

10. You're always worrying <u>about something</u>.

As you can see, these sentences have prepositional phrases, which are underlined (Lesson 29). A prepositional phrase is <u>not</u> a direct object. For example, *at the grocery store* in sentence 8 and *during the night* in sentence 9 are not being acted upon.

To sum up, only transitive action verbs have direct objects, and prepositional phrases are not direct objects.

Test yourself 39.2

Decide whether or not each sentence below has a direct object.

	Direct object?	*Yes*	*No*
Sample: Her best friend entered the room first.		✗	

Getting started (answers on p. 190)

1. We'll discuss each argument.		....	....
2. Carter worked for a lumber company.		....	....
3. Those gamblers are losing their money.		....	....
4. At 7 P.M. we left for the theater.		....	....
5. The children are enjoying Disneyland.		....	....

More practice (answers on the website)

6. I slept well last night.		....	....
7. They watch football on Sunday nights.		....	....
8. Jill and Sam have left with a friend.		....	....
9. Can you pass the butter, please?		....	....
10. She wants a big scoop of chocolate ice cream.		....	....

What about this next sentence?

11. She is a doctor.

Is *a doctor* receiving the action of *is*? Kind of a strange question, isn't it? That's because *is* is not an action verb; it's a linking verb (see Lesson 9). Sentences with linking verbs don't have direct objects, since there is no action happening in the sentence. In each sentence below, the linking verb is italicized. The underlined portion of each sentence is not a direct object, since it's not being acted upon. Instead, it's called the **verb complement**.

12. My teacher *resembles* Tom Cruise.
13. That dinner *was* delicious.
14. Her husband *became* a lawyer.

Test yourself 39.3

Decide if the underlined phrase in each sentence below is a direct object or a verb complement. To make this decision, you can: (1) ask yourself if something or someone is being acted upon, and/or (2) decide if the verb is an action or linking verb.

Sample: Bill became a member of the President's cabinet.   verb complement

Getting started (answers on p. 190)

1. Gerald has taken that course.   ....

2. Rob used this technique in his restaurant.   ....

3. Adam might withdraw his resignation.   ....

4. The mayor is sounding confident.   ....

5. We quickly got ready.   ....

More practice (answers on the website)

6. He was getting a pastrami sandwich in the deli.   ....

7. She loves her new car   ....

8. We were best friends in high school.   ....

9. I'll take you to the movies.   ....

10. He feels foolish.   ....

Test yourself 39.4

Underline the direct objects in the sentences below. Not all sentences will have a direct object.
Sample: I put the letter in his mailbox.

Getting started (answers on p. 190)

1. Our discussion was highly entertaining.

2. He had a growing family.

3. She quickly got indignant.

4. You must be the new baby sitter.

5. The sheriff arrested a suspect in the fraud investigation.

More practice (answers on the website)

6. The coach of the University of Texas football team is replacing his quarterback.

7. They walked in the woods till sunset.

8. I proposed some tentative solutions.

9. He confessed on the second day of the trial.

10. Our plane had left on time.

Test yourself 39.5

Underline the subjects and put a squiggly line under the direct objects in the sentences below.
Sample: His company was losing millions.

Getting started (answers on p. 190)

1. The soldiers fired their weapons.

2. A talented designer made that hat.

3. She had married her next-door neighbor.

4. Maria was watching her favorite soap opera.

5. These people really irritate me.

More practice (answers on the website)

6. Sonya has found the directions to the party.

7. He added salt to his soup.

8. The contestant had to make a difficult decision.

9. Rhonda is expecting her third child.

10. Last week, Martin's friends bought a present for his birthday.

Lesson 40: Indirect objects

Sometimes a noun phrase is the answer to the question: "Who or what is receiving the direct object?" This noun phrase is called the **indirect object**. The indirect objects are underlined in the sentences below.

1. Mary gave the information to Robert.
2. She told the truth to her granddaughter.
3. They bought a car for their teenage daughter.
4. The accountant is giving a present to her husband.

So in sentence 4, for instance, the noun phrase *a present* is the direct object and the noun phrase *her husband* is the indirect object, since *her husband* is receiving *the present*, the direct object.

> **Quick tip 40.1**
>
> The indirect object of a sentence can be found by answering the question: "Who or what is receiving the direct object?"

You can see that sentences that have indirect objects must also have direct objects, since indirect objects receive direct objects. The opposite is not true: sentences with direct objects don't necessarily have indirect objects.

A direct object and an indirect object each follows the verb and is referred to by the term **object**. The term object can also refer to objects of a preposition, that is, noun phrases that follow prepositions. (See Lesson 29.)

Test yourself 40.1

Underline the indirect object in each of the sentences below.
Sample: Jane baked the cake for Grant.

Getting started (answers on p. 190)

1. Holly left the plate for Luke.
2. She taught the principles to the class.
3. Big Bird is telling the story to all the children.
4. His father had bought the boat for Jonathan.
5. You will show the money to me.

More practice (answers on the website)

6. Jamie's friend sent a text message to her.
7. They bid farewell to their house guests.
8. The teenage idol is throwing a party for his fans.
9. I want to wish good luck to you.
10. My dad baked a pie for us.

Indirect objects are introduced by the preposition *to* or *for*. Some verbs, such as *tell* and *show*, use *to* to introduce an indirect object, while some verbs, such as *buy* and *leave*, use *for*.

To and *for* do not function only to introduce indirect objects; often, *to* and *for* have other functions. Take a look at these next sentences and notice the differences between them:

5. Mary gave the baby to Robert.
6. Mary carried the baby to the corner.

In both sentences, *Mary* is the subject, the doer of the action, and *the baby* is the direct object, the receiver of the action. In sentence 5, *Robert* is receiving *the baby*, the direct object, so *Robert* is the indirect object. However, in sentence 6 *the corner* is not receiving *the baby* and so it's not the indirect object. (It's the object of the preposition *to*; see Lesson 29.)

Here's a similar pair of sentences:

7. He got a gift for his wife.
8. He got a gift for his birthday.

In both sentences, *He* is the subject, the doer of the action, and *a gift* is the direct object, the receiver of the action. In sentence 7, *his wife* is receiving *a gift*, the direct object, so *his wife* is the indirect object. However, in sentence 8 *his birthday* is not receiving *a gift*, so it's not the indirect object. (It's the object of the preposition *for*.)

Test yourself 40.2

For each of the sentences below, indicate whether or not *to* and *for* are being used to introduce an indirect object. Ask yourself if the noun phrase following *to* or *for* is receiving the direct object.

	Introducing an indirect object?	
	Yes	No
Sample: I inspected the car for dents.		✗

Getting started (answers on p. 190)

1. John worked that job for fifty years.	....	....
2. The professor is showing the problem to the student.	....	....
3. His wife and child brought fruit to him at the hospital.	....	....
4. Tom has left the company for another job.	....	....
5. The visiting king thanked the president for his hospitality.	....	....

More practice (answers on the website)

6. She sent the e-mail to her sister.	....	....
7. We will remember this general for his heroism.	....	....
8. I have forwarded your message to your mother.	....	....
9. He took his friend to the theater.	....	....
10. The Black family took a ride to the countryside.	....	....

Here are sentences 1–4 again, but this time with a "partner" sentence:

9a. Mary gave the information to Robert.
9b. Mary gave Robert the information.

> 10a. She told the truth to <u>her granddaughter</u>.
> 10b. She told <u>her granddaughter</u> the truth.
> 11a. They bought a car for <u>their teenage daughter</u>.
> 11b. They bought <u>their teenage daughter</u> a car.
> 12a. The accountant is giving a present to <u>him</u>.
> 12b. The accountant is giving <u>him</u> a present.

You can see that in the second sentence of each pair, the indirect object has moved so that it comes <u>before</u> the direct object, rather than <u>after</u> it. English gives us two choices for the position of indirect objects: (a) the indirect object can occur after the direct object (which follows the verb), with *to* or *for* introducing it, or (b) the indirect object can occur before the direct object (and after the verb), without *to* or *for*.

Quick tip 40.2

An indirect object can occur: (a) after the direct object (which follows the verb), with *to* or *for* introducing it, or (b) before the direct object (and after the verb), without *to* or *for*. For example: *Joan gave a present to Bill* or *Joan gave Bill a present*. (*Bill* is the indirect object in both sentences.)

Quick tip 40.3

To help you decide if a sentence has an indirect object, see if the sentence can be changed from a pattern like *The boys left a note for their teacher* to a sentence with a pattern like *The boys left their teacher a note*, or vice versa.

Note that when the direct object is a pronoun, the two patterns are not both possible, as you can see in these next sentence pairs:

> 13a. Her best friend bought <u>it</u> for her family.
> 13b. *Her best friend bought her family <u>it</u>.
> 14a. Lucy sold <u>them</u> to her neighbor.
> 14b. *Lucy sold her neighbor <u>them</u>.

That is, when the direct object is a pronoun, it must come before the indirect object.

Quick tip 40.4

If the direct object is a pronoun, it must come before the indirect object. Example: *My sister sent it to her friend, *My sister sent her friend it.*

Test yourself 40.3

Each sentence below contains an indirect object, which is underlined. Change each sentence to the other pattern, by moving the indirect object and either deleting or adding *to* or *for*.

Sample: Sally made <u>us</u> breakfast.   Sally made breakfast for us.

Getting started (answers on p. 191)

1. The principal might show the film to <u>her students</u>.

2. Mrs. Hausen sent <u>the company</u> her check.

3. We bought the house for <u>our parents</u>.

4. The referee threw <u>me</u> the ball.

5. The artist is drawing a sketch for <u>her patron</u>.

More practice (answers on the website)

6. I am saving this seat for <u>my father</u>.

7. My colleague did <u>me</u> a favor.

8. Albert passed <u>his friend</u> a note.

9. She will read <u>her children</u> a poem.

10. The boss wished much success to <u>his new employee</u>.

Test yourself 40.4

Each sentence below contains an indirect object (not underlined). Change each sentence to the other pattern, by moving the indirect object and either deleting or adding *to* or *for*.
Sample: Steve gave Mary a package.   Steve gave a package to Mary.

Getting started (answers on p. 191)

1. He will send the poem to his fiancée.

2. The professor is e-mailing the students his comments.

....

3. That company built a ship for the navy.

....

4. She drew a picture for her son.

....

5. Amanda's friend was throwing a party for her.

....

More practice (answers on the website)

6. I sang a lullaby to you.

....

7. The company's president had shipped the order to them.

....

8. The librarian found George a good book.

....

9. The arresting officer must read his rights to him.

....

10. My aunt baked me my favorite dessert.

....

Test yourself 40.5

Underline the indirect object in each sentence below. It can occur either before or after the direct object.
Sample: Jerry made <u>me</u> that bench.

Getting started (answers on p. 191)

1. We found a dress for her.
2. Mr. Duquesne has brought him the plans.
3. The old hunter told us the story.
4. The instructor is ordering this book for the students in his class.
5. I never promised you a rose garden.

More practice (answers on the website)

6. The contractor will build a brand new deck for me.
7. Can't she give him a straight answer?
8. The realtor showed them a lovely house.
9. The economist had painted a rosy picture for his audience.
10. I got you a small present.

Test yourself 40.6

For each sentence below, underline the direct object and put a squiggly line under the indirect object, if there is one. Remember, the indirect object can occur either before or after the direct object.

Sample: That man got his friend a computer.

Getting started (answers on p. 191)

1. The children gave the teacher an apple.

2. I brought this for you.

3. The two men clasped hands.

4. This treaty will benefit all mankind.

5. She is telling the reporter the truth.

More practice (answers on the website)

6. Don't give me that!

7. We have to return this to the store.

8. At the meeting, he showed us his true colors.

9. People have been telling this story for ages.

10. I bid all of you good night.

Lesson 41: The functions of pronouns

Now that we've talked about subjects and objects in some detail, it's a good idea for us to reexamine subject and object pronouns, which we first discussed in Lesson 21.

Take a look at the noun phrase *the teacher* in each of the sentences below.

    1. The teacher went home early today.
       (*The teacher* is the subject.)
    2. The students liked the teacher very much.
       (*The teacher* is the direct object.)
    3. The parents gave the questionnaire to the teacher.
       (*The teacher* is the indirect object.)

Notice that *the teacher* has the same form whether it's functioning as the subject, the direct object, or the indirect object in a sentence. This is true for all nouns in English: they don't change form when they change function.

In contrast, there are subject pronouns and object pronouns (see Lesson 21). Subject pronouns are used when a pronoun is functioning as the subject of a sentence (see Lesson 38). The subject pronoun is underlined in the following sentences:

    4. I read the newspaper every day.
    5. She is happy.
    6. We love potato chips.

Object pronouns are used in all other contexts. The three major uses for object pronouns are: direct object (Lesson 39), indirect object (Lesson 40), and object of a preposition (Lesson 29). The object pronouns are underlined in the following sentences:

    7. My sister congratulated me on my birthday.   (direct object)
    8. The director sent her a message.   (indirect object)
    9. Mrs. Raffsky spoke to us on the phone.   (object of a preposition)

> **Quick tip 41.1**
>
> A subject pronoun is used when it is functioning as the subject of the sentence. An object pronoun is used when it is functioning as: (a) the direct object of the sentence; (b) the indirect object of the sentence; (c) the object of a preposition.

Test yourself 41.1

For each underlined pronoun below, indicate whether it is a subject or object pronoun. For *you* and *it*, you will need to look at how the pronoun is being used in the sentence.

	Subject pronoun	*Object pronoun*
Sample: I feel great.	**x**	

Getting started (answers on p. 191)

1. She laughed at the movie.	....	....
2. Don't bother me now.	....	....

3. I don't feel guilty.   ....

4. He has asked her to dance.   ....

5. Chris had been living near you.   ....

More practice (answers on the website)

6. It is not a very interesting movie.   ....

7. This does not concern us.   ....

8. He disappointed his friends.   ....

9. The critics were raving about it.   ....

10. It doesn't matter to them at all.   ....

Test yourself 41.2

Each of the sentences below contains an object pronoun, which is underlined. Indicate whether it's being used as a direct object, an indirect object, or the object of a preposition.
Sample: Audra lives very far from him.   object of a preposition

Getting started (answers on p. 192)

1. My dear friend sent me a postcard from Italy.   ....

2. A teenager sat next to me in the theater.   ....

3. Irma has bought you the cookware.   ....

4. The dog approached them.   ....

5. That family is always blaming us for their problems. ....

More practice (answers on the website)

6. They gave us their promise.   ....

7. He is renting an apartment close to me.   ....

8. I never saw it.   ....

9. He gave her an ultimatum.   ....

10. Brandon will even buy it from you.   ....

To enhance your understanding
In the past, *who* and *whom* worked the same way as subject and object pronouns. In particular, *who* was used when functioning as a subject and *whom* was used when functioning as an object:

     10. Who is running away? (subject: *Who* is doing the action.)

     11. Whom does Katie like? (direct object: *Whom* is receiving the action.)

   However, like all languages, English changes over time, and today, for all but the strictest traditional grammarians, *who* is used in all contexts, except when it directly follows a preposition (see below). So today a sentence like the following is perfectly grammatical:

     12. Who does Katie like? (direct object)

While most of us prefer to use *who* in sentence 12, it's still okay to use *whom* in these contexts. It's just not necessary to do so, and it tends to sound very formal.

Note that *whom* must be used when it follows a preposition. In the following examples, *whom* and the preposition before it are underlined.

13. <u>With whom</u> would you like to speak?
14. <u>To whom</u> may I direct your question?

Lesson 42: Implied subjects: commands

1. Open that book right now!
2. Don't even think about crossing the street here!
3. Please be careful.

We all recognize a command when we hear one. We have seen that all sentences have a subject, but where is the subject of these commands? Speakers of English readily agree that these sentences do, in fact, have a subject. The subject, though not stated, is understood or implied to be *you*. Thus, when someone says "Wash the dishes!" you know they're talking to you. Commands are also called **imperative sentences**. In writing, command sentences often end with an exclamation point (!).

> **Quick tip 42.1**
>
> The subject of commands is an understood or implied *you*.

Test yourself 42.1

Indicate the subject of each sentence below. If it's a command, specify *you* as the subject. (We won't be using exclamation points in this exercise.)

	Subject
Sample: Eat a well-balanced diet.	you

Getting started (answers on p. 192)

1. These illnesses are treatable. ....
2. The judge had made a terrible mistake. ....
3. Be supportive. ....
4. Joan's father is an architect. ....
5. Stand up for your rights. ....

More practice (answers on the website)

6. Give me a break. ....
7. I can't give it to you. ....
8. Don't raise your voice to me. ....
9. Help me out with this. ....
10. She will be planting roses in that garden. ....

186

To enhance your understanding

There are a number of ways to prove what you, as a speaker of English, intuitively know: that *you* is the implicit subject of command sentences. We present one of these arguments here.

Take a look at the following sentences:

4. I held my breath.
5. You held your breath.
6. He held his breath.
7. She held her breath.

While these sentences are grammatical, the following sentences are not:

8a. *I held your breath.
8b. *I held his breath.
8c. *I held their breath.
9a. *You held my breath.
9b. *You held his breath.
9c. *You held their breath.

Can you explain why these sentences are ungrammatical? Clearly, a person cannot hold someone else's breath. Thus the two underlined pronouns must refer to the same person. If they don't, the sentence is not grammatical, as in 8 and 9 above.

Now what about commands which contain this same expression? Look at the following grammatical and ungrammatical commands:

10. Hold your breath!
11. *Hold my breath!
12. *Hold his breath!
13. *Hold their breath!

In fact, the only pronoun allowed in the command context *Hold* _____ *breath!* is *your*. Since we know that *your* must refer to the same person as the subject, it follows that the subject in the command must be *you*. That is, even though the *you* is not actually stated, we treat a command as though the subject were *you*.

Test yourself 42.2

For each sentence below, indicate its subject (stated or understood), direct object, if there is one, and indirect object, if there is one.

	Subject	Direct Object	Indirect Object
Sample: Give the money to Harry.	you	the money	Harry

Getting started (answers on p. 192)

	Subject	Direct Object	Indirect Object
1. You can see marks in the dirt.			
2. That film sounds interesting.			
3. The congregants built the temple.			
4. Give it to me!			
5. We need this computer.			

More practice (answers on the website)

6. Don't worry about it!

7. They have been rearranging the display.

8. They sent Bill the bill.

9. Watch me!

10. Mary fell to the floor.

Answer keys: *Test yourself, Getting started* questions – Unit 13

Test yourself 38.1

1. The <u>servant</u> accompanied His Lordship.
2. <u>Jean</u> participated in the Tour de France.
3. <u>Such families</u> have often preferred to travel in style.
4. <u>They</u> could do nothing except run.
5. <u>Mr. Tower</u> quietly explained all this to his son.

Test yourself 38.2

1. <u>The Hotel Regina</u> is an attractive place.
2. <u>It</u> became the best-known symbol of Paris.
3. <u>The local merchants</u> were on his side.
4. <u>Charles</u> looked thoughtful.
5. <u>Christine</u> seemed insecure.

Test yourself 38.3

1. <u>The editor</u> looked for new ideas for the magazine.
2. <u>You</u> can rely on the experts at that company.
3. <u>Maggie</u> usually goes berry picking in the summer.
4. <u>Roger</u> is happy with his new computer.
5. <u>The workers</u> went on strike for a couple of weeks.

Test yourself 38.4

1. After that, <u>their neighbor</u> came more often to help them.
2. Fortunately, <u>that university program</u> is accredited.
3. In the morning, <u>I'm</u> planting those flowers.
4. Eventually, <u>Mr. Mulligan</u> broke the silence.
5. While running for office, <u>the candidate</u> campaigned vigorously.

Test yourself 39.1

1. You must include <u>all relevant facts</u>.
2. Bridget is asking <u>numerous questions</u>.
3. The Spanish ships needed <u>fresh supplies</u>.
4. She will watch <u>the baby</u>.
5. The townspeople have wanted <u>tax relief</u> for years.

Test yourself 39.2

	Direct object?	Yes	No
1. We'll discuss each argument.		✗	
2. Carter worked for a lumber company.			✗
3. Those gamblers are losing their money.		✗	
4. At 7 P.M. we left for the theater.			✗
5. The children are enjoying Disneyland.		✗	

Test yourself 39.3

1. Gerald has taken <u>that course</u>.   direct object
2. Rob used <u>this technique</u> in his restaurant.   direct object
3. Adam might withdraw <u>his resignation</u>.   direct object
4. The mayor is sounding <u>confident</u>.   verb complement
5. We quickly got <u>ready</u>.   verb complement

Test yourself 39.4

1. Our discussion was highly entertaining.
2. He had <u>a growing family</u>.
3. She quickly got indignant.
4. You must be the new baby sitter.
5. The sheriff arrested <u>a suspect</u> in the fraud investigation.

Test yourself 39.5

1. The soldiers fired <u>their weapons</u>.
2. A talented designer made <u>that hat</u>.
3. She had married <u>her next-door neighbor</u>.
4. Maria was watching <u>her favorite soap opera</u>.
5. These people really irritate <u>me</u>.

Test yourself 40.1

1. Holly left the plate for <u>Luke</u>.
2. She taught the principles to <u>the class</u>.
3. Big Bird is telling the story to <u>all the children</u>.
4. His father had bought the boat for <u>Jonathan</u>.
5. You will show the money to <u>me</u>.

Test yourself 40.2

	Introducing an indirect object?	Yes	No
1. John worked that job <u>for</u> fifty years.			✗
2. The professor is showing the problem <u>to</u> the student.		✗	
3. His wife and child brought fruit <u>to</u> him at the hospital.		✗	
4. Tom's has left the company <u>for</u> another job.			✗
5. The visiting king thanked the president <u>for</u> his hospitality.			✗

Test yourself 40.3

1. The principal might show the film to <u>her students</u>.
   <u>The principal might show her students the film</u>.
2. Mrs. Hausen sent <u>the company</u> her check.
   <u>Mrs. Hausen sent her check to the company</u>.
3. We bought the house for <u>our parents</u>.
   <u>We bought our parents the house</u>.
4. The referee threw <u>me</u> the ball.
   <u>The referee threw the ball to me</u>.
5. The artist is drawing a sketch for <u>her patron</u>.
   <u>The artist is drawing her patron a sketch</u>.

Test yourself 40.4

1. He will send the poem to his fiancée.
   <u>He will send his fiancée the poem</u>.
2. The professor is e-mailing the students his comments.
   <u>The professor is e-mailing his comments to the students</u>.
3. That company built a ship for the navy.
   <u>The company built the navy a ship</u>.
4. She drew a picture for her son.
   <u>She drew her son a picture</u>.
5. Amanda's friend was throwing a party for her.
   <u>Amanda's friend was throwing her a party</u>.

Test yourself 40.5

1. We found a dress for <u>her</u>.
2. Mr. Duquesne has brought <u>him</u> the plans.
3. The old hunter told <u>us</u> the story.
4. The instructor is ordering this book for <u>the students in his</u> class.
5. I never promised <u>you</u> a rose garden.

Test yourself 40.6

1. The children gave <u>the teacher</u> an apple.
2. I brought <u>this</u> for <u>you</u>.
3. The two men clasped <u>hands</u>.
4. This treaty will benefit <u>all mankind</u>.
5. She is telling <u>the reporter</u> the truth.

Test yourself 41.1

	Subject pronoun	Object pronoun
1. <u>She</u> laughed at the movie.	✗	
2. Don't bother <u>me</u> now.		✗
3. <u>I</u> don't feel guilty.	✗	
4. He has asked <u>her</u> to dance.		✗
5. Chris had been living near <u>you</u>.		✗

Test yourself 41.2

1. My dear friend sent <u>me</u> a postcard from Italy.	indirect object
2. A teenager sat next to <u>me</u> in the theater.	object of a preposition
3. Irma has bought <u>you</u> the cookware.	indirect object
4. The dog approached <u>them</u>.	direct object
5. That family is always blaming <u>us</u> for their problems.	direct object

Test yourself 42.1

	Subject
1. These illnesses are treatable.	<u>these illnesses</u>
2. The judge had made a terrible mistake.	<u>the judge</u>
3. Be supportive.	<u>you</u>
4. Joan's father is an architect	<u>Joan's father</u>
5. Stand up for your rights.	<u>you</u>

Test yourself 42.2

	Subject	*Direct object*	*Indirect object*
1. You can see marks in the dirt.	<u>you</u>	<u>marks</u>	
2. That film sounds interesting.	<u>that film</u>		
3. The congregants built the temple.	<u>the congregants</u>	the temple	
4. Give it to me!	<u>you</u>	<u>it</u>	<u>me</u>
5. We need this computer.	<u>we</u>	this computer	

☞ **FOR A REVIEW EXERCISE OF THIS UNIT, SEE THE WEBSITE**.

Coordinating conjunctions, such as *and*, *or*, and *but*, are very powerful. As we discussed in Lesson 18, they can join any two units of the same type. Here are some examples with *and*, the most common coordinating conjunction:

1. He gave tennis lessons to <u>the girl</u> **and** <u>her brother</u>.   (two noun phrases joined)
2. I <u>cooked dinner</u> **and** <u>washed the laundry</u>.   (two verb phrases joined)
3. Their <u>beautiful</u> **and** <u>charming</u> hostess soon put them at ease.   (two adjectives joined)
4. My mother listened to me <u>seriously</u> **and** <u>patiently</u>.   (two adverbs joined)
5. The monkey ran <u>up the tree</u> **and** <u>around its trunk</u>.   (two prepositional phrases joined)
6. <u>I rode my bike</u> **and** <u>Teresa walked</u>.   (two sentences joined)

In this unit, we'll take a closer look at joined noun phrases and joined verb phrases.

Lesson 43: Compound noun phrases

What do you notice about this next sentence?

1. My friend worked at the diner and his cousin worked at the diner.

While it's a perfectly grammatical sentence, we often choose to make it less repetitious and say instead:

2. My friend and his cousin worked at the diner.

Since *and*, a coordinating conjunction, is joining two noun phrases here, *my friend and his cousin* is called a **compound noun phrase**.

> **Quick tip 43.1**
>
> Two noun phrases joined by a coordinating conjunction is called a compound noun phrase.

Here are some more examples, with the compound noun phrases underlined.

3. She slipped the photograph and both letters into her pocket.
4. The senator or his assistant will attend the event.
5. I'll be traveling to Kansas and Missouri next week on business.

Test yourself 43.1

Underline the compound noun phrases in each of the sentences below.

Sample: The public discovered that the company and its subsidiaries were cheating customers.

Getting started (answers on p. 197)

1. They had walked for miles and miles.

2. Henry felt guilt and shame for what he had done.

3. Vermont has lots of old houses and rustic barns.

4. The young bride is going shopping with her mother or mother-in-law.

5. Paying for gas and electricity costs a lot more this year than last.

More practice (answers on the website)

6. Michael and I have been best friends for years.

7. Delta Airlines and Air France have flights to Paris from the U.S.

8. The lead actress or director will likely win Oscars.

9. Audi and BMW are owned by German companies.

10. The president and his foreign visitor held a joint press conference.

Lesson 44: Compound verb phrases

What do you notice about this next sentence?

1. Frank ran to the store and Frank purchased a few items.

While it's a perfectly grammatical sentence, we often choose to make it less repetitious and say instead:

2. Frank ran to the store and purchased a few items.

Since *and*, a coordinating conjunction, is joining two verb phrases here, *ran to the store and purchased a few items* is called a **compound verb phrase**.

> **Quick tip 44.1**
>
> Two verb phrases joined by a coordinating conjunction is called a compound verb phrase.

Here are some more examples, with the compound verb phrases underlined.

3. The general <u>ran forward and led the troops</u>.
4. She <u>remained calm and followed her instincts</u>.
5. His advisor <u>presents him with good ideas but rarely helps him carry them out</u>.

Test yourself 44.1

Underline the compound verb phrases in each of the sentences below.
Sample: I'll <u>phone them and listen to their ideas</u>.

Getting started (answers on p. 197)

1. They often call each other and talk all afternoon.

2. Adam wrote letters to the company and spoke to their representatives.

3. He invented the product but lost money in the process.

4. Stephen flew to Europe and visited his childhood friend.

5. I received your message yesterday but couldn't respond to it immediately.

More practice (answers on the website)

6. On Saturday nights Samantha dresses up and meets with her friends.

7. Once a month or so we stay home and order dinner in.

8. Politicians do not always walk the walk and talk the talk.

9. On hot summer days, the O'Briens drive to the beach and enjoy the sun.

10. This couple fights but always makes up.

Test yourself 44.2

Underline the compound noun phrases and verb phrases in the sentences below. A sentence may contain more than one compound phrase.
Sample: <u>He and she</u> will probably <u>leave on Friday and return on Sunday</u>.

Getting started (answers on p. 197)

1. The horse stepped back and rolled its eyes.

2. Amanda is wearing long sleeves but carrying a parasol.

3. When Kathy and her daughter travel to Boston, they always visit Harvard and MIT.

4. On Sundays Mr. Adams and his neighbor play golf and have lunch in the clubhouse.

5. He loves to cook and entertain.

More practice (answers on the website)

6. His youngest son is afraid of thunder and lightning.

7. Your husband should work hard at his job or find another one.

8. Harry and his friend often travel to Washington and visit the Smithsonian.

9. It is common knowledge that the Yankees and the Red Sox are bitter rivals.

10. That would ruin her reputation and end her career.

Answer keys: *Test yourself, Getting started* questions – Unit 14

Test yourself 43.1

1. They had walked for <u>miles and miles</u>.
2. Henry felt <u>guilt and shame</u> for what he had done.
3. Vermont has lots of <u>old houses and rustic barns</u>.
4. The young bride is going shopping with <u>her mother or mother-in-law</u>.
5. Paying for <u>gas and electricity</u> costs a lot more this year than last.

Test yourself 44.1

1. They often <u>call each other and talk all afternoon</u>.
2. Adam <u>wrote letters to the company and spoke to their representatives</u>.
3. He <u>invented the product but lost money in the process</u>.
4. Stephen <u>flew to Europe and visited his childhood friend</u>.
5. I <u>received your message yesterday but couldn't respond to it immediately</u>.

Test yourself 44.2

1. The horse <u>stepped back and rolled its eyes</u>.
2. Amanda is <u>wearing long sleeves but carrying a parasol</u>.
3. When <u>Kathy and her daughter</u> travel to Boston, they always visit <u>Harvard and MIT</u>.
4. On Sundays <u>Mr. Adams and his neighbor</u> <u>play golf and have lunch in the clubhouse</u>.
5. He loves to <u>cook and entertain</u>.

☞ **FOR A REVIEW EXERCISE OF THIS UNIT, SEE THE WEBSITE.**

Review matching exercise and answer key – Part II

Review matching exercise

Match the underlined word or words in each sentence to the appropriate term in each set.
Use each term only once.
Sample: Warren <u>gave himself an extra serving</u>.   verb phrase

Set A

compound noun phrase	object pronoun	prepositional phrase
indirect object	perfect tense	future tense
modal	predicate adjective	

1. He <u>has written</u> to you every day.

2. Mrs. McLean is sending the recipe to <u>her sister-in-law</u>.

3. He understands <u>me</u> better than anyone.

4. His companions <u>will take</u> their canoe across the river.

5. Richard was working when <u>Miguel and Sam</u> came by.

6. The building is <u>near the stream</u>.

7. It <u>might</u> be the largest museum in the world.

8. Those decisions can be <u>difficult</u>.

Set B

compound verb phrase	past participle	subject pronoun
direct object	present participle	
main verb	progressive tense	

1. I'll <u>buy the food and then cook it</u>.

2. <u>They</u> had come back to buy two copies of the newspaper.

3. Matt is <u>hurrying</u> to his office.

4. The old man was chanting <u>a song</u> she'd never heard before.

5. Molly <u>selected</u> her dress early in the day.

6. Her horse <u>was behaving</u> calmly.

7. Johnny had <u>eaten</u> a good breakfast.

Answer key: Review matching exercise – Part II

Set A

1. He <u>has written</u> to you every day.   perfect tense

2. Mrs. McLean is sending the recipe to <u>her sister-in-law</u>.   indirect object

3. He understands <u>me</u> better than anyone.   object pronoun

4. His companions <u>will take</u> their canoe across the river.   future tense

5. Richard was working when <u>Miguel and Sam</u> came by.   compound noun phrase

6. The building is <u>near the stream</u>.   prepositional phrase

7. It <u>might</u> be the largest museum in the world.   modal

8. Those decisions can be <u>difficult</u>.   predicate adjective

Set B

1. I'll <u>buy the food and then cook it</u>.   compound verb phrase

2. <u>They</u> had come back to buy two copies of the newspaper.   subject pronoun

3. Matt is <u>hurrying</u> to his office.   present participle

4. The old man was chanting <u>a song</u> she'd never heard before. direct object

5. Molly <u>selected</u> her dress early in the day.   main verb

6. Her horse <u>was behaving</u> calmly.   progressive tense

7. Johnny had <u>eaten</u> a good breakfast.   past participle

PART III: GETTING STARTED WITH SENTENCES

As you've seen, in language we combine words to form phrases. We also combine phrases to form sentences, and there are various kinds of sentences. For example, there are statements and questions, simple sentences and combinations of sentences, and negative sentences and positive sentences. In Part III, we begin to explore different kinds of sentences, looking at the functions of sentences (Unit 15), how sentences can be combined (Unit 16), and the relationships between different sentences (Unit 17). Our goal is to help you recognize some of the more common and important sentence types.

Lesson 45: Identifying sentences by function

One way that a sentence can be described is according to the job that it's doing in a conversation. Compare these sentences:

1. That clown was funny.
2. Is she a physician?
3. Please wash the dishes.
4. What an exciting movie!

You know that sentence 1 is making a statement, sentence 2 is asking a question, sentence 3 is giving a command, and sentence 4 is expressing a strong emotion. These functions are summarized in *Quick tip* 45.1.

> **Quick tip 45.1**
>
> Sentences that make a statement are called declaratives; sentences that ask a question are called interrogatives; sentences that give a command are called imperatives; sentences that express strong emotion are called exclamations.

Here are a few more examples:

5. Edward's parents live on a farm.	(declarative)
6. Have you accepted the fact that she'll never move?	(interrogative)
7. Don't believe a word she says!	(imperative)
8. That's silly!	(exclamation)

Test yourself 45.1

Identify each of the sentences below as either declarative, interrogative, imperative, or exclamation.

Sample: How old are you now?   interrogative

Getting started (answers on p. 206)

1. I'm shocked!
2. Rose and Charles are getting married in that house.
3. What a surprising announcement!
4. The weather was awful yesterday.
5. Watch out for that car!

More practice (answers on the website)

6. Didn't we have fun together?
7. What a performance!
8. Would you want to rent a movie tonight?

9. That was ridiculous! ....

10. Write that down, please! ....

Let's take a closer look at questions:

    9. Do you like learning about sentences?

  10. What do you like best?

  11. You would rather be listening to music, wouldn't you?

These sentences demonstrate three different kinds of questions. Sentence 9 is an example of a **yes/no question**, because it can be answered with just a "yes" or "no." Here are some more yes/no questions:

  12. Did you enjoy the music?

  13. Is the television working?

  14. Are you interested in applying for that job?

> **Quick tip 45.2**
>
> A yes/no question is one that can be answered by "yes" or "no."

Sentence 10 is called a **wh- question** because it begins with a wh- word, or question word.

> **Quick tip 45.3**
>
> A wh- question begins with one of the following wh- words (question words): *when, where, what, why, which, who, whom, how*. Example: *Where is the meeting?*

Notice that *how* is a wh- word, even though it doesn't begin with *wh-*.

Wh- questions cannot be answered with a "yes" or "no." Imagine the following bizarre dialogues:

  15a. What time is it?

  15b. Yes.

  16a. Where are you going?

  16b. No.

  17a. Which dress should I wear?

  17b. Yes.

You get the point.

  Here are some more examples of wh- questions:

  18. Why did they buy that house?

  19. When should we meet?

  20. How does that work?

The third kind of question, called a **tag question**, is demonstrated by sentence 11 above. Here are some more tag questions:

  21. He's having a great time, <u>isn't he</u>?

  22. It rained last night, <u>didn't it</u>?

  23. Mrs. Williams was working hard, <u>wasn't she</u>?

In tag questions, there's a regular statement followed by a tag; the tag is underlined in these examples.

Quick tip 45.4

A tag question contains a statement followed by a tag, such as *could you? aren't they? hasn't he?* Example: *She is leaving soon, isn't she?*

Test yourself 45.2

Decide if each question below is a yes/no question, wh- question, or tag question.
Sample: Why did he call his attorney?   wh- question

Getting started (answers on p. 206)

1. He's not really crazy, is he?   ....

2. Which is yours?   ....

3. Are you interested?   ....

4. Is the evidence against him compelling?   ....

5. We have seen this before, haven't we?   ....

More practice (answers on the website)

6. How did you respond to his question?   ....

7. When did they leave last night?   ....

8. Are you leaving already?   ....

9. Joan is an accomplished woman, isn't she?   ....

10. Is there anything left in the cookie jar?   ....

Answer keys: *Test yourself, Getting started questions* – Unit 15

Test yourself 45.1

1. I'm shocked!   exclamation
2. Rose and Charles are getting married in that house.   declarative
3. What a surprising announcement!   exclamation
4. The weather was awful yesterday.   declarative
5. Watch out for that car!   imperative

Test yourself 45.2

1. He's not really crazy, is he?   tag question
2. Which is yours?   wh- question
3. Are you interested?   yes/no question
4. Is the evidence against him compelling?   yes/no question
5. We have seen this before, haven't we?   tag question

☞ **FOR A REVIEW EXERCISE OF THIS UNIT, SEE THE WEBSITE.**

Lesson 46: Simple sentences

Most of the sentences we've looked at so far in this book are simple sentences, which means that they are sentences that are made up of just one sentence. But sentences can be made up of more than one sentence. Let's start by looking at a few sentences and comparing them.

1. The little boy laughed.
2. The little boy laughed and the little girl smiled.
3. The little boy laughed and the little girl smiled and their dog ran around in circles.

You can see that sentence 2 consists of two sentences joined by *and* and that sentence 3 consists of three sentences joined by *and*. Each of the sentences that make up a larger sentence is called a **clause**. So sentence 1 contains one clause, sentence 2 contains two clauses, and sentence 3 contains three clauses. Just as words combine to form phrases, phrases combine to form clauses, and clauses can combine to form sentences. A clause must contain at least a noun phrase functioning as the subject and a main verb.

Quick tip 46.1

A clause is a free-standing sentence or a sentence within a sentence; a clause or sentence contains at least a subject and a main verb.

Quick tip 46.2

A sentence can contain one or more clauses.

Here are some more examples of sentences containing only one clause:

4. That magazine looks interesting.
5. The officer followed the rules.
6. She greeted me at the door.

Notice that each contains only one subject and one verb phrase.

Quick tip 46.3

A sentence that contains only one clause, that is, one subject and one verb phrase, is called a **simple sentence**.

Are the following simple sentences?

7. on the floor
8. the extremely tall boy
9. were reading newspapers on the train

None of these contains both a subject and a verb phrase, and so these are not sentences at all; they're just phrases. You may recognize sentence 7 as a preposition phrase, sentence 8 as a noun phrase, and sentence 9 as a verb phrase. (See Lessons 28, 29, and 30.)

Test yourself 46.1

In each simple sentence below, underline the subject and put a squiggly line beneath the verb phrase.

Sample: David listened to her response.

Getting started (answers on p. 231)

1. The committee presented its ideas to Congress.

2. I stayed in bed that day.

3. Nobody moved.

4. My favorite hotel is on Park Avenue.

5. I overslept today.

More practice (answers on the website)

6. We enjoy cruising on the Mississippi River.

7. Our cousin lives about an hour from us.

8. The young architect arrives in his office at 8:30 A.M. each weekday.

9. Whales are mammals.

10. Rain is good for the environment.

Test yourself 46.2

Decide if each item below is a simple sentence or just a phrase.

Sample: walking nearby   phrase

Getting started (answers on p. 231)

1. I have never eaten caviar. ....

2. The department stores are having a sale this weekend. ....

3. Expensive antique jewelry. ....

4. Our home on the ranch. ....

5. Fresh-cut flowers on the table. ....

More practice (answers on the website)

6. Sailing around the world. ....

7. Sang my favorite song. ....

8. She is paying for her own tuition. ....

9. Exercising can leave you exhausted. ....

10. The bus is approaching. ....

What about sentences like the following?

10. That magazine and those books look interesting.

11. The officer and his men followed the rules.

12. She and her husband greeted me at the door.

The underlined part of each sentence is a compound noun phrase (see Lesson 43) and is considered to be one subject. So these sentences are all simple sentences. The same thing is true of compound verb phrases:

13. That magazine <u>looks and seems interesting</u>.
14. The officer <u>followed the rules and saved the day</u>.
15. She <u>met and greeted me at the door</u>.

The underlined parts of sentences 13–15 are compound verb phrases (see Lesson 44) and each is considered to be one verb phrase. So, again, these sentences are all simple sentences.

Lesson 47: Compound sentences

As we mentioned in Lesson 46, a sentence can contain more than one sentence within it, for example:

1. Jane put the glass vase on the table and her mother picked it up.

This is an example of a **compound sentence**. It actually contains two sentences. The first is: *Jane put the glass vase on the table*. The second is: *Her mother picked it up*. Since a sentence within a sentence is called a clause, we can also say that sentence 1 contains two clauses. Just as a simple sentence must contain at least a subject and a verb phrase, each of the sentences (clauses) within a compound sentence must contain its own subject and verb phrase.

Recall from Lesson 18 that conjunctions, like *and*, *or*, and *but*, join things. In fact, the two sentences within sentence 1 are joined by the conjunction *and*. Recall also that there are two kinds of conjunctions, coordinating and subordinating. The sentences in a compound sentence are joined together by a coordinating conjunction. As we discussed in Lesson 18, there are three common coordinating conjunctions; they are *and*, *or*, and *but*. Four less common ones are *for*, *so*, *yet*, and *nor*. (Remember FANBOYS, which contains the first letter of each.)

Quick tip 47.1

A sentence that is made up of two or more sentences (clauses) joined by a coordinating conjunction (most commonly *and*, *or*, and *but*) is called a compound sentence.

Test yourself 47.1

Each of the sentences below is a compound sentence consisting of two sentences (clauses). Underline each of the sentences which is in the compound sentence.

Sample: I felt restless after breakfast and I wandered around the house.

Getting started (answers on p. 231)

1. Andre pulled the car into the street, and Beth began reading the directions.

2. She enjoyed shopping for food, but she especially enjoyed cooking.

3. I can do this now, or I can do it later.

4. Dan does not feel well, yet he wants to go in to work.

5. We missed our flight, so we have to wait around the airport for the next available one.

More practice (answers on the website)

6. He does not like to change his mind, nor is he willing to compromise.

7. You deserve your good fortune, for you have a heart of gold.

8. The players are running onto the field, and then they are beginning to practice.

9. Stephanie likes to go to concerts, but she will not see an opera.

10. You can pay with cash, or you can take out a loan.

Test yourself 47.2

Decide if each sentence below is a simple sentence or a compound sentence. Remember that a simple sentence contains just one sentence (clause) while a compound sentence contains at least two sentences joined by a coordinating conjunction.

Sample: Wallace stared at him in the grocery store.   <u>simple</u>

Getting started (answers on p. 231)

1. He can't blame her for the problem.   ....

2. Beth left the library, and she headed straight home.   ....

3. He was watching her, but she was pretending not to notice.   ....

4. We like him a lot.   ....

5. The coach wants to win, but he will be happy with a tie.   ....

More practice (answers on the website)

6. It will be a sunny day.   ....

7. Jeremy likes his wife's new dress.   ....

8. I will have a bowl of soup, but I don't want salad.   ....

9. Sam called me at noon.   ....

10. He will be going to Penn State, or he'll study at Temple University.   ....

A compound sentence can contain more than two sentences:

> 2. Nora was Zach's stepmother but she treated him like her other children and he trusted her completely.

Here, the <u>three</u> sentences that make up this sentence are: (1) *Nora was Zach's stepmother*; (2) *she treated him like her other children*; (3) *he trusted her completely*. So the sentence *There was a glass vase on the table and Jane picked it up* contains two sentences, or clauses. The sentence *Nora was Zach's stepmother but she treated him like her other children and he trusted her completely* contains three sentences, or clauses. In fact, a compound sentence can contain any number of sentences, though we usually limit ourselves to just a few:

> 3. He turned his head away and he pretended to ignore her but he continued to listen to her and in fact he hung on her every word. (4 sentences or clauses)

Keep in mind that you can't tell if a sentence is simple or compound by how long it is; you need to see if it contains one or more than one complete sentence within it. For example, the following sentence, although it is long, is just a simple sentence:

> 4. The tall man with the violin case quickly climbed the stairs to the abandoned warehouse near the railroad tracks.

This is a simple sentence because it has just one subject, *the tall man with the violin case*, and one verb phrase – notice that there is just one verb, *climbed*. (The sentence is just long because it contains a few preposition phrases.) And the following sentence, although it is short, is a compound sentence: *John laughed and Mary cried*. It's a compound sentence because it contains two sentences that can stand alone: *John laughed*; *Mary cried*. Each of these has its own subject and verb phrase.

Test yourself 47.3

Each sentence below is either a simple or compound sentence. Identify the number of clauses in each sentence. If there is more than one clause in the sentence, underline each clause.

Sample: The bear watched his movements closely.   1

Getting started (answers on p. 231)

1. Vicki was always looking at herself in the mirror, but Mary Ann
   was extremely self-confident, and she never gave herself a second glance.   ....

2. Her father was devoted to her.   ....

3. Our firm's CEO will be flying to Chicago next week, but he'll be returning
   the same day.   ....

4. The lady in the elegant blue dress entered the well-lit room with her perky little
   dog in her arms.   ....

5. Our boat was hit with strong winds, and we had to return to our cabins.   ....

More practice (answers on the website)

6. We don't have much time left in the zoo, but we should visit the bird cage, and
   we must see the monkeys, or we should at least feed the goats in the petting area,
   but I definitely want to take a look at the elephants.   ....

7. We can catch a movie, or we can visit a museum, but we won't be seeing a
   Broadway show.   ....

8. Many people walk in the woods in autumn.   ....

9. The economy is getting worse, and many people are worried about their jobs.   ....

10. My car is getting old, and it's pretty banged up, but I hope to get another
    year out of it.   ....

Keep in mind that a compound <u>phrase</u> (Lessons 43 and 44) is not the same thing as a compound <u>sentence</u>. For example, the following sentence has a compound noun phrase (underlined):

   5. The teacher graded <u>the students' exams</u> **and** <u>their papers</u>.

We've certainly got a coordinating conjunction, *and*, in sentence 5. However, the question is, what is the *and* joining? If we look at what's on each side of the *and*, we find the following: *The teacher graded the students' exams*, which is a sentence, and *their papers*; *their papers* is not a sentence by itself. In this case, the conjunction *and* is joining two noun phrases: *the students' exams* and *their papers*. It's not joining two complete sentences, and so the sentence is not a compound sentence but is a simple sentence.

Test yourself 47.4

Decide if each sentence below is a simple or compound sentence. Remember that a compound sentence contains a complete sentence on either side of the conjunction.

Sample: Kyle turned around and stared at the screen.   <u>simple</u>

Getting started (answers on p. 231)

1. It was a scene of joy but one thing spoiled the moment. ....

2. The boxer fell to his knees but he managed to get back up. ....

3. The designer and his assistants quickly brought order to the chaos. ....

4. Matt was driving to New York with his kids and his neighbor's son. ....

5. I like to drink coffee or tea after dinner. ....

More practice (answers on the website)

6. The weather is already getting chilly, but I am not ready for winter just yet. ....

7. His speech should be brief and to the point. ....

8. You must get ready immediately or I'll leave without you. ....

9. The flight attendant offered me beef or chicken for the entrée. ....

10. She likes classical music but rarely goes to concerts. ....

Lesson 48: Complex sentences

In the last lesson, we talked about compound sentences such as:

1. <u>Beth said hello to her mother's friend</u> and <u>then she walked outside</u>.

Each of the sentences (clauses) that is part of the compound sentence plays an equal role in the sentence; one clause is not superior to or more important than the other, in terms of the structure of the sentence.

Now let's look at some other sentences:

2. Harry was only fifteen when his mother sent him away to school.
3. Mr. Edwards looked her straight in the eye although he wasn't really sincere.
4. I won't tell you the answer unless you agree to help.

Sentences 2–4 also each contain two sentences, or clauses, which are combined to make a larger sentence. However, one of these sentences is more important than the other. The more important sentence is called the **main clause**, or **independent clause**; the less important sentence, the one that is a subpart of the main clause, is called the dependent clause or subordinate clause (see Lesson 19). Each clause, whether it's a main clause or subordinate clause, has its own subject and verb phrase. Sentences that contain a main clause and at least one dependent clause are called **complex sentences**.

The main clause of each of the following sentences is in bold; the dependent clause is underlined:

5. **Harry was only fifteen** <u>when his mother sent him away to school</u>.
6. **Mr. Edwards looked her straight in the eye** <u>although he wasn't really sincere</u>.
7. **I won't tell you the answer** <u>unless you agree to help</u>.

> **Quick tip 48.1**
>
> A complex sentence consists of at least two sentences (clauses): a main clause and a dependent clause. The dependent clause is a subpart of the main clause and adds information to it. Example, with the dependent clause underlined: *Sally visited her <u>before she moved</u>*.

Recall that, in a compound sentence, the clauses are joined by a coordinating conjunction such as *and*, *or*, and *but*. In a complex sentence, the dependent clause is joined to the rest of the sentence by a subordinating conjunction. (We introduced subordinating conjunctions in Lesson 19; you may want to check back there to refresh your memory.) The common subordinating conjunctions of English are repeated here for reference.

after	even though	than	whenever
although	how	that	where
as	if	though	wherever
as if	in order that	till	whether
as though	once	unless	while
because	rather than	until	which
before	since	what	who
even if	so (that)	when	why

Quick tip 48.2

A dependent clause is joined to another clause by a subordinating conjunction such as *although, if, where.*

Quick tip 48.3

The easiest way to identify a dependent clause is to look for a subordinating conjunction and see if it's followed by a sentence. If it is, then the subordinating conjunction plus the sentence directly following it is a dependent clause.

Test yourself 48.1

For each complex sentence below, underline the dependent clause. Remember to look for the subordinating conjunction, which is the first word of the dependent clause.
Sample: Helen stared in dismay at the floor <u>after she opened the dining room door.</u>

Getting started (answers on p. 232)

1. His father is returning to London because the furniture is arriving.

2. Selma smiled at him although she had never felt less like smiling.

3. He felt a great affection for his guardian until he discovered the truth.

4. I am going to solve this crossword puzzle even if it takes me all day.

5. James accepted the job before he checked with his wife.

More practice (answers on the website)

6. Sammy passed the final exam even though he had not studied hard.

7. You are behaving as if you were the boss.

8. I will not speak to you unless you tell me the truth.

9. New Orleans has not been the same since it was devastated by a hurricane.

10. Al tries to speak French when he is in Montreal.

In the complex sentences we've looked at so far, the dependent clause follows the main clause. But sometimes the dependent clause comes before the main clause. (Again, see Lesson 19.) In these next examples of complex sentences, the dependent clauses are underlined:

8. <u>After he uttered her name</u>, an awful silence fell on the room.
9. <u>While we hurried to the restaurant</u>, the rain continued to pour.
10. <u>Even though she was a difficult woman</u>, they had a good marriage.

Test yourself 48.2

For each complex sentence below, underline the dependent clause. Remember to look for the subordinating conjunction, which is the first word of the dependent clause. The dependent clause will either be before or after the main clause.
Sample: <u>If you continue on this highway</u>, you'll end up in the wrong place.

Getting started (answers on p. 232)

1. When Elizabeth spoke, Ben listened attentively.
2. Before you blame him, think about your own responsibility.
3. You should pay for automobile insurance even if your car is old.
4. Unless the train arrives soon, we'll miss our appointment.
5. The district attorney won't rest till he finds the perpetrator.

More practice (answers on the website)

6. While you were away, important changes took place.
7. As you know, UCLA won the Pac-10 championship.
8. If you really want it, I will loan you my laptop.
9. After he was released from the hospital, he had to rest for a week.
10. She is going to succeed wherever she ends up.

Test yourself 48.3

For each complex sentence below, underline the subject of the dependent clause (not of the main clause).
Sample: I had an interesting conversation with him while <u>we</u> were walking home.

Getting started (answers on p. 232)

1. Even though the village supported the emperor, it still paid numerous taxes.
2. I like to sit on the balcony when the weather is nice.
3. George did it because he recognized the woman.
4. Once I have made up my mind, I usually do not change it.
5. Someone rang the doorbell while we were having lunch.

More practice (answers on the website)

6. Zachary was behaving as though he knew the answer.
7. She was not sure whether she should travel to that country.
8. The bus arrived at the station before I could finish the newspaper.
9. They started learning Chinese so that they could understand their in-laws better.
10. After you left, I began washing the dishes.

A complex sentence contains only one main clause, but it can contain more than one dependent clause. In the following examples, there is a main clause and two dependent clauses. The main clause is again in bold; the dependent clauses are underlined. Notice that we sometimes have flexibility in terms of the placement of each of the clauses.

11a. **Harry was only fifteen** when his mother sent him away to school, although he looked much older.

11b. When his mother sent him away to school, **Harry was only fifteen**, although he looked much older.

11c. Although he looked much older when his mother sent him away to school, **Harry was only fifteen**.

12a. **I won't tell you the answer** unless you agree to help, because this issue is confidential.

12b. Unless you agree to help, **I won't tell you the answer**, because this issue is confidential.

12c. Because this issue is confidential, unless you agree to help, **I won't tell you the answer**.

Test yourself 48.4

For each sentence below, decide if it is a simple sentence or a complex sentence. Some complex sentences will have more than one dependent clause.

Sample: Those two brothers always dress alike.   simple

Getting started (answers on p. 232)

1. The two horses thrived on the ranch because they received excellent care. ....

2. Another little girl will be arriving at the school before noon today. ....

3. The old housekeeper welcomed her warmly when her mother was present. ....

4. The general returned home with his family. ....

5. As we approached our destination, we became rather emotional. ....

More practice (answers on the website)

6. When the actor entered the stage, the audience clapped enthusiastically. ....

7. If you promise not to tell anyone, I will let you in on a secret, even though I shouldn't. ....

8. We are not going to the beach until it stops raining. ....

9. Unless you stop complaining, we are turning right around. ....

10. He likes foreign movies a lot. ....

Test yourself 48.5

For each sentence below, indicate if it is a simple sentence, a compound sentence, or a complex sentence. Be sure to determine the kind of conjunction (coordinating or subordinating) in order to help you decide.

Sample: We were always polite to one another although we were never close.   complex

Getting started (answers on p. 232)

1. She pursued her goals relentlessly but she didn't always achieve them. ....

2. I have made numerous mistakes over the years. ....

3. I won't tell you unless you agree to help because I can't take the risk. ....

4. Jason and Ilene had to renew their passports before they could leave the country.

....

5. Baby boomers were born before this century.

....

More practice (answers on the website)

6. He insisted, but I still did not believe him.

....

7. You can watch TV all night long, or you can study for your exam.

....

8. While Mr. Kagan was at work, the air conditioning stopped working at his house.

....

9. I have known him since we moved to this town.

....

10. Ashley and Brian wanted to shop at that store.

....

Complex sentences can have different kinds of dependent clauses. The ones we've talked about so far are called **adverbial clauses** because, like adverbs, they typically tell us more about a verb, adjective, or another adverb. For example, in the sentence, *Things improved after Mr. Eliot arrived*, the underlined dependent clause is telling us something about the time of the action.

In other complex sentences, dependent clauses can be used as noun phrases. Take a look at the following pair of sentences:

      13a. <u>That statement</u> is silly.
      13b. <u>What Mark just said</u> is silly.

In sentence 13a, *that statement* is a noun phrase. In sentence 13b, *what Mark just said* is a dependent clause which is functioning as a noun phrase of the main sentence. When a dependent clause is functioning as a noun phrase, it's called a **noun clause**. Here are some more sentence pairs in which the second sentence of the pair has a dependent clause (underlined) acting as a noun phrase.

      14a. I know the truth.   simple sentence
      14b. I know <u>that you're right</u>.   complex sentence
      15a. <u>It</u> remains unknown.   simple sentence
      15b. <u>Why they left town</u> remains unknown.   complex sentence

Notice that noun clauses look just like other dependent clauses: they begin with a subordinating conjunction and contain both a subject and a verb phrase. However, when a sentence has a noun clause, the rest of the sentence cannot always stand alone; it needs the noun clause to be complete. For example, in sentence 15b, *remains unknown* is not a complete sentence.

Test yourself 48.6

Underline the dependent clause in each of the complex sentences below. It will be either an adverbial clause or a noun clause.

Sample: <u>Whatever you do</u> is acceptable.

Getting started (answers on p. 232)

1. I'll stay with Jeanette until Peter comes home.

2. That my candidate will win is obvious.

3. Although Mrs. Craft was tired, she insisted on making us dinner.

4. We were quite confident that we had made the right decision.

5. They want to find out why the waitress was so rude to them.

More practice (answers on the website)

6. He did not know which highway led to the Canadian border.

7. The assistant manager knew that she was not going to be promoted this time.

8. Wherever we travel we like to visit museums.

9. I can speak Italian better than you can speak French.

10. We were tired of waiting, so we left.

We've been telling you to look for the subordinating conjunction to help you find the dependent clause. But what about these next sentences (with the dependent clauses underlined)?

16a. I know that you're right.

16b. I know you're right.

17a. You believed that the defendant was innocent.

17b. You believed the defendant was innocent.

As you can see, we can delete the subordinating conjunction *that* in a noun clause when the dependent clause follows the main clause. However, if the dependent clause comes before the main clause, the subordinating conjunction *that* cannot be deleted:

18a. That her daughter is talented has been obvious for years.

18b. *Her daughter is talented has been obvious for years.

19a. That the defendant was innocent became clear during the trial.

19b. *The defendant was innocent became clear during the trial.

Quick tip 48.4

In a noun clause, the subordinating conjunction *that* can be deleted following a main clause. Example: *I think (that) it's going to rain.*

So when you don't see a subordinating conjunction in a sentence, but the sentence has more than one subject and verb phrase, ask yourself if you can insert *that* somewhere. If so, then you'll know you have a dependent clause.

Test yourself 48.7

Underline the dependent clauses in each of the sentences below. In some cases, the conjunction *that* will have been deleted.

Sample: They knew she would escape.

Getting started (answers on p. 232)

1. They don't believe that her partner will keep his word.

2. Mrs. Webb was sure her pie would win the baking contest.

3. That Andy is the best in the class doesn't surprise me.

4. We heard you were accepted to Georgetown Law School.

5. It is true that I am going to become a partner in this firm.

More practice (answers on the website)

6. This man does not think you are a good writer.

7. Jackie always thought that one day she would be a leading actress.

8. You knew that I would be throwing a surprise party for you.

9. The landlord assumed that all his tenants would be paying rent on time.

10. The little girl pretended she was dancing with Mickey Mouse.

Test yourself 48.8

Decide if each sentence is simple, compound, or complex. Keep in mind that sometimes the subordinating conjunction *that* may have been deleted.

Sample: She told me I wasn't giving up yet.   complex

Getting started (answers on p. 233)

1. My mother changed the subject, but it was too late.   ....

2. He proposed to her when she graduated from college.   ....

3. A man from the sawmill was overseeing the project.   ....

4. I want a piece of apple pie.   ....

5. I had been hoping you could come to the game.   ....

More practice (answers on the website)

6. If you take the kids to the movies, I can get some rest.   ....

7. The president said we should all conserve fuel.   ....

8. You can do the food shopping first, or you can do your other errands.   ....

9. Justin generally eats his soup with bread and butter.   ....

10. I know the woman in the blue dress.   ....

There's another very common type of subordinating clause, called a **relative clause**. Here are some examples:

    20. I'll tell my husband, who will be home soon.

    21. The person who knows her best is Richard.

    22. Miss Livingston had her money in the bank that failed.

Since there's quite a bit to say about relative clauses, we've given them their own lesson, which is next.

Lesson 49: Sentences with relative clauses

A well-known children's story starts with the line, *This is the house that Jack built*. It continues,

This is the malt that lay in the house that Jack built. This is the rat that ate the malt that lay in the house that Jack built. The story continues until it ends with the following sentence: *This is the farmer sowing his corn, that kept the cock that crowed in the morn, that waked the priest all shaven and shorn, that married the man all tattered and torn, that kissed the maiden all forlorn, that milked the cow with the crumpled horn, that tossed the dog, that worried the cat, that killed the rat, that ate the malt that lay in the house that Jack built.*

(www.amherst.edu/~rjyanco94/literature/mothergoose/rhymes/
thisisthehousethatjackbuilt.html, retrieved November 9, 2008.)

This story gives us a good demonstration of complex sentences with relative clauses, which are a kind of dependent clause (see Lesson 48). For example, in the sentence *This is the house that Jack built*, the main clause is *This is the house*, and the dependent, relative clause is *that Jack built*. The relative clause acts as an adjective: it modifies the noun phrase *the house*, telling us more about it. This is why relative clauses are also referred to as **adjective clauses**.

> **Quick tip 49.1**
>
> A relative clause (adjective clause) is a kind of dependent clause; it provides additional information about a noun phrase in the main clause. Example (relative clause underlined): *I brought the cookies that are on the plate*.

In each sentence below, the relative clause is underlined, and the noun phrase which the relative clause is modifying is in bold. The main clause can stand on its own as a sentence without the relative clause; the relative clause just provides additional information about the noun phrase it's modifying and cannot stand alone. Like other clauses, a relative clause has its own subject and verb phrase.

1. She transferred the plate to **the tray** that she just washed.
2. Blanche thought about **the man** who was living in Italy at the time.
3. He called **the company** that usually supplies the pipes.

Test yourself 49.1

Underline the relative clause in each of the sentences below.
Sample: Mr. Sanders was wearing a suit that he bought in Italy.

Getting started (answers on p. 233)

1. He paid no attention to the newspaper which was next to him.

2. The police arrested the man whom they had been looking for.

3. Mrs. Peterson was reaching for the phone that was nearest her chair.

4. He might recognize the woman who is hosting the show.

5. Cliff bought a present that was just perfect for his girlfriend.

More practice (answers on the website)

6. I am renting an apartment that has two bedrooms.

7. She met someone whose daughter had graduated from Duke University.

8. Are you going to eat the desert that I baked especially for you?

9. He came to the party with a friend whom I haven't seen in ages.

10. You should pay for your vacation with the money that I gave you.

The relative clause doesn't necessarily follow the main sentence (clause); it can also be within the main sentence. In the following sentences, the relative clause is underlined and the main sentence (clause) is in bold. In sentences 4 and 5, the relative clause follows the main clause; in sentences 6 and 7, it's inside the main clause.

4. **I've brought the horse** who has been specially trained.
5. **We tipped the waiter** who had served us so well.
6. **The man** who was living in Italy at the time **knew all the facts**.
7. **The company** that usually supplies the pipes **has gone out of business**.

Again, if the relative clause (the underlined part) is removed, the main clause can still stand on its own as a sentence.

Test yourself 49.2

Underline the relative clause in each of the sentences below. The relative clause may be anywhere in the sentence.

Sample: A business that manufactures engines can be difficult to run.

Getting started (answers on p. 233)

1. She gave him a smile that lit up her face.

2. The professor who gives easy tests is on sabbatical this semester.

3. The approaches which are most likely to succeed are too complicated.

4. The hotel which is near the shore doesn't open until April.

5. Are you satisfied with the computer that your parents bought for you?

More practice (answers on the website)

6. The players who just entered the stadium are wearing blue jerseys.

7. Those strawberries that you brought are absolutely delicious.

8. I will vote for the candidate whose values are close to mine.

9. The gym that she belongs to is only a mile away.

10. He is still madly in love with the woman whom he married 15 years ago.

We've seen (in Lesson 48) that other dependent clauses are linked to the rest of the sentence by subordinating conjunctions. The same is true of relative clauses. Those subordinating conjunctions which link relative clauses to the rest of the sentence are called relative pronouns, and you may remember that we talked about them in Lesson 26. The relative pronoun which introduces the relative clause is underlined in the sentences below:

8. I just read a book <u>which</u> had a really exciting ending.
9. The soldier <u>whom</u> I'm writing to recently came home on leave.
10. She signed a deal with the publishing company <u>that</u> gave her the best offer.

Note that words that are relative pronouns can also be used in other ways. For example, *who* can be used as a relative pronoun, but it can also be used as a question word, as in the sentence, *Who married her?*

> **Quick tip 49.2**
>
> Relative clauses begin with one of the relative pronouns: *that, which, who, whom, whose.*

Test yourself 49.3

Each of the sentences below contains a relative clause. Underline the relative pronoun that begins the relative clause.
Sample: The student <u>whom</u> I spoke to was confused.

Getting started (answers on p. 233)

1. The hotel chain that Greg founded has since gone out of business.

2. He phoned the woman who was writing the article.

3. Jill resents the man whose father won the lottery.

4. The highway which I take to work needs repair.

5. The TV show that she likes best is on Sunday nights.

More practice (answers on the website)

6. The DVD player which you bought was way too expensive.

7. I would like to meet the woman who you raved about.

8. Students whose names are not on the class roster should see me after class.

9. We are going to patronize the pharmacy which has just opened up.

10. I don't read all the magazines that I subscribe to.

Just as a sentence can have more than one dependent clause, it can have more than one relative clause. We saw this earlier, in the sentences about Jack, and see it here as well:

11. Pablo married the woman <u>whose sister lived in a house</u> <u>which was next door to the one</u> <u>that I bought from the man</u> <u>who had first built it.</u>

Even though this sentence is very long and contains four relative clauses, it is still perfectly grammatical.

Test yourself 49.4

Underline the relative clauses in each of the sentences below. A sentence may have more than one relative clause.
Sample: The man <u>whom he had rescued</u> turned out to be the criminal <u>whom the police were looking for</u>.

Getting started (answers on p. 233)

1. She turned on the broadcast which dealt with the scandal that had recently been in the news.

2. Buck stood behind the counter which dominated his small restaurant.

3. The photographer who took the picture which appeared in the paper that was most widely read won a Pulitzer Prize.

4. I can't find the message that you sent me.

5. No one who breaks the law should get away with it.

More practice (answers on the website)

6. The cruise that we booked 6 months ago through the agent whom you recommended is leaving next week.

7. The furnace that heats the house which we purchased with the cash that we won in the lottery that we played 5 years ago needs to be replaced.

8. Did you ever compute the number of days that you have spent on the novel that you are writing?

9. Friends who keeps their word are the kinds of friends that I like.

10. The parking garage which is on the top floor of the building that is on the corner of the intersection is almost always full.

You may be wondering why relative pronouns are called pronouns. You know that pronouns replace noun phrases in a sentence. As we discussed in Lesson 26, all of the relative pronouns except *whose* do the same thing.

> **Quick tip 49.3**
>
> A relative pronoun connects the relative clause to the rest of the sentence. All of the relative pronouns (except *whose*) also replace a noun phrase in the relative clause. (*Whose* replaces a determiner.)

Let's review how *Quick tip* 49.3 works in the following sentence, whose relative clause is underlined:

    12. Blanche thought about the man **who** was living in Italy.

What noun phrase is the relative pronoun *who* replacing? The *who* refers to the noun phrase *the man*.

    Here's another example:

    13. He called the company **that** usually supplied the pipes.

In this case, what does the relative pronoun *that* replace? It replaces the noun phrase *the company*.

Test yourself 49.5

For each sentence below, underline the relative clause and put a squiggly line under the main clause.
Sample: Natalie usually wears clothes that look flattering on her.

Getting started (answers on p. 233)

1. I am meeting Mr. Arnold at the museum that he supports.

2. The label which contains the warning is not very clear.

3. The robber opened the case which contained the most cash.

4. The policy that the president is implementing should be successful.

5. I contacted the young man whose wallet I found on the subway.

More practice (answers on the website)

6. Shirley is not satisfied with the interest that she is getting in her bank account.

7. Economists who can predict the duration of recessions are rare.

8. Doctors who overcharge patients should be prosecuted.

9. I was impressed with the author who gave a lecture at the library yesterday.

10. The salesman who called was very persuasive.

Test yourself 49.6

Underline the dependent clause in each of the sentences below. It will either be a relative clause, a noun clause, or an adverbial clause.

Sample: The historian visited most of the sites that he wrote about.

Getting started (answers on p. 234)

1. The architect's design includes a window that faces the courtyard.

2. She understood what you were trying to say.

3. If you're hungry, this town has a fantastic Greek restaurant.

4. It is obvious that we have to reevaluate our plan.

5. The offer that I have given you is a fair one.

More practice (answers on the website)

6. Her cousins need to know whether she'll be going to Boston this weekend.

7. Even if you don't feel good, you should definitely attend the convention.

8. The stranger who said hello to us wore elegant clothes.

9. The salesman can't remember what he promised his customer.

10. They watched TV when they got home.

Let's take a look at the following sentence:

14. The man **whom** I interviewed was not very knowledgeable.

As we discussed above, the sentence contains a relative clause, *whom I interviewed*, which begins with the relative pronoun *whom*. Will this sentence still be grammatical if the relative pronoun, *whom*, is left out?

15. The man I interviewed was not very knowledgeable.

If you think this sentence sounds fine, you're absolutely right. Here are some more examples:

16a. The permit that the builders applied for was denied.

16b. The permit the builders applied for was denied.

17a. The celebrity who Jack photographed left the theater early.

17b. The celebrity Jack photographed left the theater early.

You will notice that when the relative pronoun is omitted, as in sentences 15, 16b, and 17b, one noun phrase is directly followed by another noun phrase: *the man + I* in sentence 15, *the permit + the builders* in sentence 16b, and *the celebrity + Jack* in sentence 17b. So if you see a sentence that has two noun phrases next to each other, check to see if the sentence would still be grammatical and mean the same thing if you put a relative pronoun between the two noun phrases; this will help you identify relative clauses.

> **Quick tip 49.4**
>
> A relative pronoun may be omitted before a noun phrase. Example: *The movie (that) I saw was exciting.*

Test yourself 49.7

Underline the relative clause in each of the sentences below. In some cases, the relative pronoun will have been deleted.

Sample: The waiter set the table he had placed outside the restaurant.

Getting started (answers on p. 234)

1. The little square in the town we visited contained benches.

2. Other famous people will be performing at the theater that my brother works at.

3. The pilot who flew the aircraft must have been well trained.

4. My neighbor owns the horse which won this race.

5. The guest I invited is sleeping on the sofa.

More practice (answers on the website)

6. We left a nice tip for the waiter who served our delicious dinner.

7. The tennis racket I bought for you was made abroad.

8. The author whose book I am reading will go on a promotional tour.

9. The thing I like best about Jill is her positive attitude.

10. The woman who is running for mayor of this city is well known.

When we look at relative clauses more closely, we find that there are actually two types: **restrictive relative clauses** and **nonrestrictive relative clauses**. Compare the following sentences; the relative clauses are underlined.

18. Bridget likes doughnuts that have chocolate frosting.
19. She likes Peter Bolton, who is her son's piano teacher.

In sentence 18, the relative clause *that have chocolate frosting* is telling us exactly which doughnuts Bridget really likes. The clause is telling us that Bridget doesn't necessarily like all doughnuts; she specifically likes those that have chocolate frosting. This kind of relative clause, which limits or restricts the noun phrase it's modifying, is called a restrictive relative clause.

In contrast, in sentence 19, the relative clause *who is her son's piano teacher* is telling us something about Peter Bolton, but if we omit this relative clause, we still know who Peter is, although we don't know the extra information that he is her son's piano teacher. This type of relative clause is called a nonrestrictive relative clause. It's always separated from the main sentence by commas. (You can think of it as being separated from the main clause by commas because it's not essential.) When we say a sentence with a nonrestrictive relative clause, we usually pause at the commas separating it from the main sentence.

Here are some more examples to help clarify the difference between restrictive and nonrestrictive relative clauses:

    20. The employees who were upset came to the meeting.

    21. The employees, who were upset, came to the meeting.

What's the difference in meaning between these two sentences? According to sentence 20, only those employees who were upset came to the meeting. The other employees didn't come to the meeting. That is, sentence 20 restricts the employees who came to the meeting to only those who were upset. Sentence 20 thus contains a restrictive relative clause.

What we know from sentence 21 is that employees came to the meeting. In addition, we know that those employees were upset. The clause provides additional information about the employees but doesn't restrict, or limit, which employees came to the meeting. There may be other employees who were also upset but who didn't come to the meeting. This clause is a nonrestrictive relative clause.

Again, notice that in sentence 21 the relative clause is separated from the main clause by commas. Sentence 21 is also said with pauses where the commas are.

Note that one can always remove a relative clause, of either type, and still end up with a grammatical sentence. However, if the restrictive relative clause is removed, some of the information needed to fully identify the noun phrase we're talking about is missing.

Quick tip 49.5

A restrictive relative clause limits the noun phrase which it is modifying; a nonrestrictive relative clause does not. A nonrestrictive relative clause is separated from the main clause by pauses, and, when written, it is separated from the main clause by commas. Examples: *The dogs which were friendly were being trained as Seeing Eye dogs* (restrictive). *The dogs, which were friendly, were being trained as Seeing Eye dogs* (nonrestrictive).

Test yourself 49.8

Decide if each relative clause, underlined in the sentences below, is a restrictive or nonrestrictive relative clause.

Sample: The laundry <u>which had just been folded</u> was on the counter.   <u>restrictive</u>

Getting started (answers on p. 234)

1. Mrs. Smith, <u>who owns the house</u>, was not interested in selling.   ....

2. A huge truck, <u>which someone had painted bright yellow</u>, stood in the driveway.   ....

3. The children <u>who had just come back from the class trip</u> were restless. ....

4. The maid broke an antique lamp, <u>which was very valuable</u>.   ....

5. The painting <u>I brought home</u> will be perfect for the den.   ....

More practice (answers on the website)

6. The bushes <u>we planted last year</u> are growing nicely.   ....

7. Brianna is mad at John, <u>who offended her family</u>.   ....

8. I am returning your bicycle, <u>which you lent me last week</u>.   ....

9. The students who made the presentation did a great job. ....

10. This road, which we have traveled many times, is treacherous. ....

Test yourself 49.9

Underline the relative clause in each of the sentences below. Then decide if it is restrictive or nonrestrictive.

Sample: Rome, which is a lovely city, was her first destination.   nonrestrictive

Getting started (answers on p. 234)

1. The Frenchman who is from Lyons completed the project. ....

2. The general, who knew nothing about the matter, nonetheless
   voiced his opinion. ....

3. A small disturbance, which was getting louder and louder,
   finally attracted our attention. ....

4. Jeremy, who was blushing profusely, asked Tatiana for some help. ....

5. Jim wasn't the person she wanted to hire. ....

More practice (answers on the website)

6. The young lady, whose hobby was stamp collecting, was charming. ....

7. The man who is having a drink at the bar looks familiar. ....

8. The taxi I called took me to the airport. ....

9. Her report, which she prepared carefully, was well received. ....

10. The children, who are playing with their new toys, are unusually quiet. ....

To enhance your understanding

Proper names are not modified by restrictive relative clauses. Here is an example:

    22a. George, who is an architect, is a good friend of mine.   (nonrestrictive)

    22b. *George who is an architect is a good friend of mine.   (restrictive)

Since the identity of a proper noun is already well defined, it makes sense that restrictive relative clauses do not modify proper nouns.

    Notice that if we want to be very specific about a proper name, to differentiate it from others with the same name, then using a restrictive relative clause is entirely appropriate:

    23. The George who is an architect is a good friend of mine.   (restrictive)

    24. The France that I am familiar with is a very lovely country.   (restrictive)

To further enhance your understanding

A relative clause can modify any noun phrase in a sentence, whether that noun phrase is functioning as a subject, direct object, indirect object, or object of a preposition. For example, in sentence 25, the relative clause refers to the direct object of the main clause:

    25. My sister likes the house which has a large swimming pool.

And in sentence 26, the relative clause refers to the indirect object of the main clause:

    26. My sister sold the house to a family that has three children.

Lesson 50: Compound-complex sentences

You know (from Lesson 47) that sentence 1 is a compound sentence:

    1. Martha left me a note but I can't find it.

You also know (from Lesson 48) that sentence 2 is a complex sentence:

    2. She answered him impatiently when he questioned her credentials.

Like all compound sentences, sentence 1 contains at least two complete sentences joined by a coordinating conjunction, in this case *but*. And like all complex sentences, sentence 2 contains a main clause with at least one dependent clause; the dependent clause begins with a subordinating conjunction, in this case *when*.

But what about this next sentence?

    3. I'll leave a message for the plumber but I'm not sure that he'll get it.

You won't be surprised to learn that sentences such as sentence 3, which are both compound (two clauses connected with *but*) and complex (two clauses connected with *that*), are called **compound-complex sentences**. These are sentences that contain at least two main clauses, and at least one of the main clauses has at least one dependent clause.

> **Quick tip 50.1**
>
> A compound-complex sentence is a combination of a compound and a complex sentence: it has at least two main clauses and at least one dependent clause. Example: *His friends were always there for William, and he appreciated the help that they often gave him.*

Here are some more examples of compound-complex sentences, with the complete sentences in bold and the dependent clauses underlined:

    4. **While the house looked nice from the outside, the floors were sagging** and **the walls were crumbling**.

    5. **The woman who lives next door is very friendly** but **I forgot her name**.

    6. **I thanked him for his efforts** but **he insisted that he hadn't minded**.

    7. **If we don't hurry, we'll have to see a different movie,** or **we'll have to come back later**.

Test yourself 50.1

Decide if each sentence below is a complex or compound-complex sentence.
Sample: He realized that they had been investigating his private life.   complex

Getting started (answers on p. 234)

1. They are walking quickly down the hall which connects their lab to the main office.   ....

2. The castle looked beautiful in the sunlight, and it dominated the countryside which was around it.   ....

3. The Mercer family has gone on the vacation which they've been planning for years.   ....

4. He was angry at his friend, but he decided that he wasn't going to tell him.

5. We don't know whether we'll succeed, but it's important that we try.

More practice (answers on the website)

6. Since you moved, a lot of things have changed.

7. Mr. Burns's son can't buy a house until he finishes medical school, but he is already saving for it.

8. I am not going to sign the contract until my lawyer looks it over.

9. We will go to the concert, but I am warning you that we will have to wait on line for tickets.

10. The mechanic said that we should check our tire pressure every week.

Test yourself 50.2

Decide if each sentence below is a simple, compound, complex or compound-complex sentence.
Sample: Her older son, whose name was Edward, moved into the city first.   <u>complex</u>

Getting started (answers on p. 234)

1. If you travel to New York, you should definitely visit Times Square.

2. He dried his face with a towel.

3. I like the view from my apartment, but it can get very noisy outside.

4. Once you arrive in Europe, you should call me.

5. It is obvious to me that you have to limit your spending, or you'll have to look for a second job.

More practice (answers on the website)

6. He is sleeping soundly, but he needs to get up soon.

7. They buy a newspaper almost every morning.

8. The game started before I got there.

9. Valerie will be happy when she gets the news.

10. I invited Carrie over and she joined me for a dinner which was delicious.

Answer keys: *Test yourself, Getting started* questions – Unit 16

Test yourself 46.1

1. The committee presented its ideas to congress.
2. I stayed in bed that day.
3. Nobody moved.
4. My favorite hotel is on Park Avenue.
5. I overslept today.

Test yourself 46.2

1. I have never eaten caviar.	simple sentence
2. The department stores are having a sale this weekend.	simple sentence
3. Expensive antique jewelry.	phrase
4. Our home on the ranch.	phrase
5. Fresh-cut flowers on the table.	phrase

Test yourself 47.1

1. Andre pulled the car into the street, and Beth began reading the directions.
2. She enjoyed shopping for food, but she especially enjoyed cooking.
3. I can do this now, or I can do it later.
4. Dan does not feel well, yet he wants to go in to work.
5. We missed our flight, so we have to wait around the airport for the next available one.

Test yourself 47.2

1. He can't blame her for the problem.	simple
2. Beth left the library, and she headed straight home.	compound
3. He was watching her, but she was pretending not to notice.	compound
4. We like him a lot.	simple
5. The coach wants to win, but he will be happy with a tie.	compound

Test yourself 47.3

1. Vicki was always looking at herself in the mirror, but Mary Ann was extremely self-confident, and she never gave herself a second glance.   3
2. Her father was devoted to her.   1
3. Our firm's CEO will be flying to Chicago next week, but he'll be returning the same day.   2
4. The lady in the elegant blue dress entered the well-lit room with her perky little dog in her arms.   1
5. Our boat was hit with strong winds, and we had to return to our cabins.   2

Test yourself 47.4

1. It was a scene of joy but one thing spoiled the moment.   compound
2. The boxer fell to his knees but he managed to get back up.   compound

3. The designer and his assistants quickly brought order to the chaos.   <u>simple</u>
4. Matt was driving to New York with his kids and his neighbor's son.   <u>simple</u>
5. I like to drink coffee or tea after dinner.   <u>simple</u>

Test yourself 48.1

1. His father is returning to London <u>because the furniture is arriving</u>.
2. Selma smiled at him <u>although she had never felt less like smiling</u>.
3. He felt a great affection for his guardian <u>until he discovered the truth</u>.
4. I am going to solve this crossword puzzle <u>even if it takes me all day</u>.
5. James accepted the job <u>before he checked with his wife</u>.

Test yourself 48.2

1. <u>When Elizabeth spoke</u>, Ben listened attentively.
2. <u>Before you blame him</u>, think about your own responsibility.
3. You should pay for automobile insurance <u>even if your car is old</u>.
4. <u>Unless the train arrives soon</u>, we'll miss our appointment.
5. The district attorney won't rest <u>till he finds the perpetrator</u>.

Test yourself 48.3

1. Even though <u>the village</u> supported the emperor, it still paid numerous taxes.
2. I like to sit on the balcony when <u>the weather</u> is nice.
3. George did it because <u>he</u> recognized the woman.
4. Once <u>I</u> have made up my mind, I usually do not change it.
5. Someone rang the doorbell while <u>we</u> were having lunch.

Test yourself 48.4

1. The two horses thrived on the ranch because they received excellent care.   <u>complex</u>
2. Another little girl will be arriving at the school before noon today.   <u>simple</u>
3. The old housekeeper welcomed her warmly when her mother was present.   <u>complex</u>
4. The general returned home with his family.   <u>simple</u>
5. As we approached our destination, we became rather emotional.   <u>complex</u>

Test yourself 48.5

1. She pursued her goals relentlessly but she didn't always achieve them.   <u>compound</u>
2. I have made numerous mistakes over the years.   <u>simple</u>
3. I won't tell you unless you agree to help because I can't take the risk.   <u>complex</u>
4. Jason and Ilene had to renew their passports before they could leave the country.   <u>complex</u>
5. Baby boomers were born before this century.   <u>simple</u>

Test yourself 48.6

1. I'll stay with Jeanette <u>until Peter comes home</u>.
2. <u>That my candidate will win</u> is obvious.
3. <u>Although Mrs. Craft was tired</u>, she insisted on making us dinner.
4. We were quite confident <u>that we had made the right decision</u>.
5. They want to find out <u>why the waitress was so rude to them</u>.

Test yourself 48.7

1. They don't believe <u>that her partner will keep his word</u>.
2. Mrs. Webb was sure <u>her pie would win the baking contest</u>.

3. That Andy is the best in the class doesn't surprise me.
4. We heard you were accepted to Georgetown Law School.
5. It is true that I am going to become a partner in this firm.

Test yourself 48.8

1. My mother changed the subject, but it was too late.	compound
2. He proposed to her when she graduated from college.	complex
3. A man from the sawmill was overseeing the project.	simple
4. I want a piece of apple pie.	simple
5. I had been hoping you could come to the game.	complex

Test yourself 49.1

1. He paid no attention to the newspaper which was next to him.
2. The police arrested the man whom they had been looking for.
3. Mrs. Peterson was reaching for the phone that was nearest her chair.
4. He might recognize the woman who is hosting the show.
5. Cliff bought a present that was just perfect for his girlfriend.

Test yourself 49.2

1. She gave him a smile that lit up her face.
2. The professor who gives easy tests is on sabbatical this semester.
3. The approaches which are most likely to succeed are too complicated.
4. The hotel which is near the shore doesn't open until April.
5. Are you satisfied with the computer that your parents bought for you?

Test yourself 49.3

1. The hotel chain that Greg founded has since gone out of business.
2. He phoned the woman who was writing the article.
3. Jill resents the man whose father won the lottery.
4. The highway which I take to work needs repair.
5. The TV show that she likes best is on Sunday nights.

Test yourself 49.4

1. She turned on the broadcast which dealt with the scandal that had recently been in the news.
2. Buck stood behind the counter which dominated his small restaurant.
3. The photographer who took the picture which appeared in the paper that was most widely read won a Pulitzer Prize.
4. I can't find the message that you sent me.
5. No one who breaks the law should get away with it.

Test yourself 49.5

1. I am meeting Mr. Arnold at the museum that he supports.
2. The label which contains the warning is not very clear.
3. The robber opened the case which contained the most cash.
4. The policy that the president is implementing should be successful.
5. I contacted the young man whose wallet I found on the subway.

Test yourself 49.6

1. The architect's design includes a window that faces the courtyard.
2. She understood what you were trying to say.
3. If you're hungry, this town has a fantastic Greek restaurant.
4. It is obvious that we have to reevaluate our plan.
5. The offer that I have given you is a fair one.

Test yourself 49.7

1. The little square in the town we visited contained benches.
2. Other famous people will be performing at the theater that my brother works at.
3. The pilot who flew the aircraft must have been well trained.
4. My neighbor owns the horse which won this race.
5. The guest I invited is sleeping on the sofa.

Test yourself 49.8

1. Mrs. Smith, who owns the house, was not interested in selling.   nonrestrictive
2. A huge truck, which someone had painted bright yellow, stood in the driveway.   nonrestrictive
3. The children who had just come back from the class trip were restless.   restrictive
4. The maid broke an antique lamp, which was very valuable.   nonrestrictive
5. The painting I brought home will be perfect for the den.   restrictive

Test yourself 49.9

1. The Frenchman who is from Lyons completed the project.   restrictive
2. The general, who knew nothing about the matter, nonetheless voiced his opinion.   nonrestrictive
3. A small disturbance, which was getting louder and louder, finally attracted our attention.   nonrestrictive
4. Jeremy, who was blushing profusely, asked Tatiana for some help.   nonrestrictive
5. Jim wasn't the person she wanted to hire.   restrictive

Test yourself 50.1

1. They are walking quickly down the hall which connects their lab to the main office.   complex
2. The castle looked beautiful in the sunlight, and it dominated the countryside which was around it.   compound-complex
3. The Mercer family has gone on the vacation which they've been planning for years.   complex
4. He was angry at his friend, but he decided that he wasn't going to tell him.   compound-complex
5. We don't know whether we'll succeed, but it's important that we try.   compound-complex

Test yourself 50.2

1. If you travel to New York, you should definitely visit Times Square.   complex
2. He dried his face with a towel.   simple
3. I like the view from my apartment, but it can get very noisy outside.   compound
4. Once you arrive in Europe, you should call me.   complex
5. It is obvious to me that you have to limit your spending, or you'll have to look for a second job.   compound-complex

☞ **FOR A REVIEW EXERCISE OF THIS UNIT, SEE THE WEBSITE.**

Lesson 51: Looking at related sentences

One interesting characteristic of language is that sentences can be related, in a consistent way, to other sentences. What do we mean by this? Let's start by looking at some related sentences which we've seen before.

1a. She <u>looked up</u> the answer.
1b. She <u>looked</u> the answer <u>up</u>.
2a. We will just <u>drop off</u> the files.
2b. We will just <u>drop</u> the files <u>off</u>.
3a. The professor <u>pointed out</u> the correct answer.
3b. The professor <u>pointed</u> the correct answer <u>out</u>.

You can see that one member of each pair is related to the other in a systematic way: the verb and its particle (both underlined) can either be next to each other or the particle can be on the other side of the next noun phrase. (See Lesson 11.) The important point here is that we can't change the structure of a sentence in any random way. For example, we can't say *She up looked the answer*.

Let's look at other examples of related sentences:

4a. Mary gave the information <u>to Robert</u>.
4b. Mary gave <u>Robert</u> the information.
5a. She told the truth <u>to her granddaughter</u>.
5b. She told <u>her granddaughter</u> the truth.
6a. They bought a car <u>for their teenage daughter</u>.
6b. They bought <u>their teenage daughter</u> a car.

Once again, you can see that these indirect object pairs are related to each other in a systematic way. (See Lesson 40.) And again, we can't just randomly change them; for example, we can't say, *Mary Robert the information gave*.

Here's one more example of related sentences:

7a. I know <u>that</u> you're right.
7b. I know you're right.
8a. You believed <u>that</u> the defendant was innocent.
8b. You believed the defendant was innocent.
9a. The residents of the village feel <u>that</u> the new highway is important.
9b. The residents of the village feel the new highway is important.

Here, while the word *that* can be deleted (see Lesson 48), we can't delete just anything. For example, we can't say *I that you're right*.

Test yourself 51.1

Change each sentence below into its related "partner," using the examples above as a guide.
Sample: His editor put down the manuscript.   <u>His editor put the manuscript down</u>.

Getting started (answers on p. 250)

1. They brought their concerns to the clergyman.

   ....

2. I have an idea you'll like this movie.

   ....

3. You should hand your ticket to the flight attendant.

   ....

4. By noon, Jackie had turned in her assignment.

   ....

5. I ordered you your favorite book.

   ....

More practice (answers on the website)

6. She knows this will disappoint her mother.

   ....

7. Please put your pens down!

   ....

8. He promised his friend a good time.

   ....

9. The accountant figured that he would spend about three hours with his client.

   ....

10. They gave money to their local chapter.

    ....

So far, the related sentence pairs we've looked at have the same meaning. For example, *She looked up the answer* and *She looked the answer up* mean exactly the same thing. But sometimes sentences are related to each other in a consistent way, even though their meanings are not the same. For example, here's a statement:

   10a. Amanda is working today.

Can you turn it into a yes/no question (Lesson 45)? The related yes/no question is:

   10b. Is Amanda working today?

No native speaker of English would make the yes/no question something like, **Working Amanda today is*. That's because there's a systematic relationship between statements and yes/no questions, even though they don't have the same meaning.

   Try another one:

   11a. That boy has eaten an enormous breakfast.

The related yes/no question is:

   11b. Has that boy eaten an enormous breakfast?

Here are some more examples:

    12a. Hank was laughing.

    12b. Was Hank laughing?

    13a. That artist had chosen to represent animals in his drawings.

    13b. Had that artist chosen to represent animals in his drawings?

    14a. You can see the old hotel near the railroad station.

    14b. Can you see the old hotel near the railroad station?

Another example of related sentences can be seen when we look at statements and tag questions (Lesson 45).

For example, here's a statement:

    15a. Molly should do that.

Can you turn it into a tag question (Lesson 45)? The related tag question is:

    15b. Molly should do that, shouldn't she?

No native speaker of English would respond with the tag question, *Mary should do that, can't they*? That's because, again, there's a systematic relationship between statements and tag questions, even though they don't have the same meaning.

Try another one:

    16a. The students are waiting to have lunch.

The related tag question is:

    16b. The students are waiting to have lunch, aren't they?

Here are some more examples:

    17a. He had mailed the letter yesterday.

    17b. He had mailed the letter yesterday, hadn't he?

    18a. Mr. Peters was wearing a hat with a wide brim.

    18b. Mr. Peters was wearing a hat with a wide brim, wasn't he?

    19a. Rebecca will wait for her.

    19b. Rebecca will wait for her, won't she?

See Lesson 53 for further discussion of yes/no questions and tag questions.

So far, we've been looking at sentence types that we've already come across in other lessons. However, there are many more sentences in English that are related. In the next two lessons, we'll take a closer look at two sets of related sentences that we have not discussed before.

Lesson 52: Active and passive sentences

So far in this book we've seen lots of sentences with the following pattern:

    1a. The witch kidnaped Esmeralda.

In this sentence, *the witch* is the subject (the doer of the action); *kidnaped* is an action verb, and *Esmeralda* is the direct object (the receiver of the action). (See Lessons 38 and 39.) This word order – subject first, then verb, then direct object – is typical of English sentences. Sentences like this, with the subject before its verb, are called **active sentences** (or are said to be in the **active voice**).

> **Quick tip 52.1**
>
> Sentences with the subject before the verb are called active sentences. Example: *Charley repaired this computer.*

What do you notice about this next sentence?

    1b. Esmeralda was kidnaped by the witch.

It has basically the same meaning as sentence 1a, but with a different structure. We can see that the noun phrase *the witch* is still the subject; however, it no longer occurs before the verb. It occurs after the verb and following the word *by*. The direct object noun phrase, *Esmeralda*, is now before the verb. Sentences with this pattern are called **passive sentences** (or are said to be in the **passive voice**).

> **Quick tip 52.2**
>
> Sentences which do <u>not</u> have the subject before the verb are called passive sentences. Example: *This computer was repaired by Charley.*

Here are some more examples of active and passive sentence pairs:

    2a. My friend mentioned his excellent reputation. (active)
    2b. His excellent reputation was mentioned by my friend. (passive)
    3a. Nellie sent the Browns a present. (active)
    3b. The Browns were sent a present by Nellie. (passive)
    4a. The bird ate the worm. (active)
    4b. The worm was eaten by the bird. (passive)

Test yourself 52.1

Decide if each sentence is active or passive. To help you decide, see if the subject (doer of the action) is before or after the verb.

Sample: The story was told by a great writer.   <u>passive</u>

Getting started (answers on p. 250)

1. The landscaper was hired by her neighbor.   ....

2. Tim chose the pastries.   ....

3. Christine had driven about thirty or forty miles that day. ....

4. Little Suzie's picture was taken by her grandmother. ....

5. We are cooking something for lunch. ....

More practice (answers on the website)

6. This investor made a lot of money. ....

7. He was appointed by the mayor. ....

8. The votes were counted by the election commission. ....

9. The soprano is singing a famous aria. ....

10. My credit card company has responded to my inquiry. ....

In order for an active sentence to have a related passive sentence, it must have a direct object. Unlike the sentences we have looked at so far in this lesson, the following sentences do not have a direct object; therefore they don't have related passive sentences.

     5. The train arrived late.

     6. We are traveling to Mexico.

     7. Harry studied.

Active and passive sentences are related to each other in a systematic way. Let's look more closely at this relationship by examining sentences 8a and 8b.

     8a. The policeman saw the criminals.   (active)

     8b. The criminals were seen by the policeman.   (passive)

We will see that there are five ways in which passive sentences like 8b differ from active sentences like 8a. We'll now discuss each of the characteristics of passive sentences.

First, as we mentioned in *Quick tip* 52.2, the subject (doer of the action) follows the verb:

     8b. The criminals were seen by <u>the policeman</u>.

Second, the word *by* precedes the subject:

     8b. The criminals were seen <u>by</u> the policeman.

Third, the noun phrase that follows the verb in the active sentence occurs before the verb in the passive sentence:

     8b. <u>The criminals</u> were seen by the policeman.

Fourth, passive sentences have a form of *be* (*am, is, are, was, were, be, being*) before the verb:

     8b. The criminals <u>were</u> seen by the policeman.

We talked about auxiliary, or helping, verbs in Lessons 31–36; the **passive *be*** is also a kind of helping verb.

And fifth, the main verb following the passive *be* is in a special form:

     8b. The criminals were <u>seen</u> by the policeman.

You may recognize this special form of the verb as the past participle form of the verb, the same form of the verb that follows the helping verb *have*. (See Lesson 33.) That is, just as each of the other helping verbs has an effect on the verb following it (see Lesson 36), the passive *be* also has an effect on the verb following it: the verb must be in its past participle form.

Use the following exercises to help you focus in on the differences between active and passive sentences.

Test yourself 52.2

In the passive sentences below, underline the passive *be* helping verb and put a squiggly line under the past participle form of the verb that follows it.
Sample: Roller-coasters are designed by that company.

Getting started (answers on p. 250)

1. Amazing results are produced by that approach.

2. Marjorie Kelly was given first prize by the judges.

3. Those words were spoken by Abraham Lincoln.

4. This actor's suit was designed by Armani.

5. One hundred new airplanes were ordered by Singapore Airlines.

More practice (answers on the website)

6. The rebels were attacked by government soldiers.

7. Columbia Pictures was bought by Sony.

8. A quick deal was struck by the negotiating team.

9. Gandhi is admired by people all over the world.

10. *The Wall Street Journal* is read by many company executives.

Test yourself 52.3

Convert each active sentence below to its related passive sentence.
Sample: The principal gave my class the award.   My class was given the award by the principal.

Getting started (answers on p. 250)

1. The tenant filed the complaint.

....

2. The advertising agency presents many ideas.

....

3. The politicians analyze the questionnaires.

....

4. Flood damaged their house.

....

5. My colleagues complimented me.

....

More practice (answers on the website)

6. This law firm hired Joan's daughter.

....

7. Charity helps the needy.

....

8. Some travelers buy flight insurance.

....

9. Hens produce eggs.

....

10. My grandfather built that house.

....

Test yourself 52.4

Convert each passive sentence below to its related active sentence.
Sample: The message was read by the old man.   The old man read the message.

Getting started (answers on p. 250)

1. Graham is touched by her remarks.

....

2. The tower was built by a well-known architect.

....

3. The silence is broken by the alarm bell.

....

4. Mexico was conquered by Cortez.

....

5. Chinese is spoken by more than a billion people.

....

More practice (answers on the website)

6. The sofa is delivered on time by the furniture store.

....

7. My finger was stuck by a pin.

....

8. The Tony Awards were broadcast by CBS.

....

9. This statue was sculpted by Bernini.

....

10. iPod was introduced by Apple Computer.

....

We've said that passive sentences contain the word *by*. Let's compare *by* in these next two sentences:

9. The two bags were lost by Dina.
10. She lives by the seashore.

Although both *by*s are prepositions, their functions are not the same. In sentence 9, *by* is in a passive sentence, letting us know that the doer of the action (in this case, *Dina*) is following. But in sentence 10, *the seashore* is not doing anything; rather, *by* is telling us about location.

Test yourself 52.5

Each of the sentences below contains the word *by*. Decide if it is being used as a marker of the passive or to indicate location.

Sample: There were too many cars parked by the school.   <u>location</u>

Getting started (answers on p. 250)

1. The trooper is pleased by the strategy.   ....

2. The building by the bank is new.   ....

3. He was confused by that new information.   ....

4. This afternoon we rested by the pond.   ....

5. The rally was attended by college students.   ....

More practice (answers on the website)

6. They don't want to buy the house by the highway.   ....

7. The lost puppy was found by its owner.   ....

8. The newlyweds were married by their hometown priest.   ....

9. The case is tried by a newly elected judge.   ....

10. She was reading by the fireplace.   ....

As we mentioned, passive *be* (in all its forms) is a kind of helping verb, occurring right before the main verb. In a sentence that has other helping verbs as well, the passive *be* is always the last one. You can see that in the following sentences, where the form of the passive *be* is underlined and the other helping verbs are in bold:

11. The letter **will** <u>be</u> answered by McCarthy.
12. The letter **has** <u>been</u> answered by McCarthy.
13. The letter **is** <u>being</u> answered by McCarthy.
14. The letter **should have** <u>been</u> answered by McCarthy.

> **Quick tip 52.3**
>
> The passive *be* helping verb is always placed after all the other helping verbs, right before the main verb. Example: *The table has <u>been</u> set by the waitress.*

Test yourself 52.6

Underline the form of the passive *be* helping verb in the passive sentences below. Remember that it will always be the last helping verb in a passive sentence.

Sample: They could have <u>been</u> seen by the reporters.

Getting started (answers on p. 251)

1. My office is being redecorated by two newcomers to the field.

2. The stop had been planned by the tour guide.

3. Her house might have been damaged by the storm.

4. This book should be read by curious students.

5. The long awaited picture will be unveiled by the painter next Sunday.

More practice (answers on the website)

6. The trash was being collected by the sanitation department.

7. You might be pleased by his generosity.

8. The Finnish runner was being overtaken by the runner from Kenya.

9. That business should have been shut down by the authorities.

10. Joseph's car must be repaired by the dealership.

Test yourself 52.7

Each of the sentences below is an active sentence with one or more helping verbs. Convert each active sentence below to its related passive sentence.

Sample: Matt should read this newspaper.   <u>This newspaper should be read by Matt.</u>

Getting started (answers on p. 251)

1. The tenants have filed the complaint.

....

2. The advertising agency is presenting the ideas.

....

3. The politicians have analyzed the questionnaires.

....

4. The author should have given a more interesting speech.

....

5. I might have forgotten the whole thing.

....

More practice (answers on the website)

6. The hotel management may be building another wing.

....

7. Someone must have noticed this.

....

8. A live band will entertain the wedding guests.

....

9. Bad weather has delayed us.

....

10. Careless campers can start forest fires.

....

The following sentences are also passive sentences, but they're different from the ones we've talked about so far.

15. The bank was robbed.

16. A landscaper was hired at last.

In these passive sentences, the *by* and the subject are missing. That is, instead of saying *The bank was robbed by someone*, we have the option of simply saying *The bank was robbed*, if we don't feel it's necessary to say by whom. This kind of passive sentence, where the subject noun phrase is missing, is called a **truncated passive**. Here are some more examples:

17. My dinner was prepared quickly.

18. That proposal has already been discussed.

> **Quick tip 52.4**
>
> A truncated passive is a passive sentence without the *by* and subject noun phrase. Example: *The proposal was discussed*.

Test yourself 52.8

Each of the sentences below is a passive sentence. Decide if it is a full passive or a truncated passive. Look for the *by* + noun phrase to help you decide.

Sample: The game was lost by the team.   full passive

Getting started (answers on p. 251)

1. The stories of his wealth have been exaggerated by others.

....

2. That bestseller was written by Tony Martin.

....

3. The bridge has been repaired.

....

4. The store is being watched.

....

5. We should have been warned by the contractor.

....

More practice (answers on the website)

6. This watch was given to me by my uncle.

....

7. Another pyramid has been unearthed.

....

8. My article will be published by a prestigious journal.

....

9. I am being paged right now.

....

10. Elephants have been hunted illegally for their ivory.

....

Test yourself 52.9

Decide if the following sentences are active or passive. Some of the passives are truncated.
Sample: The chef is making a sauce for the pasta.   active

Getting started (answers on p. 251)

1. The celebrity was spotted at eight in the morning.

2. Tom is carrying two large glasses.

3. The old man might have been looking at his host suspiciously.

4. The company was sold.

5. The stop had been planned by the tour guide.

More practice (answers on the website)

6. She was thoroughly surprised by him.

7. I might have been exaggerating.

8. The lasagna was cooked in the brand new oven.

9. The ship is circling the island.

10. Nice things were said about him.

To enhance your understanding

Let's compare another active/passive pair of sentences:

     19a. Their aunt <u>visits</u> the children every Christmas.
     19b. The children <u>are</u> visited by their aunt every Christmas.

In sentence 19a, why is the verb *visits* rather than *visit*? Since *their aunt* is one person, we say *visits*. If there were more than one aunt, we'd say: *Their aunt**s** visit the children every Christmas*. So in an active sentence, the first noun phrase, the subject, controls the form of the verb.

What happens when the direct object of the sentence, *the children*, is before the verb, as in the passive sentence 19b? You can see that the first noun phrase, *the children*, is now controlling the form of the verb: we say, *the children <u>are</u> visited by their aunt every Christmas* (because there is more than one child). Even though there's still only one aunt, *aunt* is no longer controlling the form of the verb. The important thing to keep in mind is that in a sentence it is always the noun phrase before the verb, whether or not it's doing the action, that controls the form of the verb.

Lesson 53: Positive and negative sentences

The following are all **positive sentences**:

1. I will think about it.
2. Timothy has called her.
3. The teacher was listening.

Can you turn them into **negative sentences**, using the word *not*? The related negative sentences are:

4. I will not think about it.
5. Timothy has not called her.
6. The teacher was not listening.

(Of course, native speakers often put *not* in contractions, saying, for example, *I won't think about it* instead of *I will not think about it*; we will not be focusing on the contractions in our discussion here.)

No native speaker of English would make the negative sentence something like, **I will think about not it*. That's because there's a systematic relationship between positive and negative sentences, even though they don't have the same meaning. We're not usually consciously thinking about how to make a sentence negative, but we know how to do it, and we do it in a consistent way.

Can you figure out exactly where you put *not* in a sentence when you make it negative? Here are some negative sentences, with *not* underlined and the helping verb in bold. (See Lesson 31 for a reminder about helping verbs.)

7. I **am** <u>not</u> going there next week.
8. That phone **might** <u>not</u> work.
9. She **has** <u>not</u> written to me often.

Where does the *not* go? You can see that it goes right after the helping verb.

What if a sentence has more than one helping verb? Again, the *not* in each sentence below is underlined; the helping verbs are in bold.

10. That phone **should** <u>not</u> **have** worked.
11. She **has** <u>not</u> **been** writing to me often.
12. Those people **should** <u>not</u> **have been** attending the conference.

What pattern do you notice? You can see that *not* is always placed after the first helping verb.

Quick tip 53.1

A sentence is made negative by inserting *not* after the first helping verb.

Test yourself 53.1

For each of the sentences below, insert the word *not* to make the sentence negative.
Sample: I should turn around.   <u>I should not turn around.</u>

Getting started (answers on p. 251)

1. Nate has been busy lately.

....

2. You might ask your father.

....

3. Interest rates are going up.

....

4. It could have been a hurricane.

....

5. I will be playing soccer tomorrow.

....

More practice (answers on the website)

6. George has had enough.

....

7. She could have been saying that.

....

8. He was being photographed.

....

9. This company was sued for fraud.

....

10. I can be persuaded to change my mind.

....

Now make the following sentence negative:
13. I went there last week.
You probably ended up with the following:
14. I did not go there last week.
How did *did* end up here? Let's look at some more examples to figure it out:
15a. She writes to me often.
15b. She **does** not write to me often.
16a. Many important people attended the conference.
16b. Many important people **did** not attend the conference.

If we look at one of these sentences, such as *I went there last week*, we can see that it has a main verb, *went*, but no helping verb. So when a sentence has no helping verb but we need one, for example, to make the sentence negative, we use a form of *do* as the helping verb. Notice that in that case, the tense information is not on the main verb, but on the form of *do* instead (*do*, *does*, *did*). This is exactly as expected. You may recall from Lesson 37 that tense is always indicated by the first verb; since *do*, and not the main verb, is the first verb in the sentence, it is the one that carries the tense information. This leaves the main verb in its base form. (The same is true for person and number information, distinguishing between *do* and *does*.)

Test yourself 53.2

For each of the sentences below, insert the word *not* where it is needed to make the sentence negative. Some sentences will have helping verbs; some will not, so insert the appropriate form of *do* where it is needed.

Sample: The soldier helped his comrade to his feet. The soldier did not help his comrade to his feet.

Getting started (answers on p. 251)

1. This path will lead you to the stable.

   ....

2. Frank had been walking for hours.

   ....

3. Mr. Clay returned as soon as he could.

   ....

4. The principal of this school is thinking about retiring.

   ....

5. They have a swimming pool.

   ....

More practice (answers on the website)

6. You could have been more forthcoming.

   ....

7. That company imports products from Canada on a regular basis.

   ....

8. She has been a waitress for a long time.

   ....

9. He tries to write poetry twice a week.

   ....

10. This could be happening to you.

    ....

Quick tip 53.2

In negative sentences, we use a form of *do* as the helping verb if the sentence does not have any other helping verb. Example: *He does not like spaghetti.*

There is one main verb that doesn't use *do* to form a negative sentence, even when the sentence has no helping verb: that exception is *be*. In these next examples, there is no helping verb, just the main verb *be* (underlined); you can see that no form of *do* is needed to form a negative sentence.

17a.	She **is** awake now.	(positive sentence)
17b.	She **is** not awake now.	(negative sentence)
18a.	The judges **were** in their chambers.	(positive sentence)
18b.	The judges **were** not in their chambers.	(negative sentence)

To enhance your understanding

The verb *do* has a number of different uses. Here are some examples:

19. I did not study. (helping verb)
20. I did it.   (main verb)
21. I did think of it! (emphasis)

Answer keys: *Test yourself, Getting started* questions – Unit 17

Test yourself 51.1

1. They brought the clergyman their concerns.
2. I have an idea that you'll like this movie.
3. You should hand the flight attendant your ticket.
4. By noon, Jackie had turned her assignment in.
5. I ordered your favorite book for you.

Test yourself 52.1

1. The landscaper was hired by her neighbor.   passive
2. Tim chose the pastries.   active
3. Christine had driven about thirty or forty miles that day.   active
4. Little Suzie's picture was taken by her grandmother.   passive
5. We are cooking something for lunch.   active

Test yourself 52.2

1. Amazing results are produced by that approach.
2. Marjorie Kelly was given first prize by the judges.
3. Those words were spoken by Abraham Lincoln.
4. This actor's suit was designed by Armani.
5. One hundred new airplanes were ordered by Singapore Airlines.

Test yourself 52.3

1. The complaint was filed by the tenant.
2. Many ideas are presented by the advertising agency.
3. The questionnaires are analyzed by the politicians.
4. Their house was damaged by flood.
5. I was complimented by my colleagues.

Test yourself 52.4

1. Her remarks touch Graham.
2. A well-known architect built the tower.
3. The alarm bell breaks the silence.
4. Cortez conquered Mexico.
5. More than a billion people speak Chinese.

Test yourself 52.5

1. The trooper is pleased by the strategy.   passive
2. The building by the bank is new.   location

3. He was confused by that new information.   passive
4. This afternoon we rested by the pond.   location
5. The rally was attended by college students.   passive

Test yourself 52.6

1. My office is <u>being</u> redecorated by two newcomers to the field.
2. The stop had <u>been</u> planned by the tour guide.
3. Her house might have <u>been</u> damaged by the storm.
4. This book should <u>be</u> read by curious students.
5. The long awaited picture will <u>be</u> unveiled by the painter next Sunday.

Test yourself 52.7

1. The complaint has been filed by the tenants.
2. The ideas are being presented by the advertising agency.
3. The questionnaires have been analyzed by the politicians.
4. A more interesting speech should have been given by the author.
5. The whole thing might have been forgotten by me.

Test yourself 52.8

1. The stories of his wealth have been exaggerated by others.   full passive
2. That best-seller was written by Tony Martin.   full passive
3. The bridge has been repaired.   truncated passive
4. The store is being watched.   truncated passive
5. We should have been warned by the contractor.   full passive

Test yourself 52.9

1. The celebrity was spotted at eight in the morning.   passive
2. Tom is carrying two large glasses.   active
3. The old man might have been looking at his host suspiciously. active
4. The company was sold.   passive
5. The stop had been planned by the tour guide.   passive

Test yourself 53.1

1. Nate has not been busy lately.
2. You might not ask your father.
3. Interest rates are not going up.
4. It could not have been a hurricane.
5. I will not be playing soccer tomorrow.

Test yourself 53.2

1. This path will not lead you to the stable.
2. Frank had not been walking for hours.
3. Mr. Clay did not return as soon as he could.
4. The principal of this school is not thinking about retiring.
5. They do not have a swimming pool.

☞ **FOR A REVIEW EXERCISE OF THIS UNIT, SEE THE WEBSITE.**

Review matching exercise and answer key – Part III

Review matching exercise

Match the underlined word or words in each sentence to the appropriate term. Use each term only once.

Sample: <u>After Katie escorted her mother home</u>, she went out to look for work.

<u>adverbial clause</u>

compound-complex sentence	full passive	truncated passive
compound sentence	relative clause	wh-question
imperative	tag question	yes/no question
negative sentence		

1. Alexandra met a girl <u>who lived in an apartment across the street.</u> ....
2. <u>Do you feel that you can trust him</u>? ....
3. <u>Kirk wrote out a receipt and then they signed it.</u> ....
4. <u>I have not actually seen a new version of that movie.</u> ....
5. <u>That robot can do all the things that the technician does but it can do them better.</u> ....
6. <u>Remember to bring those papers.</u> ....
7. <u>The city was rebuilt by its residents.</u> ....
8. <u>The roads were built last year.</u> ....
9. A treaty should be binding, <u>shouldn't it</u>? ....
10. <u>Why did Luke buy that house?</u> ....

Answer key: Review matching exercise – Part III

1. Alexandra met a girl <u>who lived in an apartment across the street.</u>   relative clause
2. <u>Do you feel that you can trust him?</u>   yes/no question
3. <u>Kirk wrote out a receipt and then they signed it.</u>   compound sentence
4. <u>I have not actually seen a new version of that movie.</u>   negative sentence
5. <u>That robot can do all the things that the technician does but it can do them better.</u>   compound-complex sentence
6. <u>Remember to bring those papers.</u>   imperative
7. <u>The city was rebuilt by its residents.</u>   full passive
8. <u>The roads were built last year.</u>   truncated passive
9. A treaty should be binding, <u>shouldn't it</u>?   tag question
10. <u>Why did Luke buy that house?</u>   wh-question

List of *Quick tips*

Unit 1: Nouns

Quick tip 1.1 If you can put the word *the* in front of a word and it sounds like a unit, the word is a noun.

Quick tip 2.1 Concrete nouns refer to things we can perceive with one of our senses. Abstract nouns cannot be perceived by our senses.

Quick tip 2.2 If you can put *his* in front of a word and it sounds like a unit, the word is a noun.

Quick tip 4.1 Animate nouns refer to things that are alive; inanimate nouns refer to things that are not alive.

Quick tip 5.1 If you can pluralize a noun in a sentence, it is functioning as a count noun.

Quick tip 5.2 If you can use *many* with a noun (when it is pluralized), it's a count noun. If you can use *much* with a noun, it's a noncount noun.

Quick tip 5.3 If you can use *fewer* with a noun (when it is pluralized), it's a count noun. If you can use *less* with a noun, it's a noncount noun.

Quick tip 6.1 Nouns that are actual names, for example *Mary*, are called proper nouns. Nouns that are not names are called common nouns, e.g. *girl*.

Quick tip 6.2 One way to identify a proper noun is to ask yourself: is this a noun I would capitalize, no matter where it is in a sentence? If so, it's a proper noun.

Unit 2: Verbs

Quick tip 7.1 If a word can have *should* in front of it and the phrase sounds complete, the word is a verb. Examples: *should leave, should sail, should discover, should complain. Leave, sail, discover*, and *complain* are all verbs.

Quick tip 7.2 If a word can have *to* in front of it and the phrase sounds complete, it's a verb. Examples: *to leave, to sail, to discover, to complain. Leave, sail, discover*, and *complain* are all verbs. (Note that we're not talking here about *two, too,* or the *to* that indicates direction, as in *Let's go to the park*.)

Quick tip 9.1 The forms of the irregular verb *be* are: *am, are, is, was, were, be, been, being*.

Quick tip 9.2 If you can substitute a form of *be* for a verb and the meaning of the sentence is basically the same, the verb is probably being used as a linking verb. The verb *be* and its forms are also linking verbs.

Quick tip 9.3 If you can substitute a form of *seem* for a verb and the meaning of the sentence is basically the same, the verb is probably being used as a linking verb.

Quick tip 9.4 Linking verbs are followed or modified by adjectives, while action verbs are followed or modified by adverbs.

Quick tip 10.1 Action verbs that act upon something are called transitive verbs. Action verbs that do not act upon something are called intransitive verbs.

Quick tip 10.2 If a verb (in any of its forms) can be put in one of the following slots, it is transitive: (a) What did you _____? (b) Who did you _____? If a verb cannot be put in one of these slots, it is intransitive.

Quick tip 10.3 If a verb (in one of its forms) can be put in one of the following slots, it is transitive: (a) He _____ something. (b) He _____ someone.

Quick tip 10.4 If a verb (in one of its forms) can be put in the following slot, it is intransitive: He _____.

Quick tip 10.5 Some verbs can be either transitive or transitive. These can occur in both of the following slots: (a) He _____ something / someone. (b) He _____.

Quick tip 11.1 If you can substitute a single verb for a verb and the word following it, you probably have a phrasal verb. For example, you can say, *She pointed out the truth to us* or *She showed the truth to us*. *Point out* is a phrasal verb.

Quick tip 11.2 If you can move a particle away from its verb, you have a phrasal verb. For example, since you can say both *She looked up the answer* and *She looked the answer up*, *look up* is a phrasal verb.

Unit 3: Determiners

Quick tip 12.1 There are only three articles in English: *the, a* and *an*.

Quick tip 13.1 There are only four demonstratives in English: *this, that, these*, and *those*.

Quick tip 14.1 The determiner possessive pronouns are: *my, your, his, her, its, our, their*.

Quick tip 15.1 Words of quantity, quantifiers, can act as determiners and precede a noun. Some examples are: *all, some, several*, and *much*.

Unit 4: Adjectives

Quick tip 16.1 If you can put a word between *the* and a noun (for example, *the _____ boy*), then that word is an adjective.

Unit 5: Prepositions

Quick tip 17.1 Prepositions are words, usually small, that typically indicate information about direction, location, or time. There is only a small number of prepositions in English. Some commonly used examples are *at, from, in, on*, and *to*.

Quick tip 17.2 If you can put a word in one of the empty slots in one of the following sentences, the word is a preposition: *I walked _____ the table. It happened _____ that time.*

Unit 6: Conjunctions

Quick tip 18.1 There are three common coordinating conjunctions in English. They are: *and, or,* and *but.* Four less common ones are *for, so, yet,* and *nor.*

Quick tip 18.2 A commonly used way to remember the coordinating conjunctions is to think of FANBOYS: F (*for*), A (*and*), N (*nor*), B (*but*), O (*or*), Y (*yet*), S (*so*).

Quick tip 19.1 Subordinating conjunctions connect a sentence with another sentence, which is a subpart of it. The subpart sentence is called a dependent clause (or subordinate clause). In the following sentence, the subordinating conjunction is underlined and the dependent clause is in italics: Nick decided to try to escape, <u>although</u> *he knew his chances were slim.*)

Quick tip 19.2 The subordinating conjunction is always the first word of the dependent clause.

Quick tip 20.1 Correlative conjunctions are two-part conjunctions. Common correlative conjunctions are: *both /and, either /or, if /then, neither /nor.*

Unit 7: Pronouns

Quick tip 21.1 The subject pronouns are: *I, you, he, she, it, we, they.*

Quick tip 21.2 The object pronouns are: *me, you, her, him, it, us, them.*

Quick tip 22.1 The reflexive pronouns are: *myself, yourself, himself, herself, itself, ourselves, yourselves, themselves.*

Quick tip 22.2 All the reflexive pronouns end in *-self* (singular) or *-selves* (plural).

Quick tip 23.1 There are only four demonstrative pronouns: *this, that, these,* and *those.*

Quick tip 24.1 Nominal possessive pronouns replace a whole noun (or noun phrase). For example, instead of saying *That book is <u>Sally's book</u>* we can simply say, *That book is <u>hers</u>.* The nominal possessive pronouns are: *mine, yours, his, hers, its, ours, theirs.*

Quick tip 25.1 Interrogative pronouns are question words. The interrogative pronouns are: *how, what, when, where, which, who, whom, whose, why.* Look for the question mark to help find them.

Quick tip 26.1 The common relative pronouns are: *that, which, who, whom, whose.* They refer back to a noun in the sentence.

Quick tip 26.2 Relative pronouns are a type of subordinating conjunction. A relative pronoun typically occurs soon after the noun it refers to. Example: *He liked <u>the teacher who gave easy tests.</u>*

Unit 8: Adverbs

Quick tip 27.1 Adverbs generally indicate information about location, time, degree, and manner. They provide extra information about the action in a sentence, about adjectives and about other adverbs.

Quick tip 27.2 If you don't know what else a word is (and you've eliminated the other parts of speech), it's probably an adverb.

Quick tip 27.3 Can the word go in the following slot? *Mary slept* _____. If so, it's probably an adverb. For example, *Mary slept peacefully*. *Peacefully* is an adverb.

Quick tip 27.4 Can the word go in the following slot? _____, *I gave / will give my speech*. If so, it's probably an adverb. For example, *Yesterday, I gave my speech*. *Yesterday* is an adverb. Or: *Tomorrow, I will give my speech*. *Tomorrow* is an adverb.

Quick tip 27.5 Can the word go in the following slot? *He is* _____ *happy*. If so, it's probably an adverb. For example, *He is very happy*. *Very* is an adverb.

Quick tip 27.6 Does the word end in the suffix *-ly*? Is it an adjective? If it ends in *-ly* and it's not an adjective, it's probably an adverb (e.g. *hopefully, happily, unusually*).

Unit 9: Noun phrases

Quick tip 28.1 A noun phrase can consist of a noun alone, for example *audiences, John*.

Quick tip 28.2 A noun phrase can consist of a determiner, one or more adjectives, and a noun. The determiner and adjective(s) are optional.

Quick tip 28.3 A noun phrase can consist of just a pronoun, for example *he* or *them*.

Unit 10: Prepositional phrases

Quick tip 29.1 A prepositional phrase consists of a preposition plus a noun phrase, for example *in the closet*.

Unit 11: Verb phrases

Quick tip 30.1 Every verb phrase contains a verb, for example *laughs, left*.

Quick tip 30.2 A verb phrase can consist of a verb plus a noun phrase, for example *chased the ball*.

Quick tip 30.3 A verb phrase can consist of a linking verb plus an adjective, for example *is tall*.

Quick tip 30.4 A verb phrase can consist of a verb plus a prepositional phrase, for example *drove to the mall*.

Quick tip 30.5 A verb phrase can consist of a verb plus a noun phrase plus a prepositional phrase, for example *drove her friend to the mall*.

Unit 12: Auxiliary phrases

Quick tip 31.1 The basic helping verbs of English are:
a. can may shall will must
   could might should would
b. have has had
c. am are is
   was were
   be been being

Quick tip 31.2 If a sentence has both a main verb and a helping verb, the main verb is always last.

Quick tip 32.1 One kind of helping verb is called a modal. The basic modals of English are:

can	could
may	might
shall	should
will	would
must	

Quick tip 33.1 One kind of helping verb is the verb *have*. It has three forms: *have, has,* and *had.*

Quick tip 33.2 *Have* can be used as a helping verb or as a main verb. When *have* is used as the main verb, it refers to the idea of possession. When *have* is used as the helping verb, it is always followed by another verb.

Quick tip 34.1 One kind of helping verb is *be*. It has the following forms: *am, is, are, was, were, be, been,* and *being*.

Quick tip 34.2 *Be* and its forms can be used as a helping verb or as a main verb. When *be* is used as the helping verb, it is always followed by another verb.

Quick tip 35.1 A sentence can have zero, one, or more than one helping verb. If there is more than one, they will always be in the following relative order: modal +*have* +*be*.

Quick tip 36.1 When the helping verb is progressive *be*, the next verb always has -*ing* added to its base form. Example: *is sleeping*. The -*ing* verb form is called the present participle.

Quick tip 36.2 When *have* is the helping verb, the next verb typically has -*ed or -en* added to its base form. Examples: *has eaten, have watched*. The verb form following the helping verb *have* is called the past participle.

Quick tip 36.3 When the helping verb is a modal, the next verb is always in its base form. Example: *can study*.

Quick tip 36.4 A noun that consists of a verb and the suffix -*ing* is called a gerund. Example: *Entertain-ing is fun*.

Quick tip 37.1 Time refers to a point in real life at which something occurs. Tense refers to the grammatical form of a verb.

Quick tip 37.2 Tense information is always indicated by the first verb in the sentence, excluding modals.

Quick tip 37.3 Sentences with no helping verb are in either the present or past tense, depending on the form of the verb.

Quick tip 37.4 Sentences with *will* followed by the main verb are in the future tense.

Quick tip 37.5 If a sentence has a form of *have* as a helping verb, it will have the word *perfect* as part of the name of its tense.

Quick tip 37.6 The present tense forms of *have* are *have* and *has*. The past tense form of *have* is *had*.

Quick tip 37.7 If a sentence has *will* as a helping verb, it will have the word *future* as part of the name of its tense.

Quick tip 37.8 If a sentence has a form of *be* as a helping verb, it will have the word *progressive* as part of the name of its tense.

Quick tip 37.9 The present tense forms of *be* are *am, is*, and *are*. The past tense forms of *be* are *was* and *were*.

Unit 13: Subjects and objects

Quick tip 38.1 If the main verb of the sentence is an action verb, the subject of the sentence is the doer of the action and generally comes before the verb. It can be found by answering the question: "Who or what is doing the action?"

Quick tip 38.2 If the main verb of the sentence is a linking verb, the subject is who or what the sentence is about; the subject is found before the verb.

Quick tip 39.1 The direct object of a sentence is receiving the action. It can usually be found by answering the question: "Who or what is being acted upon or receiving the action?" The direct object typically occurs immediately after the verb.

Quick tip 40.1 The indirect object of a sentence can be found by answering the question: "Who or what is receiving the direct object?"

Quick tip 40.2 An indirect object can occur: (a) after the direct object (which follows the verb), with *to* or *for* introducing it, or (b) before the direct object (and after the verb), without *to* or *for*. For example: *Joan gave a present to Bill* or *Joan gave Bill a present*. (*Bill* is the indirect object in both sentences.)

Quick tip 40.3 To help you decide if a sentence has an indirect object, see if the sentence can be changed from a pattern like *The boys left a note for their teacher* to a sentence with a pattern like *The boys left their teacher a note*, or vice versa.

Quick tip 40.4 If the direct object is a pronoun, it must come before the indirect object. Example: *My sister sent it to her friend,* **My sister sent her friend it.*

Quick tip 41.1 A subject pronoun is used when it is functioning as the subject of the sentence. An object pronoun is used when it is functioning as: (a) the direct object of the sentence; (b) the indirect object of the sentence; (c) the object of a preposition.

Quick tip 42.1 The subject of commands is an understood or implied *you*.

Unit 14: Compound phrases

Quick tip 43.1 Two noun phrases joined by a coordinating conjunction is called a compound noun phrase.

Quick tip 44.1 Two verb phrases joined by a coordinating conjunction is called a compound verb phrase.

Unit 15: The Functions of sentences

Quick tip 45.1 Sentences that make a statement are called declaratives; sentences that ask a question are called interrogatives; sentences that give a command are called imperatives; sentences that express strong emotion are called exclamations.

Quick tip 45.2 A yes/no question is one that can be answered by "yes" or "no."

Quick tip 45.3 A wh- question begins with one of the following wh- words (question words): *when, where, what, why, which, who, whom, how*. Example: *Where is the meeting?*

Quick tip 45.4 A tag question contains a statement followed by a tag, such as *could you? aren't they? hasn't he?* Example: *She is leaving soon, isn't she?*

Unit 16: Combining sentences

Quick tip 46.1 A clause is a free-standing sentence or a sentence within a sentence; a clause or sentence contains at least a subject and a main verb.

Quick tip 46.2 A sentence can contain one or more clauses.

Quick tip 46.3 A sentence that contains only one clause, that is, one subject and one verb phrase, is called a simple sentence.

Quick tip 47.1 A sentence that is made up of two or more sentences (clauses) joined by a coordinating conjunction (most commonly *and, or,* and *but*) is called a compound sentence.

Quick tip 48.1 A complex sentence consists of at least two sentences (clauses): a main clause and a dependent clause. The dependent clause is a subpart of the main clause and adds information to it. Example, with the dependent clause underlined: *Sally visited her before she moved.*

Quick tip 48.2 A dependent clause is joined to another clause by a subordinating conjunction such as *although, if, where.*

Quick tip 48.3 The easiest way to identify a dependent clause is to look for a subordinating conjunction and see if it's followed by a sentence. If it is, then the subordinating conjunction plus the sentence directly following it is a dependent clause.

Quick tip 48.4 In a noun clause, the subordinating conjunction *that* can be deleted following a main clause. Example: *I think (that) it's going to rain.*

Quick tip 49.1 A relative clause (adjective clause) is a kind of dependent clause; it provides additional information about a noun phrase in the main clause. Example (relative clause underlined): *I brought the cookies that are on the plate.*

Quick tip 49.2 Relative clauses begin with one of the relative pronouns: *that, which, who, whom, whose*.

Quick tip 49.3 A relative pronoun connects the relative clause to the rest of the sentence. All of the relative pronouns (except *whose*) also replace a noun phrase in the relative clause. (*Whose* replaces a determiner.)

Quick tip 49.4 A relative pronoun may be omitted before a noun phrase. Example: *The movie (that) I saw was exciting*.

Quick tip 49.5 A restrictive relative clause limits the noun phrase which it is modifying; a nonrestrictive relative clause does not. A nonrestrictive relative clause is separated from the main clause by pauses, and, when written, it is separated from the main clause by commas. Examples: *The dogs which were friendly were being trained as Seeing Eye dogs* (restrictive). *The dogs, which were friendly, were being trained as Seeing Eye dogs* (nonrestrictive).

Quick tip 50.1 A compound-complex sentence is a combination of a compound and a complex sentence: it has at least two main clauses and at least one dependent clause. Example: *His friends were always there for William, and he appreciated the help that they often gave him*.

Unit 17: Related sentences

Quick tip 52.1 Sentences with the subject before the verb are called active sentences. Example: *Charley repaired this computer*.

Quick tip 52.2 Sentences which do not have the subject before the verb are called passive sentences. Example: *This computer was repaired by Charley*.

Quick tip 52.3 The passive *be* helping verb is always placed after all the other helping verbs, right before the main verb. Example: *The table has been set by the waitress*.

Quick tip 52.4 A truncated passive is a passive sentence without the *by* and subject noun phrase. Example: *The proposal was discussed*.

Quick tip 53.1 A sentence is made negative by inserting *not* after the first helping verb.

Quick tip 53.2 In negative sentences, we use a form of *do* as the helping verb if the sentence does not have any other helping verb. Example: *He does not like spaghetti*.

Glossary

abstract noun: does not have physical attributes. Example: *history*. Contrast **concrete noun**.

action verb: indicates action. Example: *go*. Contrast **linking verb**.

active sentence: a sentence expressed in the active voice. Contrast **passive sentence**.

active (voice): a sentence in which the subject, defined in terms of meaning, occurs before the main verb. Example: *A better team beat us*. Contrast **passive (voice)**.

adjective: refers to a characteristic of a noun. See **attributive adjective**; **predicate adjective**.

adjective clause: see **relative clause**.

adverb: refers to a characteristic of a verb, adjective, or another adverb. It generally indicates information about location, time, degree, or manner. Example: *quickly*.

adverbial clause: a dependent clause that functions as an adverb in the main clause of a complex sentence. Example: *It is obvious where we went wrong*.

animate noun: a human or an animal. Example: *child*. Contrast **inanimate noun**.

article: a determiner that indicates whether or not a noun is a specific one known to both the speaker and the listener. The articles are: *the* and *a/an*. See **definite article**; **indefinite article**.

attributive adjective: occurs before a noun in a noun phrase. Example: *an interesting movie*. Contrast **predicate adjective**.

auxiliary verb: see **helping verb**.

auxiliary phrase: a phrase whose principal component is a helping (auxiliary) verb. Example: *have been wondering*.

base form: see **verb base**.

clause: a free-standing sentence or a sentence within a sentence. See **main clause**; **dependent clause**; **adverbial clause**; **noun clause**; **relative clause**.

common noun: refers to general categories – things other than specific names. Example: *book*. Contrast **proper noun**.

complex sentence: contains one main clause and at least one dependent clause. Example: *Meredith was driving to work when she received a phone call from her mother*. Contrast **simple sentence**; **compound sentence**; **compound-complex sentence**.

compound-complex sentence: consists of at least two main clauses (compound) and at least one dependent clause (complex). Example: *Although I like traveling with you, I am very tired and I have to finish a project in the office*. Contrast **simple sentence**; **compound sentence**; **complex sentence**.

compound noun phrase: contains two or more noun phrases joined by a coordinating conjunction. Example: *Andy and his two sons went to the park*.

compound phrase: a phrase containing two or more linguistic units of the same type (such as noun phrases, prepositional phrases, adverbs, sentences), joined by a coordinating conjunction. Example: *up the block and around the corner*. See **compound noun phrase**; **compound verb phrase**.

compound preposition: see **phrasal preposition**.

compound sentence: contains two or more sentences joined by a coordinating conjunction. Example: *You can pay me now, or you can pay me later*. Contrast **simple sentence**; **complex sentence**; **compound-complex sentence**.

compound verb phrase: contains two or more verb phrases joined by a coordinating conjunction. Example: *He likes spaghetti but rarely orders it*.

concrete noun: possesses physical attributes. Example: *table*. Contrast **abstract noun**.

conjunction: a function word that connects grammatical units such as words, phrases, and sentences. See **coordinating conjunction**; **subordinating conjunction**; **correlative conjunction**.

continuous (aspect): see **progressive (aspect)**.

coordinating conjunction: connects any two units that are the same type, such as sentences (*I go or he goes*), nouns (*milk and cookies*), verbs (*drink and drive*), determiners (*Jack's and Nancy's*), prepositions (*at or near*), adjectives (*healthy and nutritious*), or adverbs (*softly but forcefully*). The three most common coordinating conjunctions are: *and*, *or*, and *but*. Four less common ones are: *for, so, yet*, and *nor*. Contrast **subordinating conjunction**; **correlative conjunction**.

copula: the linking verb *be*. The forms of *be* are: *am, are, is, was, were, be, been, being*. Example: *She is happy*. The term is sometimes used to refer to any linking verb.

correlative conjunction: a two-part conjunction. Common correlative conjunctions are: *both / and, either /or, if /then*, and *neither /nor*. Example: *Either I cook or we order take-out*. Contrast **coordinating conjunction**; **subordinating conjunction**.

count noun: a noun that is countable. Count nouns can be used with the determiners *a/an, many* (as opposed to *much*), and *fewer* (as opposed to *less*), and can have plural forms. Example: *a book, many books, fewer books*. Contrast **noncount noun**.

declarative sentence: expresses a statement. Example: *The sun rises every morning*. Compare **imperative sentence**; **interrogative sentence**; **exclamation**.

definite article: the determiner *the*, used with a noun that has specific identity. Example: *the final exam*. Contrast **indefinite article**.

demonstrative: a determiner or pronoun whose reference is defined in context, "pointing" to something or someone. See **demonstrative determiner**; **demonstrative pronoun**.

demonstrative adjective: see **demonstrative determiner**.

demonstrative determiner: *this* and *that* (singular) and *these* and *those* (plural) when used before a noun. Example: *this morning*. Also called **demonstrative adjective**. Contrast **demonstrative pronoun**.

demonstrative pronoun: *this, that, these, those* when used alone, without a following noun. Example: *I want this*. Contrast **demonstrative determiner**.

dependent clause: the secondary clause in a complex sentence in terms of meaning and structure, forming a subpart of the main clause. Example: *Many people feel* *good in the morning after they've had a good night's sleep*. Also called **subordinate clause**. Contrast **main clause**.

determiner: one of several types of words occurring before a noun. Example: *some people*. See **article**; **demonstrative**; **possessive**; **quantifier**; **interrogative determiner**.

determiner possessive pronoun: a possessive pronoun used before a noun. Example: *our decision*. The determiner possessive pronouns are: *my, your, his, her, its, our, their*. Also called **possessive pronoun with determiner function**; **possessive adjective**. Contrast **nominal possessive pronoun**.

direct object: a noun phrase that functions as the recipient of the subject's action. In most sentences, expressed in the active voice, the direct object occurs after the main verb. Example: *We met Anne in the restaurant*. Also called **object**. Contrast **subject**; **indirect object**.

exclamation: a sentence that expresses strong emotion and does not necessarily contain a subject and a main verb. Example: *What a day!* Contrast **declarative sentence**; **imperative sentence**; **interrogative sentence**.

first person pronoun: see **personal pronoun**.

future perfect progressive tense: indicated by the modal *will* (or *shall*) and perfect *have* helping verbs followed by the *been* (past participle) form of the progressive *be* helping verb and the present participle form of the next verb. Example: *My students will have been studying*.

future perfect tense: indicated by the modal *will* (or *shall*) helping verb followed by perfect *have* and the past participle of the next verb. Example: *My students will have studied*.

future progressive tense: indicated by the modal *will* (or *shall*) and progressive *be* helping verbs followed by the present participle form of the next verb. Example: *My students will be studying*.

future tense: indicated when the modal helping verb *will* (or *shall*) is followed by the main verb. Example: *My students will study*. Also called **simple future tense**.

gerund: a noun that is derived from a verb by adding the suffix *-ing*. Example: *Cooking is fun*.

grammatical function: the role a linguistic unit plays with respect to other units within a grammatical structure. Example: the noun *Anne* functions as the subject in the sentence *Anne went to sleep*, as the direct object in the sentence *We met Anne in the restaurant*, and as the indirect object in the sentence *Someone sent a present to Anne*. Also called **grammatical relation**.

grammatical relation: see **grammatical function**.

helping verb: a verb that augments the main verb and as such belongs to an auxiliary phrase. Example: *I might call you today*. Also called **auxiliary verb**. See **modal**; **perfect have**; **progressive be**; **passive be**. Contrast **main verb**.

human (animate) noun: a person. Contrast **nonhuman noun**; **nonhuman animate noun**.

hypercorrection: producing an incorrect form by applying a general rule beyond its correct domain ("overapplying" a rule). Example: When producing **I feel badly* instead of *I feel bad*, the use of an adverb to modify action verbs is extended to linking verbs as well.

imperative sentence: a command. Example: *Give me a hug!* Contrast **declarative sentence**; **interrogative sentence**; **exclamation**.

inanimate noun: a thing. Contrast **animate noun**.

indefinite article: the determiner *a*/*an*, used before a singular noun whose identity is not specific. The *a* variant is used when the next word begins with a consonant sound; the *an* variant is used when the next word begins with a vowel sound. Example: *a mystery; an experience*. Contrast **definite article**.

independent clause: see **main clause**.

indirect object: a noun phrase that functions as the recipient of the direct object. In most sentences, expressed in the active voice, the indirect object occurs after the main verb, either before the direct object or after it. Example: *Someone sent Anne a present; Someone sent a present to Anne*. Contrast **subject**; **direct object**.

infinitive: either the verb base (example: *read*) or *to* + verb base (example: *to read*).

interrogative determiner: question word occurring before a noun. The interrogative determiners are: *which, whose, what*. Example: *Which option do you prefer?* Contrast **interrogative pronoun**.

interrogative pronoun: question word used alone, without a following noun. Common interrogative pronouns are: *how, what, when, where, which, who, whom, whose, why*. Example: *Which do you prefer?* Contrast **interrogative determiner**.

interrogative sentence: expresses a question. Example: *Are we having fun?* See **yes/no question**; **wh-question**; **tag question**. Contrast **declarative sentence**; **interrogative sentence**; **exclamation**.

intransitive verb: does not act on something; it is not followed by a direct object. Example: *I sleep*. Contrast **transitive verb**.

irregular plural: formed by means other than adding *-(e)s* to a noun. Example: *geese*. Contrast **regular plural**.

irregular verb: does not form its past tense by adding the suffix *-ed*. Example: *see* (past tense *saw*). Contrast **regular verb**.

linking verb: a verb which does not express action. Rather, its main function is to relate (link) the subject to a complement. Example: *They seemed anxious*. The most common linking verb is *be* (see **copula**). Contrast **action verb**.

main clause: the primary clause in a complex sentence in terms of meaning and structure. Example: *Many people feel good in the morning after they've had a good night's sleep*. Also called **independent clause**. Contrast **dependent clause**.

main verb: the principal verb of a sentence or phrase; it belongs to a verb phrase. Example: *I might call you today*. Contrast **helping verb**.

mass noun: see **noncount noun**.

modal: a type of helping verb that expresses categories of modality, such as possibility and necessity. Example: *I might visit you tomorrow*. See **phrasal modal**.

negative sentence: expresses negation by including the word *not* after the first helping verb. Example: *You have not been honest with me*. Compare **positive sentence**.

nominal possessive pronoun: a possessive pronoun used alone, without a following noun. The nominal possessive pronouns are: *mine, yours, his, hers, its, ours, theirs*. Example: *That book is hers*. Contrast **determiner possessive pronoun**.

noncount noun: a noun that is not countable. Noncount nouns can be used with the determiners *much* (as opposed to *many*) and *less* (as opposed to *fewer*), but not with the indefinite article *a*/*an*, and they do not have plural forms. Example: *much* *furniture*; *less furniture*; **a furniture*; **furnitures*. Also called **mass nouns**. Contrast **count noun**.

nonhuman animate noun: an animal. Contrast **human animate noun**.

nonhuman noun: an animal or a thing. Contrast **human noun**.

nonrestrictive relative clause: does not limit the reference of the noun phrase it modifies. Example: *All the students, who studied hard, did well on the final exam*, meaning that all students did well on the final exam and all students studied hard. Compare **restrictive relative clause**.

noun: commonly defined as referring to a person, place, thing, or idea. It is the principal component of a noun phrase (except when replaced by a pronoun). See **abstract noun**; **animate noun**; **common noun**; **concrete noun**; **count noun**; **human (animate) noun**; **inanimate noun**; **noncount noun**; **nonhuman animate noun**; **nonhuman noun**; **possessive common noun**; **possessive proper noun**; **proper noun**.

noun clause: a dependent clause that functions as a noun phrase in the main clause of a complex sentence. Example: *It is obvious that you are a learned woman*.

noun phrase: a phrase whose principal component is a noun, or its replacement, a pronoun. It fulfills various grammatical functions within a sentence, such as subject, direct object, and indirect object. Example: *these flowers*; *you*.

number: a grammatical category that refers to the distinction between singular (one entity) and plural (more than one entity) in nouns and pronouns. Example: *bush, I* (singular); *bushes, we* (plural).

object: refers to direct object, indirect object, or object of a preposition.

object of a preposition: the noun phrase that follows the preposition in a prepositional phrase. Example: *to us*.

object pronoun: the form of a personal pronoun that is used when the pronoun has an object function. This happens when the personal pronoun is the direct object, indirect object, or object of a preposition. Example: *George saw her* (direct object); *George sent her a message* (indirect object); *George heard from her* (object of a preposition). The object pronouns are: *me, you, her, him, it, us, them*. Contrast **subject pronoun**.

particle: the second word in a phrasal verb. It follows the verb, from which it can be separated. Example: *We looked up the answer* / *We looked the answer up*.

passive (voice): the structural configuration of a sentence in which the subject, defined in terms of meaning, does not occur before the main verb. The main verb appears in its past participle form, preceded by the helping verb passive *be*. Example: *We were beaten by a better team*. Contrast **active (voice)**.

passive *be*: the verb used in the formation of the passive voice.

passive sentence: a sentence expressed in the passive voice. See **truncated passive**. Contrast **active sentence**.

past participle: a verb form most commonly ending in the suffix *-ed* or *-en* (other forms exist). It is used in the formation of the perfect aspect and the passive voice. Example: *We were beaten by a better team*.

past perfect progressive tense: indicated by the *had* form of the perfect *have* helping verb followed by the *been* (past participle) form of the progressive *be* helping verb and the present participle form of the next verb. Example: *My students had been studying*.

past perfect tense: indicated by the *had* form of the perfect *have* helping verb and the past participle form of the next verb. Example: *My students had studied*.

past progressive tense: indicated by the *was* or *were* form of the progressive *be* helping verb and the present participle form of the next verb. Example: *My students were studying*.

past tense: indicated when the main verb is not preceded by a helping verb and has the suffix *-ed* added to its base. Example: *My students studied*. Also called **simple past tense**. See **irregular verb** for exceptions.

perfect (aspect): indicates a time period prior to another time period. It is expressed by perfect *have* plus the past participle form of the following verb. Example: *We have eaten already*.

perfect *have*: the helping verb used in the formation of the perfect aspect.

periphrastic modal: see **phrasal modal**.

personal pronoun: a type of pronoun that has different forms, depending on whether it refers to the speaker (first person), listener (second person), or anyone/anything else (third person). See **object pronoun**; **possessive pronoun**; **reflexive pronoun**; **subject pronoun**.

phrasal modal: a modal consisting of more than one word. Example: *You are able to do this*.

phrasal preposition: a preposition consisting of more than one word. Example: *across from*.

phrasal verb: a verb consisting of two words. Example: *She pointed out the truth*. See: **particle**.

phrase: a group of related words forming a grammatical unit that does not have both a subject and a main verb. A phrase may also contain a single word if that word is defined as the principal component of the phrase. Example: verb phrases may contain a number of words (*writes a message*), or just one word (*writes*). See **auxiliary phrase**; **compound phrase**; **noun phrase**; **prepositional phrase**; **verb phrase**.

plural: see **number**.

plural pronoun: see **number**

positive sentence: expresses an assertion. Example: *You have been honest with me*. Compare **negative sentence**.

possessive: indicates to whom or to what a noun phrase belongs. See **possessive pronoun**; **possessive proper noun**; **possessive common noun**.

possessive adjective: see **determiner possessive pronoun**.

possessive common noun: functions as an adjective when preceding a noun. Example: *The girl's shoes*.

possessive pronoun: see **determiner possessive pronoun**; **nominal possessive pronoun**.

possessive pronoun with determiner function: see **determiner possessive pronoun**.

possessive pronoun with nominal function: see **nominal possessive pronoun**.

possessive proper noun: functions as a determiner in a noun phrase. Example: *Mary's red shoes*. See **proper noun**.

predicate adjective: occurs following a linking verb in a verb phrase. Example: *The movie was interesting*. Contrast **attributive adjective**.

preposition: a function word before a noun phrase that typically indicates information about direction, location, or time. Example: *from the kitchen*. See **phrasal preposition**.

prepositional phrase: a phrase consisting of a preposition and a noun phrase. Example: *in the store*.

present participle: a verb form ending in the suffix -*ing*. It is used in the formation of the progressive aspect.

present perfect progressive tense: indicated by the *have* or *has* form of the perfect *have* helping verb followed by the *been* (participle) form of the progressive *be* helping verb and the present participle form of the next verb. Example: *My students have been studying*.

present perfect tense: indicated by the *have* or *has* form of the perfect *have* helping verb and the past participle form of the next verb. Example: *My student has studied*.

present progressive tense: indicated by the *am*, *are*, or *is* form of the progressive *be* helping verb and the present participle form of the next verb. Example: *My students are studying*.

present tense: indicated when the main verb is not preceded by a helping verb and its form corresponds to the verb base or verb base followed by -*(e)s* (*be* is a notable exception). Example: *My students study*; *My student studies*. Also called **simple present tense**.

progressive (aspect): information that the duration of the action or state signified by the main verb extends over a period of time. It is expressed by progressive *be* jointly with the present participle of the following verb. Example: *We are eating dinner*.

progressive *be*: the helping verb used in the formation of the progressive aspect.

pronoun: a function word that replaces (stands in for) a linguistic unit, most commonly a noun phrase. See **demonstrative pronoun**; **interrogative pronoun**; **personal pronoun**; **relative pronoun**.

proper noun: refers to a specific name; begins with capital letters. Example: *New York*. Contrast: **common noun**.

quantifier: a determiner that indicates amount or quantity. Example: *all topics*.

reflexive pronoun: replaces the second of two noun phrases that refer to the same person or thing within the same clause. The reflexive pronouns are: *myself, yourself, himself, herself, itself, ourselves, yourselves, themselves*. Example: *Harry saw himself in the mirror*.

regular plural: formed with the suffix -*(e)s* added to nouns. Example: *gardens, boxes*. Contrast **irregular plural**.

regular verb: forms its past tense by adding the suffix -*ed* to the verb base. Example: *walk* (past tense *walked*). Contrast **irregular verb**.

relative clause: a dependent clause that adds information about a noun phrase in the main clause of a complex sentence. A relative clause is introduced by a relative pronoun, which may be omitted before a noun phrase. Example: *The ice-cream (that) you bought for me tastes delicious*. See **restrictive relative clause**; **non-restrictive relative clause**.

relative pronoun: a subordinating conjunction which introduces a relative clause and refers back to the preceding noun phrase. Example: *He liked the teacher who gave easy tests*. The common relative pronouns are: *that, which, who, whom,* *whose*. Other relative pronouns, such as *whatever, whoever, whomever, whosever* (all ending in *-ever*), represent, rather than refer back to, a noun phrase. Example: *They can travel with whomever they choose*.

restrictive relative clause: limits the reference of the noun phrase it modifies. Example: *All the students who studied hard did well on the final exam*, meaning that all and only those students did well on the final exam who studied hard. Compare **non-restrictive relative clause**.

second person pronoun: see **personal pronoun**.

sentence: minimally contains a subject and a main verb, except for exclamations and imperatives. See **active sentence**; **clause**; **complex sentence**; **complex-compound sentence**; **compound sentence**; **declarative sentence**; **exclamation**; **imperative sentence**; **interrogative sentence**; **negative sentence**; **passive sentence**; **positive sentence**; **simple sentence**.

simple future tense: see **future tense**.

simple past tense: see **past tense**.

simple present tense: see **present tense**.

simple sentence: made up of just one sentence (contains only one clause). Example: *Paris is the capital of France*. Contrast **compound sentence**; **complex sentence**; **compound-complex sentence**.

singular: see **number**.

singular pronoun: see **number**.

subject: a noun phrase that functions as the performer of an action verb or the topic of a linking verb. In most sentences, expressed in the active voice, the subject occurs before the verb. Example: *Anne went to sleep*; *Anne is a dentist*. Contrast **direct object**; **indirect object**.

subject pronoun: the form of a personal pronoun that is used when the pronoun functions as the subject. The subject pronouns are: *I, you, he, she, it, we, they*. Example: *He is happy*. Contrast **object pronoun**.

subordinate clause: see **dependent clause**.

subordinating conjunction: connects the main clause and the dependent clause in a complex sentence. Example: *Many people feel good in the morning after they've had a good night's sleep*. Contrast **coordinating conjunction**; **correlative conjunction**.

tag question: a statement followed by a question "tag." Example: *She is leaving, isn't she*? Contrast **yes/no question**; **wh-question**.

tense: the form of a verb through which a grammar indicates information about time. See **future tense**; **future perfect tense**; **future perfect progressive tense**; **future progressive tense**; **past tense**, **past perfect tense**; **past perfect progressive tense**; **past progressive tense**; **present tense**; **present perfect tense**; **present perfect progressive tense**; **present progressive tense**.

third person pronoun: see **personal pronoun**.

transitive verb: acts on something; it is followed by a direct object. Example: *I threw the ball*. Contrast **intransitive verb**.

truncated passive: a passive sentence in which the subject, defined in terms of meaning, is not expressed. Example: *The proposal was discussed*.

verb: the principal component of a verb phrase. It indicates action or state of being. See **action verb**; **helping verb**; **intransitive verb**; **irregular verb**; **linking verb**; **main verb**; **phrasal verb**; **regular verb**; **transitive verb**; **verb base**.

verb base: the form of a verb that contains no grammatical information. It occurs in the infinitive expression, among others. Example: *to go*.

verb complement: a unit that occurs after a linking verb and refers back to the subject. Example: *The patient seemed anxious*.

verb phrase: a phrase whose principal component is a main verb. Example: *saw a movie*.

wh-question: begins with a wh-word (interrogative pronoun). Example: *Where is the meeting?* Contrast **yes/no question**; **tag question**.

yes/no question: can be answered with a "yes" or "no." Example: *Is today Sunday?* Contrast **wh-question**; **tag question**.

Index